ARTFUL TRUTHS

Artful Truths

THE PHILOSOPHY OF MEMOIR

Helena de Bres

The University of Chicago Press   *Chicago and London*

The University of Chicago Press, Chicago 60637
The University of Chicago Press, Ltd., London
© 2021 by The University of Chicago
All rights reserved. No part of this book may be used or reproduced in any
manner whatsoever without written permission, except in the case of brief
quotations in critical articles and reviews. For more information, contact
the University of Chicago Press, 1427 E. 60th St., Chicago, IL 60637.
Published 2021
Printed in the United States of America

30 29 28 27 26 25 24 23 22 21   1 2 3 4 5

ISBN-13: 978-0-226-78813-5 (cloth)
ISBN-13: 978-0-226-79380-1 (paper)
ISBN-13: 978-0-226-79394-8 (e-book)
DOI: https://doi.org/10.7208/chicago/9780226793948.001.0001

Library of Congress Cataloging-in-Publication Data
Names: De Bres, Helena, author.
Title: Artful truths : the philosophy of memoir / Helena de Bres.
Description: Chicago : London ; University of Chicago Press, 2021. |
Includes bibliographical references and index.
Identifiers: LCCN 2020045758 | ISBN 9780226788135 (cloth) |
ISBN 9780226793801 (paperback) | ISBN 9780226793948 (ebook)
Subjects: LCSH: Autobiography. | Autobiography—Philosophy. |
Autobiography—Moral and ethical aspects.
Classification: LCC CT25 .D39 2021 | DDC 808.06/692—dc23
LC record available at https://lccn.loc.gov/2020045758

♾ This paper meets the requirements of ANSI/NISO Z39.48-1992
(Permanence of Paper).

FOR JORIS, ANGELA, JULIA, AND CAS

Contents

ONE

What Is Memoir?

At the beginning of his *Class: A Guide through the American Status System*, Paul Fussell reports that when he told people he was writing a book about social class in America, it was as if he'd said "I am working on a book urging the beating to death of baby whales using the dead bodies of baby seals."[1] I didn't quite get that response when I informed people at parties that I was writing a book on the ethical and metaphysical issues that arise when writing a memoir, but the replies were always animated. Some people—usually men—sniffed "oh, *memoirs*, I don't read them." Others rolled out a combination of "everyone's writing a memoir these days, aren't they?" "did you hear about that guy who faked his?" "I can't remember what I did last Tuesday," and "I could never do that to my family." Some dove right into the questions I was starting to mull over myself: "what's the difference between a memoir and an autobiography?" "isn't the border between fiction and nonfiction pretty fuzzy?" "does it matter if a memoir is true if it's a work of art?" and "do you have a right to tell your story even if it hurts others?" Then there were the people—my favorites—whose eyes lit up, who launched into a list of all their favorite memoirs ever, and who got out their phones so they could note down as many more titles as I could manage to recommend after two martinis.

At first I was surprised by the intensity of these reactions, because I hadn't thought that the average person, neither memoir writer, nor professional theorist of literature, would be so personally invested in what is, in the end, simply a literary genre, and one we've had around for hundreds of years. Having written the book, though, I now get it. Memoir nestles right up against deep, perplexing, and consequential questions about the nature of the self, the mind, memory, truth, art, ethics, friendship, and the meaning of a human life—just to list a few. These questions aren't of merely theoretical interest. Many among my early audience arguably had more of a grip on the far-reaching personal significance of what I was studying than I did at the time.

Those in the more dismissive camp who suggested to me that memoir was a "fad" were at least on to something. Literary writing about the self, in the form of memoir and personal essays, has surged in popularity over the past thirty years. The trend began in the late eighties, with a set of best-selling coming-of-age memoirs, including *The Liars' Club* (by Mary Karr) and *This Boy's Life* (by Tobias Wolff). It gathered current in the nineties, with more works in the same traditional vein (including Frank McCourt's blockbuster *Angela's Ashes*) and, later, more daring experiments by writers like Dave Eggers (*A Heartbreaking Work of Staggering Genius*) and Lauren Slater (*Lying*). And the flood reached what some would call natural disaster status by the early 2000s, dragging with it James Frey's fraudulent addiction "memoir," *A Million Little Pieces*, and Toni Bentley's *The Surrender*, a heartfelt personal manifesto for anal sex. Then the internet took off, and with it a growing deluge of personal essays, written for online magazines and blogs by the famous and not so famous and shared enthusiastically on Twitter.

Just how unprecedented the boom is is unclear. Definitions in this area are tricky, so it's hard to state uncontroversially when exactly what we today call "memoir" began. But people have recorded and reflected on their lives in written form since antiquity, and literary personal narration (the kind that aims at the status of art) dates back to at least Montaigne's *Essays* in the sixteenth century. There was a craze for autobiographical narratives in America in the eighteenth century, in Britain in the nineteenth, and in the United States in the 1960s–1970s. To that extent, the present enthusiasm for personal nonfiction is nothing new. That said, the current boom does have some distinctive features.

More people are publishing memoirs today than ever before, and the market for memoirs is now as strong as that for novels. The authorship of published memoir has shifted from mostly older White men to an increasingly young, female, non-White and otherwise diverse set of writers. Whereas in the past people tended to write just a single autobiography, we're now in an age of serial partial-life memoirs (Kathryn Harrison has written five, so far). And we're arguably seeing a period of particularly intense innovation in the form. Works like Maggie Nelson's *The Argonauts*, Geoff Dyer's *Out of Sheer Rage*, Alison Bechdel's *Fun Home*, and the "lyric essays" championed by John D'Agata have moved us ever further away from traditional linear narrative toward fragmentary and hybrid forms incorporating elements of poetry, theory, criticism, and visual art.

Finally, accompanying the current memoir boom has been a genuinely novel, albeit quieter, boom in writing *about* autobiographical literature. For much of its history, memoir was viewed by scholars, critics, and writers as a poor cousin to fiction, drama, poetry, and even biography. For many, memoir seemed too unimaginative, too self-involved, too tasteless, to merit serious attention. Writing in the *New Yorker*, Daniel Mendelsohn called the genre "the black sheep of the literary family," the "drunken guest at a wedding."[2] But these attitudes have shifted over the past few decades. Interest in autobiography has exploded in a range of academic disciplines, including literary studies, cultural studies, anthropology, history, and psychology, and courses in nonfiction have multiplied in MFA programs. The result has been a large number of critical studies, anthologies, practitioners' guides, and craft essays by writers.

You might think, then, that we have plenty enough written on this subject already, but I'm not so sure about that. Wannabe memoirists interested in learning how to write a memoir are well served by books like Brenda Miller and Suzanne Paola's *Tell It Slant*, Dinty W. Moore's *Crafting the Personal Essay*, Thomas Larson's *The Memoir and the Memoirist*, Mary Karr's *The Art of Memoir*, and Phillip Lopate's *To Show and to Tell*. A memoirist or reader who wants to understand the development of the genre over time and its various subtypes, distinctive devices, and characteristic preoccupations can get a lot out of two recent accessible guides to those subjects—Ben Yagoda's *Memoir: A History* and G. Thomas Couser's *Memoir: An Introduction*—along with the many scholarly articles and monographs available. And those who want to understand and evaluate particular memoirs and essays have a raft of critical books and reviews to choose from.

But there are important and intriguing questions about memoir and the writing of memoir that don't get treated, or treated much, in any of these kinds of books. The questions I have in mind are philosophical, rather than primarily practical, historical, descriptive, or evaluative. A brief tour of the main contents of the book you're reading now will give you a sense of what I mean by that.

One philosophical question concerns what memoir is, exactly, and, relatedly, what distinguishes it from other forms of literature. A natural way of contrasting memoir and personal essays with novels and short stories is to claim that the former are nonfiction and the latter are fiction. But that turns out to be a controversial suggestion. Some have argued that, because there's no such thing as a unified and stable self to write about, or because memory is highly fallible, or because all narratives are constructions, all memoir is really just another branch of fiction. Are they right? Moreover, what's at stake in answering this question? Why does it matter how we class things in the literary realm?

A further philosophical question concerns the role of truth in memoir. If memoir is different from fiction (I'll be arguing that it is), that'll be because it succeeds at making true rather than false claims about the self and the world. But what kind of truth are we talking about here, and why should a memoirist aim for it? Goethe wrote: "Truth belongs to all written accounts of one's life, either in relation to matters of fact or in relation to the feeling of the autobiographer, and God willing in relation to both."[3] That's an admission that the factual truth and what's often called the "emotional truth" may sometimes diverge. When they do, which should the memoirist go with? A further question relates to the possibility that Goethe ignores: it's open to memoirists to fudge both the facts and their feelings. So why shouldn't they? What's the source of this alleged truth-telling obligation we place on memoirists anyway?

Another set of philosophical questions centers on memoirists' ethical obligations not to their readers but to their subjects. It's almost impossible to write memoir without including sensitive personal material about your family, friends, lovers, colleagues, or acquaintances. Some argue that the moral obligation to tell the truth, the moral right to free expression, the value of assisting others through your story, or the aesthetic commitment to creating a full and compelling narrative are all that matter here. But it's hard to sustain that hard-line view in light of the very real possibility of injuring loved (or hated) ones by writing about them. We might also wonder whether memoirists have responsibilities to *themselves* not to write about certain subjects, or about certain subjects in certain ways. What are the ethical constraints on what writers do in these areas, and how should they be balanced against writers' other more literary aims?

Finally, there's the classic, all-purpose philosophical question: why even bother? Writing a good memoir is difficult, exhausting, and time-consuming, and in many ways still a misunderstood and disrespected endeavor. Why would anyone do it? Or, to put it more philosophically, are there any *good* reasons for doing it—as William Gass asks, "any motives for the enterprise that aren't tainted with conceit or a desire for revenge or a wish for justification? To halo a sinner's head? To puff an ego already inflated past safety?"[4]

These questions are philosophical, in the sense that they don't concern how to write or read memoir, but how to understand what it is that you're doing when you do those things. They ask, not "is this true?" but "what would it mean for this to be true?" Not "what am I writing?" but "why am I writing it?" Not only "does this constitute betrayal?" but also "if it does, what are the implications of that for what I should do?"

Doing philosophy *of* memoir in this way is different from doing philosophy *in* memoir.[5] Unlike the latter, it doesn't involve analyzing the metaphysical, epistemic, or ethical themes that authors treat in particular works. It doesn't ask, for instance, "What's Augustine's theory of time?" in his *Confessions*, "Should Rousseau have packed his kids off to the orphanage?" as he describes in his, or "What can we draw from Thoreau's *Walden* about a life well lived?" Philosophy *of* memoir involves analyzing the conceptual issues that are raised, not just by one memoir, but by all memoirs, by their very nature.

Someone looking for developed and accessible answers to these questions in the existing literature on memoir won't have much luck. Despite the recent trend toward life writing in other academic disciplines, philosophers of literature have written very little about memoir.[6] Memoirists and scholars in literary studies and related disciplines have ventured into this territory more often, but, because their priorities and backgrounds are nonphilosophical, not generally at great length or in great depth—and not in a way that's easily available to a nonacademic audience.[7]

I'm a philosophy professor as well as a memoirist, so it's maybe no surprise that I feel the force of these questions intensely. The meta mode is the default mode in my day job, so when I write about my own life after hours, I often find myself wondering about the assumptions that underlie the activity I'm engaging in. But I'm not alone in finding the neglected issues I'm raising here perplexing and urgent. I've gathered from conversations with memoirists at creative writing workshops that the same questions come up regularly in their own work and classes, and that a compact, comprehensive, and clear discussion of them by a philosopher with an active involvement in creative writing and a good working knowledge of memoir would be helpful. Since that book didn't exist, but I did, I decided to write it.

This book, the result, is mainly aimed at writers, teachers, students, and critics of memoir, as well as those who love to read memoirs. There's a lot of philosophy in it, but it requires no previous knowledge of philosophy. I've avoided the more abstract and technical issues that are likely to interest mainly my philosopher colleagues, to focus instead on the kinds of questions that are of active interest to memoirists and essayists as they write. (This has produced an idiosyncratic picture of the philosophical landscape in places, but I think the gain in clarity and digestibility is worth it. The notes at the end point to further reading for those interested in more scope and detail.) And I've tried to show throughout how the questions that I treat intersect with many classic and contemporary memoirs that readers will know and love.

It's also my hope that even those who aren't (yet) particularly interested in memoir may get something out of this book. When it comes down to it, memoir is just a particularly extended, articulate, and well-crafted version of a semi-universal human practice. We humans are a storytelling species, and most of us tell and listen to personal narratives every day of our lives. So even those who don't write down their life stories or read those of others are likely to relate to much of what I write here.

I didn't realize until finishing this book that, though it isn't itself a memoir, it falls into one of the classic subgenres of the form. What's known as the "apologia" is a defense of the author's past conduct against criticism and challenge. The memoirs of politicians often fall into this category, as do memoirs, like Jean-Jacques Rousseau's, that are initially presented as "confessions" but end up adopting a self-justifying tone.

This book, it turns out, is an apologia for memoir itself, and, by extension, for individual memoirists. Each of the chapters can be read as responding to a common set of criticisms that have been lobbed at memoirists over the centuries: that their enterprise is naive, foolhardy, and quixotic; that they're liars and cheats; that they would throw their mothers and ex-lovers under the bus for fame and fortune; that they're narcissists and exhibitionists; that their artistry is facile and fake. I love memoir and don't accept these charges against memoirists as a group. But showing them to be unfounded takes a lot of philosophical work. I've done it for the genre, and I've done it for myself—and if you write or read memoir, I've done it for you, too.

The Definition of Memoir

To get a better grip on the subject, we need to have an idea of what the term "memoir" means. The rest of this introduction will narrow in on that question, which is more complex and controversial than you might think.

If asked what a memoir is, most of us would probably come up with something like this: memoir is a nonfiction prose narrative, written in the first person, by oneself about one's past experience. That definition isn't bad: it includes most of the canonical examples of the form. But it needs correction and elaboration to adequately cover the full ground.

Let's take the corrections first. For one, a memoir doesn't need to be written (exclusively) in prose. Wordsworth's *Prelude*, which traces the development of its author's personality and worldview, is an autobiographical narrative written in verse, and feels distinctively memoirish. So does Kristen Radtke's *Imagine Wanting Only This*, though, as a graphic memoir, it consists as much of images as words.

Nor does a memoir need to be narrative, at least in the sense of including an extended, event-filled plot line. Some memoirs (as discussed below) are primarily meditative rather than action oriented.

And while memoirs are generally written in the first person, that hardly seems crucial. *The Education of Henry Adams*, authored by Henry Adams himself, is in the third person. And there's recently been a trend of memoirs written wholly or partly in the second person, including Carmen Maria Machado's book-length *In the Dream House*, alongside many personal essays.

What does seem closer to being central is that a memoir is a non-fiction account of the author's own past life. But those features require qualification and spelling out.

Memoirs undoubtedly examine *the author's singular life*, rather than exclusively the life of another (that's biography) or the lives of many (that's history). But the boundaries between memoir, biography, and history are porous. Many memoirs treat other individuals in as much detail as the author. Edmund Gosse's classic *Father and Son*, for instance, is an extended portrait of his father and their relationship. Other memoirs delve deeply into the social and historical context in which the author lived. Sarah Broom's *The Yellow House* weaves together the lives of several generations of her family with the broader story of Black New Orleans, up to and through Hurricane Katrina. And in hybrid memoirs—which merge personal history with, say, literary criticism, philosophy, biography, or travelogue—the explicit focus might be on an inanimate or abstract object, with the author and the author's personal life largely a vehicle and occasion for the ride. In *To the River*, Olivia Laing explores the cultural history of the river Virginia Woolf drowned in, as she walks down it; in *Lonely City*, she combines meditations on the concept of loneliness with biographical material on a set of twentieth-century outsider artists who lived and worked in New York City, as she winters in it. We see the river and the city through Laing's eyes, and get snippets of the events that led her to these places, but much of her personal history and activities remain opaque to us.

What makes such books memoirs is that they nonetheless consistently filter facts about other characters and external events and objects through the author's own consciousness and use them to reveal aspects of the author's self. We get an intensely personal, subjective picture: even when the author-protagonist is ostensibly in the background, their presence is insistent. And, as Roy Pascal writes, "All these objective identities, these other people, become forces within the writer and are referred back, implicitly more than explicitly, to the writer, whom their impact shapes and who develops in subtle response to them."[8] When an interviewer suggested to Broom that she was "selfless" for devoting the first quarter of *The Yellow House* to a time before her birth, Broom resisted, replying: "I needed to establish how people thought about home and place and their relationship to New Orleans, and why they made the choices they did. Their story is, in fact, my story."[9] And it's Laing's persistent emphasis on her own evolving reactions to the topics she treats, and their relationship to her personal history, that makes her books memoir rather than simply history, criticism, or biography (albeit maybe a limiting case).

Similarly, while it's true that memoirs necessarily treat the *past*, they also treat the present (the time of writing). This is so not just in the obvious sense that some memoirs discuss events and relationships that are recent and ongoing or include sections resembling current self-portraits. The deeper point is that all memoirs, to a greater or lesser extent, incorporate the contemporary perspective of the author: what Virginia Woolf called the "I now" alongside the "I then."[10] A narrative memoir often switches back and forth between narration in what Sue Silverman terms "the voice of innocence" (expressing what the author felt at the time) and commentary in "the voice of experience" (expressing what the author feels now about what happened at the time).[11] Memoirs aren't so much about the past, then, as retrospective: they include both the past and the person looking back at it.

A memoir is an *account* of the past, yes, but not in the sense of a mere chronicle (a "factual written account of important or historical events in the order of their occurrence" as the *New Oxford American Dictionary* puts it). Memoirists are out not just to record the past, but also to evoke and interpret it. Their work requires shaping the raw material of their experience into a coherent and engaging form that allows for both of those things. This often means breaking from linear chronology and always means using creative and imaginative language. It's this shaped quality, along with its retrospective nature, that distinguishes memoir from a diary, which is written on the fly, in a scrappy, disunified, and often artless way.

A trickier criterion is the claim that a memoir is a *nonfiction* account. We'll be discussing the giant can of metaphysical worms that claim opens up in the following chapter. Here I'll just make a brief but important point. To call a memoir "nonfiction" isn't to claim that everything (or, arguably, anything) written in it is true. Instead it's to claim that the author *presents* its contents as true. The memoirist may be mistaken or lying about everything addressed in the book. But, in calling it a memoir, they're entering into what Philippe Lejeune calls an "autobiographical pact" with their audience.[12] They're committing themself publicly to the claim that they've made a sincere attempt to tell the truth, to the best of their ability.

The entering into of this pact is what distinguishes memoirs from autobiographical novels, which include substantial material closely reflecting the author's life. Such books remain novels rather than memoirs not because they contain less truth, but because their authors, by calling them novels, have declined to commit themselves publicly to the claim that they and their protagonists are the same people. (I go into some reasons for this decision in chapter 2.)

How do we work out whether an author has signed an autobiographical pact or not? If the author explicitly calls their work fiction, that's a clear sign that they haven't. But many writers have written mock memoirs: novels or stories in which the fictional narrator claims to offer a truthful account of their actual experience. (*Robinson Crusoe*, *Jane Eyre*, and *The Adventures of Sherlock Homes* are examples.) Looking at the text alone, it's often impossible for a reader to distinguish such a thing from an actual memoir. Is it, or isn't it? Lejeune suggests that we solve this taxonomical problem not by stalking the author in real life to ask them, but simply by referring to the title page of the book. If the author listed on that page shares an identical name with the narrator and protagonist in the rest of the text, he claims, we have in our hands an autobiography (unless a subtitle announcing "a novel" or "a fiction" is present), though it may well be a faked one. If the author has a different name, we have something else.

All of the above is true of memoirs in general, but it doesn't yet get at some crucial features of contemporary memoir. To understand those, it'll help now to distinguish between three broad types of autobiographical writing.

One, which I'll call "autobiography," is a full-life narrative, recounted in strict chronological order, focused on external events, and written, often, by an author who's already established a public reputation (usually in politics, war, business, the arts, or entertainment.) Autobiographies can't cover an entire life, of course—only your biographer can do that, after your death—but they attempt to capture the large majority of its progress so far, starting at the author's birth.

Although autobiographies continue to sell well, they aren't popular among literary memoirists these days. One reason is that the form is felt to express a dated and unappealing outlook and sensibility. The autobiographer is associated with the "great man" (traditionally, autobiographers were usually male) who thinks of himself as the powerful agent of his destiny. The reason his story is so linear—a series of billiard balls moving forcefully into the future—is that he himself is at the cue, setting them decisively and tidily rolling. Many of us today can't stomach the arrogance, unearned certainty, and implicit sexism built into that picture.

Another reason contemporary memoirists tend to criticize and avoid autobiography is that it's seen as a relatively unreflective and reticent form. The writer's focus on recounting public actions and events leaves little room for either in-depth interpretation of those things or for a fleshed-out treatment of private life. (This is what Virginia Woolf had in mind when she complained that the problem with most memoirs of her time was that "they leave out the person to whom things happened."[13]) The author is often concerned with presenting themself in a positive light, justifying their decisions and explaining away their mistakes, and therefore keeps clear of more vulnerable moments, searching psychological analysis, or deep insight. Autobiographies also often stay at a high level of generality, tending toward summary rather than detailed and lifelike scenes. All in all, the autobiography leans too close to the chronicle or the argument, aiming more for documentation and self-justification than art.

A second type of autobiographical writing, which I'll call "modern memoir," aims to avoid these problems. A modern memoir is a selective, not necessarily linear, account, focused on the inner life of, often, a nonpublic figure. Rather than aiming for comprehensiveness, it narrows in on a particular aspect of the author's experience: a relatively short time period, specific event, or select theme. Modern memoirs are structurally more experimental than autobiographies, more likely to move back and forth in time. They're centrally interested in exploring the interiority of the author, and often the author's private life and intimate relationships, and they aim for an engaging, conversational voice imbued with (some aspect of) the author's personality. They privilege rumination on the meaning of experiences, and memory itself (not merely things remembered) is often part of their subject. When it comes to events, modern memoirists are ultimately focused less on "what?" than on "who?" and "why?" but when they do treat events, they aim for specificity over generality and vivid drama over summary. And they're open to a broader range of authors: you don't need to have done anything impressive to justify writing a modern memoir, other than having lived an ordinary human life. Memoirists like to locate large significance in apparently small things.

As far as general outlook goes, modern memoirists tend to be more uncertain in their pronouncements than autobiographers and humbler in their self-presentation (on the page, anyway). They're more comfortable with ambiguity and unanswered questions, and when questioning they like to go deep. Many of them aim to show fundamental change or a gain in insight in the protagonist as their narrative develops, in contrast to the more static picture of the personality and worldview offered in autobiography.

A third type of autobiographical writing is the personal essay.[14] Like modern memoirs, and unlike autobiography, personal essays are selective, often nonlinear, persistently personal and reflective and open to the nonfamous. They differ, most obviously, in being much shorter and therefore devoted to an even slimmer piece of life. They're also less likely to have a strong narrative focus than either of the other two forms. (Montaigne, the progenitor of the essay as we know it, wrote "there is nothing so contrary to my style as an extended narration."[15]) Essays always involve a steady progression, an adventure of sorts, but the plot is often the development of the author's ideas or the rounding out of a complex self-portrait, rather than the recounting of a series of actions. In Edward Hoagland's words: "Essays . . . hang somewhere on a line between two sturdy poles: this is what I think, and this is what I am."[16] Some modern memoirists have taken the writing workshop dictum "show, don't tell" overly to heart, treating ideas, in William Gass's phrase, "like a cockroach in a picnic basket"[17] and skimping on the genre's intellectual possibilities. Essayists are less likely to do that.

Maybe because of their lesser narrative orientation, of the three forms of autobiographical writing that I've distinguished here, essays are the least likely to focus on the past. While some retrospection is necessary if they're to be included in the broader memoir camp, they may mainly be concerned with the author's present and future.

Personal essays are closer to autobiography than modern memoir in the one sense that many of them are less insistently focused on the self, at least on the surface. They often turn the bulk of their explicit attention to other persons, events, artworks, or ideas. Even when they do this, though, they remain instances of autobiographical writing, either because the author's personality is vividly present in the voice used to discuss these external subjects (unlike in the case of formal, impersonal, expository essays) or because the aim of the discussion is in part to explore and convey that personality. Often both.

It's difficult to draw a firm line between these three types of autobiographical writing. The boundaries between them have always been fuzzy. (For instance, some linear full-life narratives told by public figures have involved substantial personal reflection. In fact, that's strongly true of the two most influential works in the history of literary personal narration—Augustine's and Rousseau's *Confessions*—which, to that extent, have more in common with modern memoirs than autobiographies.) And the boundaries have arguably been getting fuzzier, if anything, over time. We've recently been experiencing both what David Lazar calls a "memoirization" of the essay (an uptick in autobiographical content, scenes, and dialogue in short idea-oriented, pieces) and an "essayification" of the memoir (an increase in philosophizing in long-form personal narratives).[18]

Not only are the three forms I've outlined above difficult to disentangle, but there are other forms of autobiographical and auto-biographical-ish writing that also share several of their features. Within the broader category of "literary nonfiction," we can point to "immersive" or "New" journalism (think Truman Capote, Hunter S. Thompson, Joan Didion), literary-clinical case studies that highlight the author's perspective (think Oliver Sacks), autoethnography (in academic anthropology), and particularly personal forms of travelogue, celebrity profile, art or social criticism and food or nature writing. And within the broader category of "self–life writing" (which somewhat overlaps), we can point to diaries, journals, letters, blogs, reminiscences, and interviews, among other things. None of these forms satisfy all the criteria I've listed above, but some of them satisfy some of them, and they sometimes make guest appearances within the sorts of texts I've been discussing.

This three-way distinction, then, doesn't rigidly and exhaustively divide up the terrain. What it's useful for is indicating the center of gravity of this book. In what follows I'm interested in modern memoirs and personal essays rather than autobiographies, and the closer that other forms of writing (including autobiographies) approach those two ideal types, the more interested I am in them.

For the sake of concision, I won't be too particular from now on about which terms I use. I'll treat "memoir" and "autobiography" as synonyms in the rest of this book, and use "memoir" to refer to both book-length works (the standard usage) and short-form mini-memoirs, in the form of personal essays. Other theorists use these terms in different ways, but I hope that what I've said here will make clear enough what I have in mind.

Memoir as Literature

One final clarification before we move on to the heart of the book. A natural thought is that a further feature distinguishing modern memoirs and personal essays from autobiographies is the fact that they're more literary. Nabokov expressed this view with characteristic force and snobbishness in 1950. When the publisher of his forthcoming memoir *Speak, Memory* warned him that the book would be competing with "the abnormally large number of memoirs and autobiographies" coming out that Christmas, Nabokov replied: "a profusion of memoirs and autobiographies by generals, politicians, musicians, rat-catchers, farmers etc. can hardly have any bearing on the sales of my book, since it is primarily a work of literature and the fact of its being an autobiography is really quite inessential."[19]

Similarly, it's natural to suspect that what divides the specific examples of memoir that critics tend to focus on (say, Jean-Paul Sartre's *Words*) from those that they don't tend to focus on (say, Jill Langham's *How I Became the Dancing Queen of Palm Springs: A Memoire of Body, Mind and Spirit Transformation*) is the superior literary quality of the former.

That distinction is certainly at work in this book. I don't have a problem with nonliterary memoirs per se. (That book by Jill Langham is on my bookshelf—though admittedly because someone gave it to me.) But I'll be focusing my attention here on the subset of memoirs that I think count as literature.

What's the basis of, and rationale for, this classification? What does it mean to call a memoir "literary," and why should we find literary memoirs especially interesting?

Defining "literature" is even harder than defining "memoir." We can all point to uncontroversial examples of literary and nonliterary objects (Shakespeare's plays vs. the telephone directory or a tree), but most of us would struggle to specify the criteria driving our selections. A literary work has to be written, in a language that someone other than the author can understand. (That rules out the tree, as well as the gobbledygook your toddler wrote in crayons on the wall last week.) But it's very hard to pin down what makes something literature not just in the broad sense of a written text (the telephone directory) but in the narrower sense of art (Shakespeare).

Literary theorists have proposed many different accounts of what the characteristic features and functions of literature-understood-as-art are. They take one of two broad tacks. Those known as essentialists aim to identify a set of features—say, of style or content—internal to written texts that mark them (and only them) out as literary works.[20] The difficulty with this approach is that the features pointed to are often either too narrow or too broad in scope (sometimes, in different ways, both) to cover all the examples we intuitively want to include.

Some people are tempted to claim, for instance, that genuinely literary works are fictional. But that doesn't cover the whole category of what's known as "creative nonfiction" or much poetry. And it does cover fictions that don't seem to count as art (for instance, jokes or philosophical thought experiments). Others single out "fine writing" as the crucial feature: eloquent, poetic phrasing that departs from ordinary speech in including distinctive sonic or musical effects, complex syntax, and figurative language. But that excludes Carver- and Hemingway-esque prose that uses short, direct, apparently artless sentences, and doesn't go in for many (at least surface) metaphors. Writing like that can be very well done, in the sense of carefully crafted and effective, without being eloquent. (It's worth noting here that even poetry doesn't necessarily use "poetic" language: prose poems can be, you know, prosaic.) The "fine writing" criterion also throws part of its net too wide: some examples of history, philosophy, and science writing are eloquent and metaphorical, but fail to count, intuitively, as literature. Essentialist claims that literature is distinctively creative, imaginative, complex, layered, or deep fail for the same reason.

Those known as antiessentialists argue that this whole approach is doomed. There's no feature internal to a literary work that makes it count as literature, they claim. Instead, what makes a work literary is a matter of external or relational factors. The most influential approach in this camp is the institutional theory of art first advocated by Arthur Danto.[21] Danto argued that it's possible for there to be no perceptible difference between a work of art and an object that isn't art. Take, for instance, Marcel Duchamp's infamous art installation of 1917. Duchamp found a porcelain urinal somewhere in Paris, signed it, and submitted it to an art exhibition with the title *Fountain*. This urinal looked no different from a urinal you might have found in a public toilet at the time, but it's viewed by art historians as one of the most significant landmarks of twentieth-century art. When placed in a gallery setting, those historians argue, this plain urinal gained symbolic and conceptual meaning that elevated it into an art object.

How? The basic idea is that when an object is set in the context of an ongoing institution or practice (in this case, the "artworld") it can direct our attention in a novel way. When a piece is presented as art, we, the audience, are encouraged to consider it with a particular and intense kind of attitude—one that looks below the surface for nonobvious aesthetic, intellectual, or ethical qualities—that we've become accustomed to employing with other objects in the artworld.

On this account, a work of literature is a written text that's intended by its author to produce certain valuable responses in an audience that adopts a certain set of reading techniques in responding to the work.[22] A written text *isn't* a work of literature when it isn't intended to produce the relevant valuable responses. And a written text is a *bad* work of literature when it tries, but fails, to produce the relevant valuable responses for those who adopt the relevant techniques. A good literary work both invites literary attention and rewards it.

The debate between essentialists and antiessentialists is complex, and I can't hope to resolve it here. Thankfully, I don't need to. Both types of account justify singling out certain texts as literary and certain others as not (and they'll often converge on roughly the same examples). Moreover, both types of account justify including memoir within the general category of literature.

Some have doubted that memoir counts as literary, because it shares some central features with instances of what we think of as nonliterary prose: life writing that's mainly scholarly, documentary, or therapeutic. But many examples of memoir clearly satisfy the criteria singled out by both essentialist and antiessentialist approaches to literature. Memoir can be daringly original, subtly crafted, linguistically inventive, beautiful, symbolic, true to life, emotionally moving, psychologically insightful, intellectually profound, morally serious, visionary, and enduring in relevance—to list just some of the features that essentialists have pointed to as necessary or sufficient for literary value. And much memoir is intended by its authors to evoke certain characteristic responses in an informed audience within the context of an ongoing social practice of aesthetic engagement. It's memoirs that satisfy the criteria of one or other of these types of accounts that I want to focus on here.

But why, you might wonder? What's so special about literature, anyway? One reason for my focus on literary memoirs is that I'm a literature lover, and these are the memoirs that I love. The other reason is that I'm a philosopher, and literary memoir raises some especially interesting philosophical questions.

While each of the following chapters can be read independently, they share a through line, captured in the title of the book. The central dilemma of memoir, from a philosophical perspective, is this: is it possible to genuinely aim at representing the truth while also engaging in the imaginative invention we associate with art?

Critics of memoir as a genre argue no. Some claim that memoir is all artless truth. The writer Aleksandar Hemon, for instance, has diagnosed the present memoir boom as "a crisis of the imagination."[23] Others claim that memoir is all truthless art. They're likely to endorse André Maurois's assertion that "Memory is a great artist. For every man and for every woman it makes the recollection of his or her life a work of art and an unfaithful record."[24]

This book is founded on the idea, and the hope, that truth and art are less antagonistic in this genre than critics like this claim. But they raise serious and important questions: the tension between art and truth is real in memoir, as the following chapters will attest. The consolation is that the same tension is also a major part of memoir's charm. The writer and reader of memoir are out not merely for truth, nor merely for art, but for artful truths. It's that sly conjunction that makes the endeavor both the philosophical minefield and the rich source of pleasure and insight that it is.

TWO

Is All Memoir
Really Fiction?

Defining memoir isn't straightforward, as the previous chapter showed. But one thing memoir clearly *isn't* is fiction, right? Novels and short stories are one thing, memoirs and personal essays are another, and the key reason why is that the former are fiction and the latter are nonfiction. To drag this suggestion out: if something's nonfiction, it's not fiction, and if something's fiction, it's not nonfiction. So at least we've got that.

Well, maybe not. The boundary between fiction and nonfiction, as the terms are used in practice, is more controversial than a glance at the words themselves would suggest. Many people—general readers as well as literary theorists—have argued that much of what we refer to as nonfiction contains a large amount of what we might well call fiction (and vice versa). The less ambitious version of this claim states that *some* memoirs *happen to* contain *some* fictional elements. For instance, the fiction writer Sherwood Anderson persisted in referring to his grandmother in his memoirs as Italian, even after finding out she wasn't. ("But she was German," his brother Karl protested. "And so she was maybe to you," Anderson replied. "If you prefer that your own grandmother be an old German, all right. Shall a man who has spent all of his life creating people not have the privilege of creating his grandmother?"[1]) The more ambitious and controversial claim is that *all* memoirs *necessarily* contain a *very large* amount of fiction, to the point that we might as well admit that memoir, as a genre, just is fiction.

When people state that all memoir is really fiction, they're often not just making a descriptive claim, or suggesting, in a neutral way, that we tidy up our terminology. Instead they present the assertion as a major criticism of the genre. Memoir, by its nature, purports to be nonfiction: a good-faith attempt at a factual record of the actual experience of real human beings. That connection to the real world, rather than to a made-up world, is a core part of what memoir claims to be up to. But memoir can't succeed in its nonfictional ambitions, the challenge goes, so it's set up to fail: to write a memoir is to aim at a goal that's impossible to reach.

We can call this the "fictionalist" challenge to memoir. Why might someone make it? There are many answers to that question, connecting to fundamental debates in metaphysics (the theory of what is ultimately real), epistemology (the theory of knowledge), and aesthetics (the philosophy of art). This chapter will look at fictionalist arguments relating to each of those three areas in turn, consider some responses to them, and assess what remains of the challenge at the end.

Metaphysics: What Self?

I guess I won't send that note now, for the mind is such a new place, last night feels obsolete.

EMILY DICKINSON[2]

Though memoirs vary in the emphasis they place on the author, it's safe to say that the author's self—its nature and development over time—is always *a* theme in a memoir, and very often the central one. In her classic guide to the genre, *The Situation and the Story*, Vivian Gornick writes: "The question clearly being asked in an exemplary memoir is 'Who Am I?'"[3] The search to answer that question, to understand who and what one has become, provides much of the motivation for and content of such canonical works as Augustine's *Confessions*, Malcolm X's *Autobiography*, Simone de Beauvoir's *Memoirs of a Dutiful Daughter*, and Gornick's own *Fierce Attachments*.

Given this self-oriented bent, it looks like a fundamental and central assumption of memoir is that the author's self is a real thing that extends over a considerable portion of time. (At the very least, from the beginning of the events recounted in the book to the completion of the writing of the book.) Memoirists and their readers standardly assume—generally without bothering to think about it—that the character referred to as "I" at the beginning of the book is essentially the same character referred to as "I" throughout and at the end of it (even if the character's nonessential properties — say, the color of their hair, their job, many of their beliefs and desires — change along the way). Because memoirists and readers also standardly assume that that "I-character" refers to a real person, existing out in the world at the time of writing, they seem to assume the same thing of the real person referred to. In short, memoirists and readers appear to assume that the memoirist has a stable self that persists over time, and of which this book or essay is the true (or attempted-true) written account.

The metaphysical version of the fictionalist challenge denies that assumption. A very radical and sweeping version of this denial is the claim that there is no real world, period. We'll get to that (briefly) below, but will start at the somewhat shallower end of the pool. The less radical challenge claims that, regardless of what we say about the world in general, there's certainly no such thing as a unified and stable self. Because memoirists aim, apparently, to tell the story of such a self, their story can't possibly be true. All memoirs are fictions precisely because the things at their heart — singular and enduring selves — are fictions too.

This line is often associated with postmodern literary theory: the work of, say, Derrida, Barthes, Foucault, and Lacan. You can certainly find it there, but the underlying philosophical claim — the denial of a unitary and persisting self — wasn't invented in mid-twentieth-century France.[4] It's a core part of most strains of Buddhism, reaching back to the sixth century BC, and of the thought of Hume in the eighteenth century and Nietzsche in the nineteenth. In the Western tradition, these thinkers are arguing against a very old picture of the self that we owe originally to Plato. In the *Phaedo*, Socrates argues that each of us has a *psyche*, an invariant and eternal essence that preexists our bodies and survives their change and decay. It's this psyche that ensures unity among the various sensations, perceptions, memories, ideas, and emotions that we experience at any moment and continuity as those various experiences pass. It constitutes us as coherent, stable individuals, internally integrated and distinct from other objects and persons around us. And beyond giving us that everyday existential assurance, it grounds some of the things that matter most deeply to us in life: our sense of ourselves and others as autonomous beings with long-term commitments, projects, and relationships, who are morally responsible for our actions, and who can survive major physical and psychological changes while alive, as well as possibly our own deaths.

The Platonic idea that humans possess a freestanding, persisting essence became central to the Jewish and Christian doctrines of the soul and gained a new twist in the thought of René Descartes in the seventeenth century. The Cartesian innovation was to abandon talk of the soul and locate this essential self in the mind. "I know that I exist," Descartes wrote in 1641, "The question is, what is this 'I' that I know?"[5] His answer, summed up in that famous catchphrase of his, was that the "I" was an immaterial substance whose essence is thinking.

The Platonic-Judeo-Christian-Cartesian model of the transcendent ego began to take a beating with the rise of materialism in the eighteenth century. Enlightenment scientists and philosophers increasingly argued that all that exists is matter: no room here for mysterious nonextended substances, whether understood as *psyches*, souls, or minds. With this development, the problem of how to account for the unity of the self, both at any given moment and across time, became acute. The ancient philosopher Plotinus had warned of this in the third century AD. Because it's in the nature of matter to be divisible, he argued, if the human body were only matter, it'd be made up of a multiplicity of souls, including "say, a soul of the finger."[6] Without a unifying immaterial soul-substance, he wrote, human lives would be "meaningless."

John Locke tried to solve the problem by arguing that a unified and persisting self didn't require an immaterial essence, but could be provided by a complex of relations between purely material parts.[7] Locke agreed with Descartes that what's essential to us is our minds, but he saw those minds not as indivisible substances, but as composed of a multiplicity of individual mental states ultimately reducible to physical stuff. What makes these states those of a single person—you—both at a time and over time, Locke argued, is that they're nonetheless connected to each other in a special manner. Your mental states interact with each other in ways that they don't with my mental states. In particular, you have memories right now of sensations, perceptions, and emotions you had in the past. You remember that sunny day in 1992 when you frolicked with your dog Zippy in the

Pacific Ocean, and I don't. That's what holds you together over time and distinguishes you from me.

This emphasis on psychological connectedness, whether in the form of memory or other casual connections between mental states, has been the dominant view of the self in Western philosophy ever since. It's unclear, though, that it really solves the problem that Plotinus warned us about. Locke's view seems to imply, for instance, that our selves go out of existence whenever we fall asleep (since the crucial unifying connection of memory is inactive while you're sleeping). It also seems to imply that if you can't remember your childhood, whatever happened back then happened to someone else, not you. Comforting for some of us in the local case, maybe, but at a more general level, unsettling.

Philosophers in Locke's time and since have offered many different variants of the psychological continuity view that avoid these particular objections. But the basic problem with all of them is the same. Much of our mental life is so complex and transient that pointing to partial and temporary connections between particular bits of it can't guarantee the more robustly unified and extended sense of self that most of us both assume we have and desperately want to retain.

To bring the above brief history up to the present century, Galen Strawson has argued that, at most, the self lasts for a few seconds.[8] In order for a self to be appropriately unified, he suggests, it has to be graspable introspectively all at once. But we only have this kind of unified experience for up to three seconds. On Strawson's "Pearl view," then, what we think of as a single self is really a succession of very many selves, succeeding each other, one at a time, like pearls on a string. This picture is so extraordinarily distant from our usual understanding of the self that, though it does claim that selves are real, it sure *feels* like it doesn't. "I don't suppose the Pearl view will be much liked," Strawson writes.[9] Right.

One response here is to retreat to the transcendental ego model and posit a soul, but for many of us these days, as committed secular materialists, that's not a realistic option. So here's where we get the suggestion that the self is not a real thing, but a fiction. David Hume argued, a few decades after Locke, that when we attend to our inner life we never perceive the mind itself directly; all we find is a "bundle" of perceptions, one succeeding another:

For my part, when I enter most intimately into what I call *myself*, I always stumble on some particular perception or other, of heat or cold, light or shade, love or hatred, pain or pleasure. I can never catch *myself* at any time without a perception, and can never observe anything but the perception. When my perceptions are re-mov'd for any time, as by sound sleep; so long am I insensible of *myself*, and may truly be said not to exist.[10]

We might conceive of the mind as, in a sense, the "theater" in which these "actors" appear, Hume suggests, but we have no evidence of its independent existence: there "are the successive perceptions only, that constitute the mind; nor have we the most distant notion of the place, where these scenes are represented, or of the materials, of which it is compos'd." The idea that there's some kind of "simple and continu'd self" beyond and behind this flux of experience, Hume concluded, is best understood as an illusion. Friedrich Nietzsche argued for essentially the same view. There's no single dominant subject housed in each human body, he suggested, but instead "a plurality of subjects, whose interaction and struggle lie at the bottom of our thought and our consciousness in general." The idea that "several similar states [are] the effect of one substratum" is, again, merely a fiction.[11] We humans do think, of course—Descartes was right about that—but that thinking is merely a process, and one that doesn't require a thinker.

The claim that the self is a fiction doesn't imply that we should eliminate all thought and talk of it. The idea of the self might after all be a *useful* fiction, which is how Hume and many Buddhists see it.[12] An analogy helps here. Philosophers have argued that modern physics gives us no reason to believe that "middle-sized objects," like chairs, apples, or lions, are real in any ultimate sense. Instead they're reducible to force fields of atoms and empty space. If we want to be precise about carving nature at its joints—the traditional task of metaphysics—we should talk about those atoms and fields, then, not the clumsier categories that unscientific "folk physics" has given us. But for everyday purposes, we have little choice but to stick with the categories of folk physics. We humans have a major interest in recognizing and manipulating what we clumsily conceive of as middle-sized objects, and human cognitive equipment is bad at keeping track of individual atoms. So though it's false that chairs, apples, and lions are ultimately real, it's a helpful convention to adopt the fiction that they are. Similarly, though it's false that we each have a unified self that endures over a lifetime, human activities and interactions go much more smoothly when we adopt the fiction that we do have one. Technically, you're a force field of atoms too, one in constant flux. But if we both think of you that way, it's going to be hard to get this grocery run finished and persuade you to take your turn cooking dinner tonight.

Buddhists characteristically warn us that we shouldn't take this fiction too far, though. It's useful up to a point to pretend that we're more than an impermanent, impersonal series of multiple physical and mental parts. But if we invest too deeply in that picture and become overly attached to our persistence, frustration and despair will result. The enlightened human atom-aggregation wears its faux personhood lightly.

For many of us, the idea that the self is a *useful* fiction, rather than one we should ditch, might be marginally comforting, but remains very disturbing. It also just seems plain implausible. Our practice of treating ourselves and others as entities that persist over a lifetime doesn't feel like merely a helpful convention, but an absolutely basic feature of human life. We might be wrong about this—our feelings aren't a great guide to the ultimate reality of things across the board—but it's tempting to think that what's going wrong here isn't our naive views about our true nature, but the concept of the self that these no-self theorists are operating with. Mightn't there be an alternative understanding of what the self *is* that would line up better with our introspective sense that we each have a real and persisting one, while staying within the bounds of materialism?

One option here is to go for what's known as a "narrative" conception of the self. There are several variants, but the basic idea is that to be a self is to interpret your present experience in the context of an ongoing life narrative. A self, understood this way, doesn't view itself or its life as a mere succession of events, but as an unfolding story made up of projects, relationships, and activities that stretch back into the historical past and, imaginatively, into the future. Selfhood, in this sense, is strongly connected to choice and agency, the leading of a purposeful life over time. On some narrative approaches, selfhood requires a highly explicit and well-defined life story, actively organized around a unifying theme, goal, or canonical plot arc. But in the less demanding and more plausible versions, that isn't necessary: a rough, and roughly articulable, sense of the shape of your past and your hopes for the future that informs your sense of the significance of your current experiences will do the trick.[13]

The narrative view can seem confused. How can telling a narrative *make us* a self, when there pretty obviously needs to be a self in place already to tell the narrative in question? Narrative theorists reply by distinguishing between someone who's merely a conscious, experiencing subject and someone who's a person. All humans who are alive and not in a coma are the former, but becoming the latter is an achievement rather than a given. Children begin as merely centers of consciousness, but as they develop they're socialized into seeing their experiences in narrative terms, and—as a necessary part of that—themselves as individuals who continue over time. It's this narrative self-conception that permits them to lead their later lives as fully fledged agents, capable of planning and taking responsibility for their actions. As Marya Schechtman puts it: "Some, but not all, individuals weave stories of their lives, and it is their doing so that makes them persons."[14]

According to narrative theorists, it's this richer notion of a person, rather than of merely a passive experiencing subject, that most of us have in mind when referring to the "self." When people talk about their "personal identity," they point not to their bare capacity to experience or to think, but to exactly the sorts of historical experiences, ongoing commitments, and future plans that the narrative view highlights. Another welcome feature is that, on the narrative view, selves are less isolated and independent than they are on the Cartesian picture: full-blown selfhood emerges only in the company of other persons.

Although adopting the narrative conception certainly allows you to construe the self as a coherently integrated entity that persists over time—that's the whole point of it—it's less obvious that it allows for selves to be *real* entities. Narrativists may be right that we learn to see ourselves as unified and enduring selves as children, but seeing yourself as something and being that thing are, in principle, rather different.

Is the self real, then, on the narrative approach, or not? There's disagreement on this. Some argue that the self described by the narrative view is just as much a fiction as the self that appears in the views of Hume, Nietzsche, and the Buddha: a construction that we create to unify and organize our experience, but that reflects no ultimate reality. Others argue that, insofar as the narrative self is in fact constructed, it has a genuine existence. Waterslides, banknotes, and parties are constructed by humans too, this line goes, and we don't go around calling them "mere fictions."

This disagreement turns on a deeper dispute over what it means to say that something is real.[15] On one view, which we can call "minimal realism," all that's required for something to be real is that it exist. On another view, "robust realism," mere existence isn't enough. To be *really* real—to have reality in the fundamental sense—something has to exist objectively, not subjectively. What does "objective existence" amount to here? It means that the continued existence of the thing in question doesn't depend on human wishes or intentions.

Money is a nice example of something that satisfies the condition of minimal realism, but not robust realism. Money exists, for sure: there's likely some in your bank account right now. But money doesn't objectively exist, in the sense at issue here, because if we all collectively decided to abandon the money system, it would cease to be. The continued existence of money depends on our continuing to have a particular set of beliefs and intentions about what it means and how to use it. The same goes for state laws, nations, colleges, and marriages. Each of these things is a psychologically constructed entity: a thing that exists and has real consequences, but that is ultimately subjective, mind-dependent. It's the psychological aspect, not the mere fact of being constructed by humans, that's crucial for the distinction here. Waterslides are constructed by humans, but not psychologically constructed: we made them out of matter and can't simply wish them out of existence now that the job is done. According to robust realism, waterslides are therefore genuinely real, but money isn't.

The self on the narrative view looks more like money than a waterslide. The view implies that we would cease to have selves if we stopped thinking of ourselves as narrative beings. So whether or not you call the narrative self "real"—really real—depends on whether you're a minimal realist or a robust realist when it comes to metaphysics. Robust realists will note that the self posited by the narrative view doesn't objectively exist and therefore call it unreal. But it's open to minimal realists to argue that that self does exist, insofar as we create and use it from childhood on, and that that's real enough to count.

The same applies to the Hume-Nietzsche-Buddhist view that the self is a fiction. A fiction can't satisfy robust realism, but it might satisfy minimal realism. Literary characters, for instance, aren't robustly real: Heathcliff and Cathy depend fully on the workings of our minds. But Heathcliff and Cathy are arguably minimally real: they exist in a way that characters who haven't yet been made up don't. This means that the sharp contrast we tend to make in everyday language between fictional entities and real entities is contentious. For minimal realists, fictions can be real, provided they exist. Hume, Nietzsche, and Buddha certainly believe that the fiction of the self exists—Hume and Buddhists, at least, are inclined to celebrate that fact, given what a useful fiction it is. So it's open to us to read them as minimal realists about the self.

The aim of the above discussion wasn't to settle the question of what the self is and whether or not it's real. I've covered only three families of views on those questions, and each in nothing like the detail required for that purpose. Instead, the aim was to get enough of a grip on the ongoing metaphysical debate about the self to draw out its implications for the nature and viability of memoir as a genre. What can we say, now, about that?

It'll help at this point to lay out the metaphysical version of what I earlier called "the fictionalist challenge" as a more formal argument. As I understand it, the argument goes like this:

1. All memoirs centrally assume the existence of a unified and stable self.
2. There is no such thing as a unified and stable self.
3. If there is no such thing as a unified and stable self, the self is a fiction.
4. (Therefore) The self is a fiction.
5. (Therefore) All memoirs centrally assume the existence of a fiction.
6. (Therefore) All memoir is fiction.

Set aside for now the worry that the leap from claim 5 to claim 6 is pretty big. Sure, the existence of one fiction—even a central one—

might not be enough to make the whole genre fictional. But we're addressing the fictionalist challenge bit by bit in this chapter, and it may be that there are enough fictions in place by the end of it to collectively secure that sweeping conclusion. Claim 6 is there just to remind us where the overall challenge is meant to be heading.

The most straightforward option for those who want to defeat this version of the fictionalist challenge is to simply deny claim 2. Philip Lopate writes, in this vein, "I have long held the personal essay to be one of the last bastions of the orthodoxy of the unitary self: those of us who are drawn to practicing this form tend to believe in our possessing a core reality or self, and we would cling to this conviction even if critical theory disproved it beyond doubt."[16] One helpful thing we've learned above is that if you want to take this route and insist that human selves cohere and endure over a lifetime, you don't need to believe in the traditional immaterial soul or Cartesian ego (though you can if you want to). Instead, you can adopt the narrative conception of the self as something progressively developed, in a purely terrestrial way, in the course of human socialization. Moreover, if you endorse minimal realism, you can insist that this narrative self is genuinely real, despite being a psychological construction.

A less straightforward option is to point to an ambiguity in claim 5. One way of reading that claim is as saying that all memoirs centrally assume that something that isn't real is in fact real. If that were true, it would indeed seem that the stories told in memoirs were substantially false, and the conclusion that the genre was essentially fiction wouldn't be too far off. Another way of reading claim 5, though, is as saying that all memoirs assume that a fiction—a make-believe construction—exists. They assume, in other words, that the fiction of the self *is a thing*—an illusion or pretense that's an actual feature of our world (real, that is, in the minimal realist sense). If *that's* what claim 5 means, the conclusion of the argument doesn't follow. Memoir can be seen as telling the true, nonfictional story of our collective fiction of the self. Doing so doesn't involve implying that the fiction itself is true—that is, that there really is a unified and stable self behind the flux of human experience. So if it turns out that claim 2 is true and there isn't such a self, that fact alone won't transform memoir into fiction.

What would it mean for a memoirist to tell the true story of the fiction of the self? One way is to simply attempt to describe what it feels like, from the inside, to live a standard human life. Even if our inner lives are in fact just a bundle of perceptions, as Hume suggested, or a pearl string of selves, as Strawson suggests, it sure feels to many of us, from a first-person perspective, like we have greater unity and continuity than that. In recounting their story, the memoirist can claim to be accurately describing the phenomenology of human experience. They can remain neutral on whether or not that phenomenology tracks anything that's ultimately real (in other words, they can accept or reject claim 2 of the argument). Traditional memoirs can plausibly escape the charge of being fiction in this way.

An alternative way to tell the true story of the fiction of the self is to attempt to unmask—at least partially—the self *as* fiction in the course of the story. More experimental modernist and postmodernist memoirs can be interpreted as taking this route. In his memoir *Roland Barthes by Roland Barthes*, Roland (guess who?) Barthes dramatizes what he takes to be the fundamental discontinuity of human experience. The book eschews traditional chronology, narration, and thematic development, instead taking the form of a fragmentary autobiographical journal, made up of short entries and images about diverse and apparently disconnected subjects that resonate and repeat. The book also comments throughout on what Barthes takes to be the misguided metaphysics of standard autobiography. ("I do not say: 'I am going to describe myself' but 'I am writing a text, and I call it R.B.' I shift from imitation (from description) and entrust myself to nomination. Do I not know that, *in the field of the subject, there is no referent?*"[17]) The title implies that what Barthes is doing in this work is creating himself (in a sense) out of nothing, much as Hume and Nietzsche suggest each of us does off the page when fictionalizing ourselves a self. In both cases, all we really have is a fictional persona: as Barthes writes of his text, "It must all be considered as if spoken by a character in a novel."[18] Similarly, Goronwy Rees writes at the beginning of his memoir that "at no time in my life have I had that enviable sensation of constituting a continuous personality" and refers to the genre as "the art of creating a self which does not exist."[19] Mary McCarthy, who wrote two memoirs, suggested similarly: "It's absolutely useless to look for [the self], you won't find it, but it's possible in some sense to make it."[20]

A third and final option in responding to the fictionalist challenge is to deny claim 1, and argue that not all memoirs assume the existence of a unified and stable self—whether as a real feature of the world, a fact of first-person experience, or a useful collective fiction. Some memoirs depict the inner life, instead, as pervasively diffuse and erratic. (This strategy bleeds into the previous one, but differs in that it needn't depict or comment on our desperate attempts to create an artificial self out of the chaos.) The general picture is common in twentieth-century literature across the board. In Virginia Woolf's novels, characters are both intrapersonally discontinuous and interpersonally continuous. Not only do their inner lives fluctuate, but, Terry Eagleton suggests, they "tend to blur into each other, as feelings and sensations pass like vibrations from one individual to the next."[21] In Samuel Beckett's work, some characters have no distinctive individuality at all: Vladimir and Estragon are featureless and interchangeable with each other.

Though this picture of the fragmented self reaches its twentieth-century apex in the modernist novel and play, you can also find it in memoirs of the time, including those of a less self-consciously experimental character. In his autobiography, Malcolm X depicts his life as a series of stages, in each of which he has a different name or nickname: Malcolm Little, Homeboy, Detroit Red, Satan, Malcolm X, and El-Hajj Malik El-Shabazz. On looking back on these stages, he says: "I still marvel at how swiftly my previous life's thinking pattern slid away from me, like snow off a roof. It is as though someone else I knew of had lived by hustling and crime. I would be startled to catch myself thinking in a remote way of my earlier self as another person."[22] And in essays, the picture of the fluid, transient, and discontinuous self stretches back to the very beginning of the genre. Montaigne's mercurial self is in evidence both in individual pieces—he's the master of shape-shifting digression—and across the *Essays* as a collection. (He writes in one: "I do not portray being: I portray passing."[23]) You could say that Montaigne and Charles Lamb, in the similarly fluid *Essays of Elia*, were modernist or even postmodernist in this respect centuries before it was cool.

My view is that, given the multitude of promising options here, the metaphysical version of the fictionalist challenge fails. There's enough of a self out there in the world to satisfy all but a hard-line robust realist. And, even if you are a hard-line robust realist, there's enough flexibility in the genre of memoir to make the project of autobiography distinct from fiction.

Metaphysics: What World?

Although an essay may offer insights into the truths of human being, it will never yield the capital-t Truth, for the not-so-simple reason that no such entity exists.

NANCY MAIRS[24]

For some, the fictionalist claim that there's no stable and unified self sounds plausible, but also like it rather understates the matter. The fundamental problem with drawing a line between memoir and fiction, this more sweeping challenge asserts, isn't that the self isn't real, but that the whole world isn't real. More precisely, the world isn't robustly real: it doesn't exist objectively, independently of our minds and conceptual schemes. (This is a very radical view: if you consider it a nonstarter, you can safely skip this section and move on to the next.) The most famous exponent of this position is Bishop Berkeley, who published his theory of "subjective idealism" in 1710. If a tree falls in the forest and no one's there to hear it, does it make a sound? No, says Berkeley. Moreover, in such a case, there's not only no sound, but no tree, and no forest. "To be is to be perceived."[25]

This denial that the world objectively exists is sometimes phrased as a denial that truth (or "Truth") exists. I take it that's what memoirist Nancy Mairs is doing above. Why is the claim that there's no mind-independent world often equated with the claim that there's no such thing as truth? The connection is supplied by the most intuitive and popular account of what truth is, known as the "correspondence theory." This theory is traceable to Aristotle and was formalized in the early twentieth century by Bertrand Russell. The basic idea is that a belief or statement is true if, and only if, it corresponds to the facts: to the way things actually are. True beliefs or statements "mirror" the world. If that's what truth is, there pretty clearly needs to be a real world out there for the notion of truth to have any purchase. No real world, no real relation between beliefs and the world, no real truth.

The correspondence theory of truth and the realist theory of metaphysics that underlies it are associated with a principle known as "bi-valence." This states that every belief or sentence is either true or false. There's no murky middle ground, and no "true for me" and "true for you." Some beliefs or sentences may be vague or ambiguous, but once we really pin down what's being thought or said, there's an objective fact of the matter about whether or not they're true—period. Those, like Mairs, who suggest that there are "truths" but no "Truth" can be interpreted as rejecting bivalence.

It's relatively common to be an antirealist about a particular thing or domain of things, say, colors, numbers, fictional characters, or moral rightness and wrongness. It's much more unusual to be a *global* antirealist, of the Berkeley type—or a global antitruthist, of the Richard Rorty type. (Rorty referred to "philosophy professors who are seeking the truth, not just a story or a consensus but an honest-to-God, down-home, accurate representation of the way the world is" as "lovably old-fashioned prigs"; he also said that "the very idea of a 'fact of the matter' is one we would be better off without."[26]) Unlike these guys, the large majority of us believe that there are concrete things out there whose continued existence doesn't depend on our thoughts and intentions. And the large majority of us believe that our statements about those things are, objectively, either true or false: that is, we endorse bivalence. Responding to the antirealist strain in the culture, memoirist Mary Karr writes impatiently "someone either assaulted the woman in question, or not. It was binary."[27]

Why, then, do some feel tempted—when discussing the nature and viability of memoir, and elsewhere—to endorse global antirealism? One possibility in some cases is that they're confusing epistemic considerations with metaphysical ones. It's undeniable that the truth about the world and ourselves is hard to access (the next section of this chapter will be all about that). If you're very pessimistic about our capacity to know the truth, it's an easy slide from that to the claim that there's no such thing as truth. But that slide really ought to be resisted. Most of us recognize that there's a big difference between knowledge being impossible and truth being impossible, or between my not knowing a thing and there not being a fact of the matter about that thing. I don't know right now which bottles are in my liquor cabinet, so I don't know whether I can make a Manhattan tonight. But that fact alone doesn't imply that there's an indeterminate number of bottles in my liquor cabinet, or that the statement "Helena can make a Manhattan tonight" is neither true nor false. Nor does the fact that you've done a recent inventory and know there's whiskey, vermouth, and bitters in there, but I think you're wrong about that, mean that the sentence "Helena can make a Manhattan tonight" is true for you and false for me. I can make the Manhattan or I can't: our beliefs about that fact are irrelevant to it.

What I've just said is controversial. Some antirealists argue that truth itself is partly an epistemic matter. For instance, philosophers who endorse the competitor to the correspondence theory of truth that's known as "verificationism" argue that if we can't in principle verify or test a claim, that claim is neither true nor false. Truth just *is* verifiability, and verifiability is in large part a matter of the state of our minds, not just the world. For the verificationist, if my liquor cabinet is in another galaxy none of us can get to, the claim "there is a bottle of whiskey inside Helena's liquor cabinet" is neither true nor false. For the verificationist global antirealist, the whole world is, metaphorically speaking, in that other galaxy.

Maybe Nancy Mairs is rejecting bivalence because she's a verificationist. But, given what she says in the remainder of the passage I've quoted, it seems more likely that her rejection of capital T Truth is driven by something else. She contrasts the relativism she endorses with a vision of the world governed by a divine authority who imposes strict rules on us about how to behave. The idea seems to be that belief in truth and objective reality commits you to a supernaturalist metaphysics, a divine command theory of morality, and a very bossy monotheistic God. I'm not quite sure how she got there, but the general idea that there's a connection between realism and truth and authoritarianism and intolerance is surprisingly widespread. So it's worth noting that, as a logical matter, the connection is totally absent. It's perfectly consistent to believe that the world exists independently of the ways we think of or describe it and to respect the rights of others to think of, describe, and act in that world as they please. Claiming that something is objectively true is not, in itself, disrespectful to those who disagree, a denial of their inner experience or an act of coercion or violence toward them. (Though, of course, some particular claims can have content that is any or all of those things.)

Maybe there is no mind-independent, robustly real world: plenty of philosophers have claimed as much. But the particular reasons just mentioned are bad grounds for thinking so. It's also worth noting that, even if there isn't a robustly real world, there could still be truth. The correspondence theory ties truth closely to realism, but there are other theories out there. One classic alternative is the "coherence theory," which states that a belief is true if, and only if, it's part of a coherent system of beliefs. On this view, beliefs don't need to mirror the world; they just need to relate to each other in a suitably consistent way. Idealists who want to preserve the notion of truth will find this theory attractive; those who defend the correspondence theory will consider it a nonstarter.[28]

What are the implications of all of this for our question? The global antirealist version of the fictionalist challenge to memoir argues that all memoirs assume that the world is objectively real, but it isn't, so all memoir is fiction. The basic lines of defense here are the same as those given above in response to antirealism about the self. First, the world might be objectively real, and/or truth possible: some of the common reasons for denying those things aren't persuasive. Second, even if the world isn't objectively real, memoirists can plausibly claim to be telling the true story of the fiction of the world, by straightforwardly describing what it feels like from the inside to be a metaphysical realist. Finally, the defender of memoir as nonfiction can argue that some memoirs, at least, actively portray the world as objectively unreal, presenting their protagonists as trapped within the not-so-funhouse of the mind. If Berkeley had written a memoir, he might well have written it that way. Moreover, if he'd lined up his sentences carefully, and appealed to the coherence theory of truth, he could consistently have claimed that it was a true account of his life—and, as such, something different in kind from a novel.

Epistemology: What Knowledge?

No matter how dutifully we record what we see around us, the common denominator of all we see is always, transparently, shamelessly, the implacable "I."

                              JOAN DIDION[29]

Let's assume, at least for the sake of argument, that both the world and the self objectively exist, and that there are honest-to-God truths to tell about them. Even so, the fictionalist challenge to memoir would still have bite if we humans can't access those truths. If every attempt by a personal writer to give an accurate account of their life is just a wild and doomed stab in the dark, any essay or memoir that results would seem to have no closer relationship to the truth than a short story or novel. Here's where the philosophical terrain shifts from metaphysics to epistemology: considerations about what knowledge is, and what we can and can't hope to know.

It'll help to get one sweeping worry out of the way first. As Didion points out, there's no getting around the fact that all experience of the world is mediated by the experiencer's individual consciousness—that's just what experience is. The world doesn't imprint itself on our minds, directly, without us getting in the way. We *are* those minds, and we see and record the world using everything we've got inside them, including our preexisting beliefs, desires, and values. We live our lives with our me-glasses on, and there's no taking those glasses off.

People sometimes appeal to this undeniable fact—the subjectivity of experience—to argue that objective representations of the past are impossible. Every attempt to accurately describe the world, they suggest, is inevitably corrupted by the observer's idiosyncrasies. There's a radical and a less radical version of this claim. The less radical version says that we make observations and then later interpret those observations in accordance with our beliefs, desires, and values. The more radical version says that our distinct beliefs, desires, and values cause us to actually see distinct things at the very moment of observation. The most common variety of this radical version focuses on values in particular. Our perceptual capacities, the line goes, are essentially constrained by our moral beliefs, ideologies, or group affiliations, to the point that, say, a Black progressive and a White conservative (who are identically positioned in all other respects) will literally *see*—not just interpret—the same event differently.

The idea that all perceptual observation is value-laden in this radical way is not very compelling. (Alexandria Ocasio-Cortez and Donald Trump are standing directly in front of a rose bush in the White House garden. Is it really plausible that their distinct values and social identities cause them to see different plants?) But even if that claim is true, it doesn't follow from it that no one can ever access the objective truth. If some values are objectively well grounded, people who observe the world with those values in mind are getting an undistorted view of the situation.

Ah! you might think here. But no values *are* objectively well

grounded, either because there's no such thing as moral truth or because there's no way to objectively verify it. That train of thought
raises large questions that would take us far afield here, so I'll just say
two brief things in reply. First, this position depends on an endorsement of moral nihilism or radical moral skepticism, views that don't
have a lot going for them on closer examination.[30] If you're confident
that it's never OK to be racist, you already don't accept either of those
positions. And, second, it's worth thinking about what you're committing yourself to saying if you take this whole line we're talking about
(whether in its radical or less radical version). Do you really want to
claim that, because Einstein's perspective was unavoidably subjective,
$E = mc^2$ is too?

I don't, so I'm not persuaded by the alleged link between the subjectivity of experience and the impossibility of objective representations of the past (or present). What this challenge does helpfully
do, though, is focus our attention on what the goal of the human
thinker—and the human memoirist—ought to be. We can't hope to
use our minds as an interpretation-free mirror, or present our memoir as offering a fully neutral view from nowhere. Instead, what we
should be after is a well-grounded, unbiased interpretation of our
experience. As Stephen A. Ward puts it, "The central question thus
is not, 'How can I report only the facts and avoid values and interpretation?' but 'How well does my report, as an interpretation, satisfy objective criteria of evaluation?'"[31] Memoirists—like historians,
scientists, journalists, and the everyday person—should aim for a set
of epistemic values: including conscientious gathering and interro-
gation of evidence, careful consideration of alternative hypotheses
and counterarguments, active awareness of the workings of their
own prejudices and blind spots, and willingness to revise cherished
views in response to persuasive objections. Work that lines up with
these values satisfies our best methods and standards of verification.
It counts as objective, on a straightforward and plausible understanding of that term. It's objectivity for humans, if you like, and for human
purposes that's objectivity enough.

I may make factual omissions, transpositions, errors in dates; but I cannot
be mistaken about what I felt, nor about what my feelings led me to do; and

this is what principally concerns me here. The particular object of my confessions is to make known my inner self, exactly as it was in every circum-
stance of my life. It is the history of my soul that I promised, and to relate it
faithfully I require no other memorandum; all I need do, as I have done up
until now, is to look inside myself.

JEAN-JACQUES ROUSSEAU[32]

The upshot of the previous section is that the best epistemic version of
the fictionalist challenge to memoir isn't that all memoir necessarily
springs from a subjective point of view (sure it does—so what?). Instead, it's that memoirists are very unlikely to provide *well-supported*
subjective interpretations: takes on the past that are appropriately
grounded in strong evidence and unbiased methods of inquiry. This
can be presented as just one instance of a more general problem:
maybe all human interpretations, on any subject, are inevitably highly
distorted. But most fictionalists about memoir don't go around calling
all science, all biography, all work in the humanities, fiction. People
seem to think distortion is especially likely when it comes to writing
about yourself.

To some this might seem strange, since there's a long tradition
in philosophy of thinking that self-knowledge, of a certain kind, is
actually pretty easy (or at least eas*ier* than knowledge of the external
world, including of other minds).[33] Some—like Rousseau above, following Descartes—have gone as far as to say that our knowledge of
our own mental states is infallible: we simply can't be wrong about
whether or not we have a certain sensation, feeling, desire, or belief. If
you believe that you believe P, or feel F, or desire D, or have sensation
S, you're inevitably right about that self-ascription. Why? Well, you've
got an error-free method for getting at the truth in this department.
All you have to do to determine whether or not you have belief P or
feeling F or desire D or sensation S is "look inside yourself," as Rousseau puts it. The model here is of introspection—the "inward gaze"—
as a kind of inner sense, which gives us access to our mental states
much as perception gives us access to the world outside our minds.

Along with being infallible, Descartes suggested that our knowledge of our mental states is direct and immediate. In order to work
out whether or not you believe that you're in California, you don't
need to go through a lengthy process of evidence gathering, reasoning, or reflection. By flicking on that inner searchlight, you just know

instantly that you believe it (though knowing that you *are* in California—knowing that you know it—is of course another matter).

So should contemporary philosophers lean on tradition here and insist that memoirists are in fact in a better position to know themselves than scientists are to know the external world? No. The idea that introspection gives us immediate and infallible knowledge of ourselves is plausible only for a narrow range of mental states (if those.) It works best in the case of sensations and trivial beliefs. Descartes may be right that, provided you possess the necessary concepts and are reasoning clearly, if you believe you're in pain, then you are in pain, and if you believe you believe it's raining, then you do believe it's raining. But the mental states that memoirists (and the rest of us) are most interested in—our deepest convictions, emotions, desires, abilities, and character traits—are much more complex and opaque than this. It seems quite easy to be mistaken about whether you genuinely do believe that all races are equal, or whether you really are over her, or whether you actually do want to move to Los Angeles, or whether you truly are good with children, or whether you are in fact a jerk. Working out the truth about these things isn't plausibly a matter of simply looking "inside" and observing them. You often have to do quite a bit of reflection to get clearer on the matter: maybe observing your own behavior (seeing how you act around people of other races over time), using your imagination (what happens internally when you visualize her dating someone else?), or asking other humans about it (what do your friends think about whether you'd be happier in LA? Does your therapist seem to be gently suggesting that you're a jerk?). Not only is this kind of self-knowledge not immediately accessible, you're also not guaranteed to get it right, maybe ever. There's a reason why Descartes focused on such trivial forms of self-knowledge as knowing that you're currently thinking. It's plausible that the kind of substantial self-knowledge that's at issue in memoir is just as hard, if not harder, to get by than knowledge of the external world.

Nietzsche certainly thought so. He wrote in *The Genealogy of Morals*: "Of necessity we remain strangers to ourselves, we understand ourselves not, in ourselves we are bound to be mistaken, for of us holds good to all eternity the motto, 'Each one is the farthest away from himself.'"[34]

Why do we fail to know ourselves in these ways? Answering that question might help us get a grip on how pervasive the phenomenon really is, and therefore on how much of a problem it poses for memoir.

―――――

"I did that," says my memory. "I could not have done that," says my pride, and remains inexorable. Eventually–the memory yields.

NIETZSCHE[35]

One reason we might fail to know ourselves is that we don't want to know ourselves: or, at least, we only want to know ourselves if the knowledge will make us feel good, and we're not so sure it will. Nietzsche suggests that a large chunk of our self-ignorance is "motivated" in this way. We don't just fail to know the truth about ourselves, we're deceived about it, and the deceiver is us. The idea that self-deception of this kind is pervasive probably goes a long way toward explaining the sense that memoir is less likely to get at the truth than other forms of (alleged) nonfiction. You might have some reason to deceive yourself about what really happened during the French Revolution—who knows? People are wild. But you certainly have much *more* reason to deceive yourself about what happened leading up to your divorce. Rousseau famously claimed in his *Confessions* that he was excavating his mental interior with the utmost courage, honesty, and disinterestedness, but his text doesn't exactly bear that out. (As John Barbour puts it, "The pattern is one of inordinate attention to rather minor moral issues, along with trivialization, minimalization, and avoidance of what seem the truly significant matters. His partial awareness of unacknowledged guilt continues to haunt him, prompting further confessions that fail to set his conscience at rest."[36])

The ubiquity of self-deception has been a commonplace belief in our culture since Freud's theory of repression. It's rare these days to sign up for the whole Freudian program, including suppressed infantile longings to sleep with or kill your parents. But many of us accept the basic Freudian/Nietzschean thesis that much human action is generated by drives that are not only hidden, but intentionally so, from and by the actor, for reasons of psychic comfort.

Is self-deception a thing? The concept is so widely employed that it can seem perfectly straightforward. But looked at more closely, self-deception can appear deeply paradoxical, to the point that its genuine existence is thrown into doubt.[37] Deceiving someone else is easily understandable in a way that deceiving yourself isn't. We can make ready sense of the idea that you believe that p but concurrently make me believe that $not\text{-}p$. (You believe you're having an affair, but make me believe you aren't. It happens all the time in the suburbs!) But how can *I* believe that p and concurrently make myself believe that $not\text{-}p$? (I believe you're having an affair, but make myself believe, at the exact same time as believing that you are, that you're not. What?)

There are really two paradoxes lurking here. One, the "static paradox," notes the logical impossibility of p and $not\text{-}p$ both being true. A basic principle of rational thought is the law of noncontradiction, according to which contradictory propositions can't both be true in the same sense at the same time. The concept of self-deception implies that I can believe a logical impossibility—that you both are and aren't having an affair—but who can do that?

The "dynamic paradox" points to a psychological rather than a logical impossibility. It's built into the standard concept of self-deception, unlike mere error, that the deceiver intentionally causes her own false belief. I'm not just inadvertently mistaken about you being faithful to me, I *make* myself believe it's true, though I know it's false. But how can that work in practice? If I genuinely believe that something is false, it's hard to see how I can persuade myself that it's true: the intention to do so necessarily undercuts itself.

Rescuers of the concept of self-deception have some options here. The static paradox can be addressed by appealing to the idea that the mind is made up of several semi-independent subsystems, some of which might believe p and some $not\text{-}p$. While the mind as a collection of these subsystems might be said to believe in both p and $not\text{-}p$ at the same time, no individual subsystem need do so. (This is no weirder than saying that the nation of the USA can both believe that climate change is real and that it isn't, but that the individual citizens Chad and Pinky can't.) Since the mind's individual subsystems, by hypothesis, aren't aware of the contradiction at the level of the collective and are themselves internally consistent on the matter, the law of noncontradiction isn't violated and the static paradox is resolved.

The dynamic paradox can be addressed by claiming that the self-deceiver doesn't actually believe in p and *not-p* at the same time, whether in subsystems of their mind or in their mind as a collective. On this line, the whole picture of self-deception as lying to oneself is misleading. Instead, the person we (inaptly) refer to as a "self-deceiver" simply believes p while blocking what would ordinarily count as good evidence for *not-p*. They want to believe p so badly that they ignore, avoid, misrepresent, or misinterpret anything that suggests *not-p*. They do this so well that not only do they never come to believe *not-p*, but they may not ever even consciously entertain *not-p*. They're refusing to *face* the truth, you might say, rather than lying to themself about it. On this picture, what we call self-deception remains motivated, but it isn't intentional, since the person doesn't willfully and avowedly deceive themself. That seems psychologically possible, contra the dynamic paradox, even if it remains irrational.

These solutions bring in train their own problems, but arguably work well enough to rescue self-deception as a genuinely possible (though maybe inappropriately named) phenomenon. An empirical question then arises of how common it actually is in practice. The specific repression hypothesis advocated by Freud hasn't fared so well empirically. In their survey of the psychological literature, Timothy Wilson and Elizabeth Dunn argue that "a patchwork of studies depicts a mental architecture that would allow repression to occur," but that "no single study has demonstrated all the necessary criteria to establish the existence of repression definitively."[38] As for evidence of self-deception more broadly, well, it's difficult to directly assess whether or not someone is deceiving themself, because that requires identifying the belief that is, by hypothesis, being held unconsciously or being avoided. It's in the nature of self-deception for that belief to be hidden from the person who holds, or ought to hold, it, and it's unlikely to be all that more visible to an external observer, especially a stranger in a lab coat.

There's substantial empirical support, though, for the more general idea that some of our lapses in knowledge about ourselves are motivated. Numerous studies have shown that our self-assessments and autobiographical memories exhibit an egocentric bias. We skew the facts about ourselves and our pasts in a direction that makes us feel better about ourselves and our lives. In *The Seven Sins of Memory*, Daniel L. Schacter provides a nice catalog of some of these creatively self-serving acts.[39] When interviewed about the source of our successes and failures in life, we tend to attribute the former to ourselves and the latter to others. When college students are led to believe that introversion predicts academic success and are then asked to report past experiences of acting as introverts or as extroverts, their memories lean heavy on the introversion.[40] When Europeans and North Americans are asked to compare their earlier selves to their current selves, they tend to diss those callow youths and their quality of life, presumably out of a deep-seated desire to see their lives as having improved over time. None of this definitively demonstrates the presence of self-deception per se, but it's certainly suggestive.

There's something eerily fascinating about the idea of systematically deceiving yourself—and something gratifyingly knowing about diagnosing someone else as doing it—but much self-ignorance is arguably a lot more boring than this. Often the self-unaware seem to have no ulterior psychic motive: the truth isn't unpleasant, or anxious-making or unflattering. They just don't have it.

In some cases, what's going on here can be broadly described as "failures of critical reasoning." You might have strong evidence about your feelings, values, or character right in front of you, but not get around to drawing the relevant conclusions, or draw the wrong conclusions, due to simple inattention or error or absent conceptual resources. Your heart rate rises and you lose the power of speech whenever Ananya is in the room, but you fail to conclude that you're in love, because you're too busy writing your grant proposal, or you interpret your arousal as fear, or you believe you're straight. There's evidence from multiple domains of your life that you care deeply about social inequality, but you haven't introspected enough to make the connection and draw the obvious conclusion that you're an egalitarian rather than the right-winger you were raised to be. You delight in the sufferings of others, but you're not familiar with the concept of Schadenfreude, so you fail to infer that it's a standing disposition of yours. Et cetera.

Another possibility in this broad camp is that you're operating with a faulty background theory about which conclusion follows from the evidence you have. According to what's known in social psychology as the "fundamental attribution error," for instance, we're all inclined to overestimate the role of internal factors (preferences and character traits) in explaining our actions, when actually external situational factors do much of the work. If asked why we selected a particular product from a range, for example, we'll say it's because we liked it best, though experimenters can clearly demonstrate that it's actually because they positioned it to the right. The failure here isn't not knowing *what* you want, but not knowing *why* you want it. Psychologists Nisbett and Wilson argue that humans are pretty bad at this across the board: we routinely misidentify the factors driving our evaluations, choices, and behavior.[41]

Non-egocentric biases can be at work in these cases of absent or faulty inferences.[42] One is *confirmation bias*: a tendency to look for and retain evidence that's consistent with our existing beliefs. Another is *consistency bias*: a tendency to remember our past experiences, feelings, and beliefs as similar to our current ones. (One study showed, for instance, that people who fall more in love with their partner over time exaggerate the extent of their earlier feelings, whereas those who fall less in love underestimate them.[43]) Another is *hindsight bias*: a tendency to interpret the past in accordance with our knowledge of how things turned out later (which George Gusdorf, incidentally, refers to as "the original sin of autobiographers"[44]). Another is *stereotype bias*: a tendency to interpret individual events in line with generalizations we've developed about the past. But there need be no *egocentric* bias at work. Each of the above are examples of self-knowledge not being direct and immediate in the Cartesian way—there's a connection between evidence and knowledge that's being scrambled somehow—but also of self-ignorance not being obviously motivated by self-interest in the way Nietzsche emphasizes.

In the remaining cases, our lack of knowledge about ourselves and our lives isn't based on faulty reasoning from the evidence, but on a simple lack of evidence. A salient source of this for memoir is straight-up forgetting. We all know that memories fade over time, but one striking result of the psychological research is how quickly they fade: often within minutes, hours, or days. We tend to retain at best the gist of an event, with specific details—time, venue, attendees, dialogue—disappearing rapidly. When the event in question is high in emotional intensity, neurologist Jonathan Mink suggests, often almost all we retain is the emotion.[45]

When asked later to report on what happened, rather than reaching into the storehouse of the mind and retrieving the event whole, we extract the few key elements we retained at the time, and engage in reconstructions to fill in the gaps. Research has shown that these reconstructions are often informed by emotions and beliefs that weren't active at the time, but spring from our current emotional state, our recall of similar or recent events, and our general knowledge and hypotheses about the world. Suggestively, neuroscientists have shown that remembering makes use of the same areas of the brain as imagining.[46]

The room for error to creep in here is, of course, enormous. We can misremember the details of actual events and also claim to remember events that never happened but that we only thought about, imagined, or heard about from someone else. Again, much of this selective and creative recall may be innocent, unintentional, and unmotivated—more like confabulation than self-deception. But maybe not, for the memoirist, any less troubling for that.

———

It was a sort of epistemological crisis. How did I know that the things I was writing were absolutely, objectively true? My simple, declarative sentences began to strike me as hubristic at best, utter lies at worst. All I could speak for was my own perceptions, and perhaps not even those.

ALISON BECHDEL[47]

Most of us don't need to read the psychological literature or Nietzsche to believe that we're prone to lapses and errors in knowledge, due to some combination of memory and reasoning limitations and cognitive or emotional biases. It's a real problem, for sure, but how big a one? Should we all be in crisis, like Bechdel?

Given the multiple studies demonstrating failures of autobiographical recall, it's somewhat reassuring that the empirical experts are relatively sanguine on this point. Ulric Neisser, known as the "father of cognitive psychology," writes: "We can never do full justice … to 'historical truth,' because what really happened was too rich for anyone's memory to preserve. But it is relatively easy to remember events in a way that is accurate with respect to some overall characteristic of the situation; such a recollection always has some degree of validity even if it suggests nested details that are by no means accurate themselves."[48] Michael Ross and Anne E. Wilson concur: "The research on autobiographical recall does not indicate that biased recollections are more common than accurate recollections, or that people's implicit theories are generally false."[49] Daniel Schacter sums up his survey of the literature with the claim that "memory is a mainly reliable guide to our pasts and futures, though it sometimes lets us down in annoying but revealing ways."[50] As for philosophy, at the end of his careful recent discussion of the terrain, Quassim Cassam comes out as only a "moderate pessimist." While a significant amount of ignorance about what we believe, want, and are (and why) is normal for the average human, Cassam suggests, there's no need to follow Nietzsche to the hyperbolic conclusion that self-knowledge is impossible.[51]

For the average human, OK. But are memoirists a special case? There are several reasons for thinking that autobiographical writers are more likely to confabulate and self-deceive than others. First, memoirs generally go through multiple drafts, involving extended, obsessive rumination on the author's part. It's troubling, then, that studies suggest that the more frequently you recall an event, the further the recollection shifts from accuracy, and that merely repeating a statement can increase your conviction of its truth.[52] Second, memoirists are clearly strongly motivated to record their lives, often on the basis of intense emotions about their pasts. This forcefully raises the specter of "motivated" distortions such as self-deception and egocentric bias. Third, many memoirists have a talent for rich imagery, lifelike narration, and imaginative language: they appear to experience and recall things intensely. It's worrying, then, that evidence suggests that the more vivid a memory, the more likely you are to believe that it's accurate, whether or not it is.[53] People who produce false childhood memories have been shown to score higher on scales measuring vividness of visual imagery than people who don't.[54] Similarly, when people are asked to imagine a past event they can't initially recall rather than merely reflect on whether it occurred, their memories of the event skew false. Putting all this together: the idea of an exceptionally ruminative and imaginative person spending months or years rewriting the story of a past they're deeply personally invested in, in rich and detailed scenes, can start to seem like a sure route to fabrication rather than self-revelation.

Before the memoirists among us start to panic, it's worth considering some factors on the other side. For one, it's quite possible that those who write memoirs are partly led to do it because they have special talents in the memory department. If the page is any evidence (and of course that's contentious here), some memoirists are border-line *hyperthymestic.* That term refers to a condition with two defining characteristics: "spending an excessive amount of time thinking about one's past, and displaying an extraordinary ability to recall specific events from one's past."[55] Hyperthymestics report vividly "seeing" past events involuntarily, with minimal prompting and no conscious effort. One woman claims to recall every day of her life since age four-teen: "Starting on February 5th, 1980, I remember everything. That was a Tuesday."[56] That doesn't seem like a bad description of Nabo-kov, as he presents in his masterful memoir, *Speak, Memory.* The book begins with a lushly detailed first-person scene of the author as an infant at the vanished family estate in imperial Russia, and goes on from there. "I see again my schoolroom in Vyra, the blue roses of the wallpaper, the open window ... The mirror brims with brightness; a bumblebee has entered the room and bumps against the ceiling."[57] We can't all be Nabokov, but it wouldn't be altogether surprising if memoirists were on average more Nabokov-ish in this respect than the average person.

Second, the same traits that lead some memoirists, or all memoir-ists some of the time, to distorting navel-gazing might also lead them to the truth. Most memoirists get into the business because they're strongly committed to discovering the truth about themselves, their relationships, and their lives. And staying in the business requires sustaining that search, often at significant personal cost, for months, years, or decades at a time. If we understand self-deception as a re-fusal to confront the truth about yourself, on the face of it the great memoirists are the least self-deceiving of us all. They make some of humanity's most valiant attempts to stop avoiding, ignoring, and mis-interpreting the facts about their inner lives and past actions, and to employ instead some of the same epistemic virtues and practices that we look for in objective journalism, history, and science. Memoirists are also often highly aware of the pitfalls along the road: they're not generally naive about memory's gaps and kinks. Many of them ap-proach their subject with epistemic humility, including frequent ac-knowledgments in their writing of their uncertainty when faced with the opacity of the self. To the extent that their claims about their lives include those qualifications, the claims are less apt to be false.

No one, to my knowledge, has tried to test whether memoirists are less or more self-knowing than the average, but I'd be surprised if there were a significant lean either way. The above factors seem likely to balance themselves out. If I'm right about that, and memoirists are just like the rest of us, the fictionalist challenge to memoir again seems unpersuasive. We don't need to know everything about ourselves in order to know quite a lot, and that quite a lot is enough to maintain a real distinction between memoir and fiction.

This point might hold even in those cases, like Rousseau's, where the memoirist is clearly self-deceived. We learn a lot about Rousseau from the way he desperately tries to conceal himself. The miracle of the *Confessions* is that of an author who claims to be offering the unvarnished truth about himself, manifestly isn't, but thereby, in an unintentional act of genius, does indirectly do it. Barbour writes: "The way a writer characterizes herself inevitably reveals a great deal about her character ... at the moment of writing. Characterization reveals character, although what is revealed may or may not correlate with the author's own understanding of his character, either in the past or the present."[58] Though we might despair of the epistemic capacities of humans, it's always possible for a memoir, in this respect, to know more than its author.

Aesthetics: What Story? Who?

I was meant to know the plot, but all I knew was what I saw: flash pictures in variable sequence, images with no "meaning" beyond their temporary arrangement, not a movie but a cutting-room experience. In what would probably be the middle of my life I wanted still to believe in the narrative and in the narrative's intelligibility, but to know that one could change the sense with every cut was to begin to perceive the experience as rather more electrical than ethical.

JOAN DIDION[59]

For memoir to escape the fictionalist challenge, it has to be the case that a real world, including a real self, objectively exists, and that the memoirist is capable of gaining the self-knowledge needed to make well-supported, unbiased interpretations of that world. But that alone isn't enough. The memoirist also has to transfer their interpretation of their life to the page without distortion creeping in at that stage. The act of not merely thinking about, but writing your life—of forming it into a story, usually for others to read—has its own distinctive temptations and dangers. However good a grip we might gain on the truth about ourselves and our lives, we have aesthetic reasons for losing sight of it when writing about them.

One set of concerns here centers on the demands and seductions of narrative. Much, though not all, self–life writing is narrative in form. It presents (part of) the author's life in the form of a story: a representation of a sequence of events, from a certain point of view, with a certain coherence and implied significance. Narratives impose three core requirements that risk distorting the truth.

First, narratives have to be *selective.* Laurence Sterne's nine-volume comic novel *Tristram Shandy,* a fictional failed autobiography, dramatizes this requirement to hilarious effect. The faux-memoirist narrator is determined to recount the entirety of his life from his conception on, with the result that he doesn't even make it to his own birth until three volumes in. Tristram Shandy bears out Russell Baker's suggestion that whereas "the biographer's problem is that he never knows enough," "the autobiographer's problem is that he knows much too much. He knows absolutely everything; he knows the whole iceberg, not just the tip."[60] The solution to that problem, of course, is to sift through the raw material of your life and include only some of it in the text. But the selection process introduces obvious risks of misrepresentation. Just as you can lie in life by omission as well as commission, you can unintentionally skew the facts in your memoir by, say, including the fourth husband and—for reasons of space!—failing to mention the rest.

Second, narratives have to be *unified.* They don't need to stick to linear time, but they do need to hold together in some recognizable way: using causal, analogical, or thematic connections and integrating any micronarratives into a broader macronarrative. The events described need unity of some sort if the reader isn't to get lost or impatient and give up, and the unity of belonging to the life of a single person isn't enough. *Tristram Shandy,* again, provides the antimodel. Tristram's effort to include literally everything in his memoir doesn't just result in an interminable colossus, it also produces a jumbled, fragmentary structure, with the narrator repeatedly inserting a digression upon a digression, for pages on end. The problem here, for the memoirist bent on truth, is that the average real life probably looks more like *Tristram Shandy* than the average memoir. Much that happens to us in life is just random and chaotic, and few of us end up with a nice bow tied on the mess.

Third, narratives have to be *intelligible*. A story aims to communicate not just a unified series of events, but their significance: it offers an interpretation of the sequence, from a certain perspective, designed to elicit understanding in the narrator's audience. One effective way to do this is to structure the story on culturally familiar lines. Many memoirs use plots, governing metaphors, and archetypal figures that appear in other literary works, art forms, or myths. A traditionally popular method is to construct an autobiography on the model of the eighteenth- and nineteenth-century *Bildungsroman*, tracking the protagonist's gradual progression from innocence to enlightenment after facing a series of obstacles along the way. But even memoirists who consider that trope tired and unrealistic can find themselves reproducing established models: interpreting their lives via a limited set of conventional forms. The worry, of course, is that the fit is forced. Nabokov claimed that "the following of … thematic designs through one's life should be … the true purpose of autobiography."[61] But most memoirists relate at some point to Didion's suspicion that any narrative line she detects in her life may be just an artificial imposition on a set of essentially meaningless experiences.

The narrative demands for intelligibility and unity are particularly seductive. It's not just our readers who want our life stories to make sense. We authors want them to as well, because if our life stories make sense we can maybe convince ourselves that our lives do too. As a result, it's likely that while writing memoir we're subject to powerful desire-directed internal suggestion alongside the external suggestions of narrative form. The French existentialists are famous for pressing the line that seeing your life in narrative terms is a form of *mauvaise foi*. We urgently want there to be order, meaning, and unity *in* the world, independently of us. But there's no such thing: God is dead, nature is all accident, and the universe is fully indifferent to us. Our attempts to read significance and harmony where none exists are futile, self-deceiving, and absurd. Roquentin, the protagonist of Sartre's first novel *Nausea*, describes at length the "disgust" and "nausea" produced by an unintelligible and meaningless universe, alongside its ineffective remedy: "This is what fools people: a man is always a teller of tales, he lives surrounded by his stories and the stories of others, he sees everything that happens to him through them; and he tries to live his own life as if he were telling a story."[62]

A similar set of worries applies to the memoirist's employment of a persona. All forms of autobiographical writing, some more obviously than others, involve the use of a distinctive voice that, in Gornick's words, is a "fusion of experience, perspective and personality," "pulled from [the] self, and then shaped to [the] writer's purpose."[63] Sometimes this persona is essentially the same as the protagonist or "I"-character; other times there's more distance between the two, as when the narrator takes an ironic distance on their former or current self. The establishment of a distinctive persona is a large part of how an author creates a coherent, intelligible, and engaging narrative. But personas are also at work in nonnarrative forms of autobiographical writing, like lyric and discursive essays.

It's to the tradition of the personal essay that we owe some of the finest examples of artfully fashioned personae in the house of literary nonfiction. Essayists often revel in the multiplicity and fluidity the genre allows, both within individual pieces and across the author's oeuvre. E. B. White wrote that the essayist "can pull on any sort of shirt, be any sort of person, according to his mood or subject matter";[64] Edward Hoagland wrote that "The artful 'I' of an essay can be as chameleon as any narrator in fiction."[65] Essayists are frequently open about the artificiality of the act. Nancy Mairs claims "I am not the woman whose voice animates my essays. She's made up";[66] Montaigne remarks: "Even so one must spruce up, even so one must present oneself in an orderly arrangement, if one would go out in public. Now, I am constantly adorning myself, for I am constantly describing myself."[67] The concern, of course, is precisely that personas, like narratives, are constructed rather than found. Developing a persona in a text is an *impersonation*, all these memoirists are suggesting. Shouldn't that worry us seekers of truth?

Both the concerns about narrative and the concerns about personas reduce to a broader concern about the artfulness of memoir.

Memoirists have certain aesthetic aims, and use the materials of life and the self to pursue them. They can't achieve their aims if they merely list the events of their lives in order (even if that were a realistic possibility). As Gornick suggests, they need to fix on a story in the situation they're describing, as well as the right persona to tell it. Doing that requires the imagination, creativity, and technical mastery we associate with art. Even the apparently least artful styles, like the meandering digressiveness characteristic of many classic personal essays, are intentional constructions. The essayist Carl H. Klaus writes, in an essay on essays, that his written record of the track of his thoughts

is a contrivance of sorts. Not the thoughts and memories themselves, but my self-conscious decision to include them here as an example of the mind's meanderings, and then to jog my memory for other recollections, and then to work over the sequences, syntax and wording of those memories and thoughts to suggest the movement of a mind interacting with itself. Seemingly on an associative ramble but with a destination in mind. Seemingly in an extemporaneous style but deliberately revised to create that illusion.[68]

For the result to have literary merit, the process also requires openness to the promptings of language, which may have its own designs. J. M. Coetzee refers to "an automatism built into language: the tendency of words to call up other words, to fall into patterns that keep propagating themselves. Out of that interplay there emerges, if you are lucky, what you recognize or hope to recognize as true."[69]

If you are lucky.

All of the above can be neatly summed up in Ben Yagoda's claim that "once you begin to write the true story of your life in a form that anyone would possibly want to read, you start to make compromises with the truth."[70]

A very similar set of critiques emerged in the philosophy of history in the 1970s and 1980s, as postmodernist thought made its sweep across the humanities and arts as a whole. Looking at how that debate played out can help us assess the strength of the aesthetic version of the fictionalist challenge to memoir.

The most developed version of what's known as "historical con-
structivism" is that of Hayden White, in, among other places, his 1973
book *Metahistory*.[71] White argues that historical scholarship is less
like a science and more like an art, because it centrally involves interpretation, largely in the form of narration. Like memory, and like
memoir, historical writing is a constructive process, in which the historian selects a subset of past events, imaginatively fills in the gaps,
and orders the lot into a unified and coherent story. These historical stories, like the life stories told by individuals, are markedly conventional. (Specifically, White argues, they fall into the set of master genres—tragedy, romance, comedy, and satire—identified by the
literary theorist Northrop Frye.) Alongside these literary plot structures, historical narratives employ further poetic devices, including
metaphor, synecdoche, metonymy, and irony. All of this is a creative
act on the part of the historian, an imposition on the historical record.
The past doesn't come to us story-shaped or metaphor-rich: in itself,
it has no pattern, design, or significance. That means that different
historians—or the same historians over time—can and do provide different narrative interpretations of the same events, none of which can
be said to uniquely fit the facts. White concludes that historical writing, despite its scientific pretensions, reduces to fiction.

White is careful to clarify that he's not an antirealist about the
past. He accepts that stuff really did happen back then; it's the idea
that *stories* happened that he rejects. He also isn't an antitruther
about history: he believes that historical interpretations can be true
or false. But the kind of truth at issue, for White, isn't correspondence to the world or even coherence among beliefs. Instead it's what
you might call "literary" or "narrative" truth: the aptness and veracity
found in a good metaphor. Truth in history is possible, then, but only
when understood as the kind of truth we get in literary works. Such
metaphorical truth can provide genuine insight, White insists—not
all historical narratives are distorting—but we should call the vehicle
of that truth what it is: fiction.

In a 1990 paper, Noël Carroll offers two main lines of response
to White that transfer nicely to the fictionalist debate over memoir.[72] The first points to a set of faulty inferences in the constructivist
argument. White either asserts or implies that each of the following features of an interpretation transform it into fiction: inventive-

ness, selectivity, imaginativeness, multiplicity, conventionality, literary quality—and, sweeping all this together, narrativity. But none of those connections necessarily holds. A quick run-through shows that each of these things can be present without an immediate diagnosis of fiction. Photos and films are invented rather than found, but that doesn't make them fictional representations of the past. I select only some things to tell you about my vacation, but that doesn't mean that what I do tell you is made up. The fact that neuroscience shows imagination to be key to remembering doesn't show that all memories are false. The availability of multiple good stories about last Friday night doesn't demonstrate that one or all of them are fiction: each story can just be highlighting a distinct aspect of the same complex course of events. And your description of what you've been up to recently may be Homeric, but some weekends genuinely are epic, and nonfigurative, nonliterary language may not be enough to capture the literal (not metaphorical) truth about them.

There's a nice evocation of that last point in Tobias Wolff's autobiographical novel, *Old School*. When a teacher suggests to Robert Frost that contemporary writing can and should do without traditional form, Frost replies:

I lost my nearest friend in the one they called the Great War. So did Achilles lose his friend in war, and Homer did no injustice to his grief by writing about it in dactylic hexameters . . . Such grief can *only* be told in form . . . Without it you've got nothing but a stubbed-toe cry—sincere, maybe, for what that's worth, but with no depth or carry. No echo. You may have a grievance but you do not have grief.[73]

We can sum all of this up by saying that the presence of a narrative doesn't by itself indicate the presence of a fiction. Narrative, with all its characteristic features, can certainly *add* something to a representation, but what it adds isn't best understood as fictional, or as requiring a distinct, "literary" notion of truth.

Carroll's second line of response to White questions the assertion that the world isn't story-shaped. Sure, we're all familiar with cases where people impose a narrative line on an experience where it doesn't belong. Whether we're everyday paranoiacs or full-blown conspiracy theorists, we can "overread" the collective or personal past, detecting in its accidents some covert plot or deep significance that's in actual fact absent. But is *all* narrativizing like this? Carroll thinks not. Some narratives track real form, structure, and pattern in the past. Not only do we sometimes tell stories about ourselves and then enact them in the world—a core premise of narrative clinical therapy—but many courses of events in life unfold "in terms of causes, reasons, complications and consequences, and elucidating these relations between actions and their background conditions need not be exercises in fiction."[74]

A similar move can be made in response to the claim that a memoirist's persona is constructed rather than discovered. To say that a memoirist's persona is contrived isn't to say that it's *fully* contrived. Phillip Lopate suggests that, though "it's true that we make up our selves from moment to moment ... we have far less leeway in remaking ourselves and our personae on the page than we might first imagine."[75] Some essayists' personae are in fact remarkably stable across individual essays and decades, and sound very much like the author's in-person presentation. Lopate claims this of himself: "In my case (*pace* those who insist the self is multivalent), that voice is singular. I don't hear *voices*; at this stage of life I'm too rigid and set in my ways."

If neither of these strategies seems persuasive, there's also always the option of using your memoir to display and/or critique the human tendency to misleadingly narrativize and impersonate, both on the page and off. Given that the tendency is real and widespread, this is just another instance of the possibility discussed above of a telling a true story of a fiction. A central theme of Sartre's memoir, *The Words*—which Paul Eakin calls an "anti-narrative narrative"[76]—is the corrupting influence of literary narratives on the young Sartre's self-conception. As for personas, Margo Jefferson says, of her memoir about growing up in an affluent Black American family: "I'd been brought up in ... a world where you might have to switch persona at any moment, depending, for example, on what my mother's needs were, here's what Betty Anne down the street needs, here's what my teacher needs. In *this* situation, I have to confess to a certain awareness, a certain kind of knowledge. In *this* [other] situation, I have to play innocent. That's theatrical, but that's also psychological and factually accurate, this constant construction of different performing selves."[77] As a result, she says of writing her book, "I was very, very intent on not wanting the illusion of one tone, one narrative overview ... I knew there had to be a lot of personae."[78]

Finally, as in *Roland Barthes by Roland Barthes*, the memoirist can follow the example of some of the great works of modernist fiction and abandon narrative and standard characterization altogether.

Who Cares?

Memoir certainly has what we might call "fictive" qualities. Even memoirs that aren't novelistic in the sense of employing detailed and dialogue-rich scenes are still inventive, imaginative works of literature that employ conventional narrative, poetic, and linguistic devices. But it's a further step from noting these similarities to saying that memoir just *is* fiction, and I've argued above that none of the standard arguments for that claim are persuasive.

Fine! you might say at this point. Whatever! Who really cares whether memoir is fiction or not? What's this obsession with categorizing books as one thing or another and drawing firm lines to mark the boundaries? Why can't each book just be read on its own terms? The genre-bending Geoff Dyer is known for expressing this kind of impatience. In his *Paris Review* interview, he objects immediately to being classified as a nonfiction writer. When asked whether he distinguishes between his novels and his nonfiction, he says "I think of all of them as, um, what's the word? Ah, yes, *books*."[79]

It's not only writers of nonfiction who question the point of segregating fiction from nonfiction. There's recently been a surge in what's referred to as "autofiction": literary works that are presented as fiction, but are almost indistinguishable (for the reader) from a nonfiction account of the author's life. In, for example, Sheila Heti's *Motherhood*, Karl Ove Knausgaard's *My Struggle*, Rachel Cusk's *Outline* series, Teju Cole's *Open City*, and Chris Kraus's *I Love Dick*, the narrator-protagonist has the same name, profession, history, and, apparently, personality and views as the author. While these books are often seen as highly novel, the trend goes back to the 1970s, when Serge Doubrovsky coined the term "autofiction," and the broader genre-blurring they involve goes back even further than that. The genealogy of the modern memoir and the novel are highly intertwined. As Ben Yagoda notes in his history, the first memoir boom was set off by the fictional autobiography *Robinson Crusoe*, and the first-person voice of an autobiographically inclined narrator has continued to dominate the novel ever since.

Why not just let things be messy, then? Or, more radically, why not dispense with genre terms entirely? There are several different reasons why that would be a bad idea.

The first is aesthetic. Thomas Couser argues that genre terms are mainly useful because they provide guidance on how to read an author's work.[80] Identifying whether a work is fiction or nonfiction, or poetry or prose—or, within these broad genres, whether it's an apology, a confession, a novella, a satire, a lyric, or an elegy, and so on—can help us understand what the work is doing and what its aims are. Each of these genres and subgenres is made up a set of conventions, and knowing that the work in front of us is engaging with those conventions—whether by following them or playing against them— can deepen our comprehension and appreciation of it. The ultimate goal isn't to classify works, Couser suggests, but to clarify them.[81]

Things can misfire, of course. Sometimes genre conventions narrow rather than broaden our understanding. Couser notes, for instance, that writers of illness memoirs have traditionally felt constrained to respect the convention of a happy ending: acceptance, increased insight, or growth, if not healing. That's hard to do truthfully when the course of events is progressive debilitation or a painful death. Porochista Khakpour sold her memoir, *Sick*, on the basis of a proposal promising the traditional recovery arc. But after a car accident six months later that compounded her existing health conditions, she abandoned the original plan and wrote a memoir that's partly a commentary on the distorting pressure ill memoirists feel to narrate their recovery.[82]

There can be value, then, in particular cases, in shaking things up, working against the conventions and shifting their boundaries. But, as a general matter, the existence of genre is helpful—and can serve the aesthetic purposes even of a resolutely hybrid writer who finds genre terms stifling and rejects them. Dyer says that refusal to "segregate" his books "is part of what the books are *about*."[83] But if we're to get that aim, and understand Dyer's books as hybrids, we have to recognize the subgenres they're hybrids of. Part of the pleasure of reading Geoff Dyer is the sense of having your expectations upended. No expectations, no pleasure—or at least less of it.

To accept that genre terms are useful in general isn't to accept that the distinction between fiction and nonfiction is, specifically. How might knowing that a work is nonfiction rather than fiction, or vice versa, help to orient readers? What can it do for us? (Why did I write this chapter?)

One thing that plausibly happens when we approach a text as fiction is that we're more inclined to look for a deeper significance, design, or theme behind the events, dialogue, or descriptions portrayed. Nonfiction—whether memoir or history or something else—can also be rich in pattern, metaphor, and theme (that was one of the points made in the previous section). But it's reasonable to expect that some passages are present simply to record what happened, without signifying anything larger beyond that. While it's open to a novelist or short story writer to give *everything* a deeper resonance or subtext, it takes a truly mystical or paranoid memoirist to do that.

One thing that happens when we read a text as nonfiction, on the other hand, is that we're more attentive to the truth or falsity of the claims being made. We take the author's statements as assertions about how the world was or is, and as a result we're alert to their plausibility, consistency, and congruity with how we ourselves understand the world. Again, works of fiction can also be read as advancing a worldview or argument. But a novel or short story doesn't ask us directly to *believe* its statements, only to entertain them as hypotheses, and sometimes not even that. Some fictional works aren't out to offer insight about the real state of the world at all. The contrast here is strongest with essays that have a strong expository component: the aim there is to explain and argue, not portray someone explaining and arguing. Recognizing this can help us focus (in part) on the content of what's being said, rather than, say, what the author might be suggesting about people who think that way, or the style of the language being used to express it.

When we read something as "autofiction," finally, we're led to reflect on a set of philosophical themes common in autofictional texts (and discussed in this chapter): the nature of writing, the reality and accessibility of the self, and the relationship between literature and truth.

All of these are examples where attention to the boundary between fiction and nonfiction, rather than artificially simplifying matters, adds valuable complexity to our reading. But retaining a distinction between the two genres isn't only important for that literary reason. It also matters morally.

Labeling something as fiction allows for various forms of distancing. It blocks inferences from the text back to the views or experiences of the author and to the lives of people the author knows. (In the case of autofiction, these inferences may be all but irresistible, but we're on notice throughout that the author is denying themself the capacity for direct assertion and retaining the liberty to invent, adorn, and exaggerate.) Sophisticated readers know and accept that memoirists employ artistic license too, but for the most part they take memoirists at their word. For that reason, memoirists are much more committed to the truth of what they write, and much more responsible for the effects of what they write on other real people.

It's *valuable* to retain a literary world where these two forms of writing are possible: writing about hypothetical worlds and writing about the actual world (and, relatedly, making speculative suggestions and making direct assertions). They're each important, and when we disregard the difference between fiction and nonfiction we undermine the long-term viability of both. But, in addition, it's ethically *dangerous* to have a literary world where the two forms of writing aren't clearly distinguishable from each other. When people treat something fictional as nonfictional, serious injuries can result. All of which will be the subject of the rest of this book.

The fictionalist challenge argues that while memoir aims by its nature to be nonfiction, it's inevitably fiction and therefore constitutes an impossible project. Some memoirists, at least in certain moments, accept this conclusion. Essayist Carl H. Klaus says in an interview: "We do, in fact, aspire to write like ourselves even though we know that in some sense this is an impossibility ... It's a paradoxical thing."[84] Similarly, the pioneering theorist of autobiography Philippe Lejeune writes:

It's better to get on with the confessions: yes, I have been fooled. I believe that we can promise to tell the truth; I believe in the transparency of language, and in the existence of a complete subject who expresses himself through it; . . . I believe in the Holy Ghost of the first person. And who doesn't believe in it? But of course it also happens that I believe the contrary, or at least claim to believe it [. . .] Telling the truth about the self, constituting the self as complete subject—it is a fantasy. In spite of the fact that autobiography is impossible, this is no way prevents it from existing.[85]

For the reasons given in this chapter, I'm more sanguine than these two about the possibility of memoir: the act of telling the truth about yourself and your life on the page. Like Lejeune, I believe in the objective reality of the self and the world, the possibility of truth and knowledge, and the capacity of literature to capture and express all of that. The difference is that I don't think I'm fooling myself when I do. I also suspect that most memoirists and their readers, when they're not distracted by theorists, feel the same way. Adam Gopnik writes:

Academics' insistence that memoirs are fictions is unpersuasive to readers . . . The effort to communicate experience rather than to invent it, the feeling that, however distilled and removed it might be, it is still removed and distilled from a river of experience that the author cannot quite dam and alter as he wishes, is the secret of the memoir's appeal.[86]

If that's so, those of us who love memoirs might be well advised, even if we don't believe that memoirs are nonfiction, to adopt the nonfictional fiction that we do.

THREE

Should Memoirists Aim to Tell the Truth?

One upshot of the previous chapter is that the central aim of most memoirs—to tell a true story about the author's past experiences—is, in principle, achievable. Nothing about the self or the world or the mind or art rules that goal out as impossible from the get-go. But another upshot of that chapter is that the aim is, in practice, very tricky to fulfill. The lures of self-deception, the glitches of cognition, the fallibility of memory, the insidious pressures of narrative and literary craft: all of these can get in the way of an unbiased and fact-tracking interpretation of the personal past. Clear-eyed memoirists have to accept that, however hard they try to avoid it, their memoirs will contain factual inaccuracies, errors of judgment, self-serving justifications, unexplained lacunae, and unsupported leaps of faith. Failures like that are, to some degree, built into the game.

One possible emotional response to this situation is to agonize over your inability to meet the stringent standards of the truth. Another possible emotional response is to relax those standards (or, equivalently, your commitment to them). If we can never hope to tell the whole truth and nothing but the truth in autobiography, maybe knowingly telling some untruths isn't such a big deal. Perhaps memoirists should just use the facts of the past as a kind of helpful literary prompt and then tell the story any way they please. This isn't journalism, science, or scholarship, after all. We're talking about art!

There's a forceful presentation of that latter position in John D'Agata and Jim Fingal's controversial book *The Lifespan of a Fact*. (The focus is on non-autobiographical nonfiction, but the main points carry.) The book has a complex backstory. In 2003, *Harper's Magazine* rejected a narrative essay they'd commissioned D'Agata to

write for them, on grounds of factual inaccuracy. D'Agata then submitted the essay to the *Believer*, which handed it over to their own
fact-checker, Fingal. After seven years of back-and-forths between
John and Jim, the magazine eventually published the essay in 2010.
It then morphed into D'Agata's 2011 book *About a Mountain*, which,
as one reviewer nicely sums it up:

uses the federal government's highly controversial (and recently rejected) proposal to entomb the U.S.'s nuclear waste located in Yucca Mountain, near Las
Vegas, as [D'Agata's] way into a spiraling and subtle examination of the modern
city, suicide, linguistics, Edvard Munch's *The Scream*, ecological and psychic degradation, and the gulf between information and knowledge. Acting as a counter-
point to Yucca is the story of a teenager named Levi who leapt to his death off Las
Vegas' Stratosphere Motel.[1]

D'Agata and Fingal then decided to publish their protracted disagreement over the essay in the form of a 2012 book, which was converted
into a Broadway play by the same name in 2018. Halfway through this
not-all-that-unusual march from life to essay to book(s) to theater,
the story became much more unusual, shifting almost entirely from
the original set of subjects to the much more abstract question of the
extent to which veracity matters in narrative nonfiction.

    The Lifespan of a Fact (the book, not the play) consists of D'Agata's
original submission to the *Believer*, along with marginalia recording Fingal's extensive and highly detailed queries to D'Agata and
D'Agata's increasingly frustrated and impassioned replies. On the
basis of his own research and speculations, Fingal disputes such matters as which precise roads the teenager, Levi, took to the Vegas hotel,
which space in the parking building he parked his car, whether he
would have taken the elevator or the stairs, the color of the carpet,
whether the casino restaurant served roast potatoes or fries, how
crowded the hallway was, what the clouds were like, and the exact
minute the sun set on the night of Levi's suicide. It's easy to sympathize with D'Agata's complaint to Fingal that "your nitpicking is
absurd and it's ruining this essay."[2] But it's also easy to sympathize
with Fingal's complaint to D'Agata that he's "willfully manipulating
facts"[3] and "saying things that you know are blatantly untrue."[4]

    As the conflict escalates toward the end of the book, D'Agata types,

"Jim, please keep in mind that we are talking about the name of a slot machine here," and Jim replies, "We aren't talking about a slot machine, John, and you know it."[5] True enough: what's at stake for both men is nothing less than the integrity of narrative nonfiction as a genre, but the two have very different views about what that integrity consists in. D'Agata doesn't find Fingal's obsession with historical accuracy merely unnecessary; he finds it inimical to his literary aims. "Rules of any kind do not apply to art, they don't belong in art," he writes. "Art is supposed to change us, to challenge us, and yes, even to trick us."[6]

Most memoirists don't go for either of these extremes. (It's not even clear that D'Agata goes for one of them. He comes across in his book as an ardent asshole for art, but a direct result of his stated position is that it's hard to know if he actually means it.[7]) The large majority of literary self-narrators accept that total fidelity to the truth is undesirable and allow for some imaginative reconstruction along the way. Fudging the color of the carpet doesn't bother them. But they insist all the same that there are limits on acceptable invention. Being indifferent to veracity is a major sin in an autobiographer, they urge. We don't want to be that guy who faked a holocaust memoir! Or that guy who faked a three-month prison sentence just to sell his book and get on Oprah.[8] We don't even want to be that guy, John D'Agata, who committed the more minor but still troubling act of fiddling with the date of a boy's suicide in print. Don't be that guy!

This middle-of-the-road position is so plausible and widely accepted that it's tempting to just leave it at that. But, as stated, it leaves unanswered some tricky questions that no memoirist can avoid bumping into when sitting down to write. If we're aiming for a midway point between legalistic literal mindedness and freewheeling invention, as the standard response to the D'Agata-Fingal debate suggests, where exactly does that midpoint lie? Which departures from the truth are acceptable, which aren't, and why? The aim of this chapter is to shed some light on those questions, by discussing why truth-telling matters to us both in life and in memoir.

Truth-Telling and Literary Truth

Perhaps it never did snow that August in Vermont; perhaps there never were flurries in the night wind, and maybe no one else felt the ground hard-

ening and summer already dead even as we pretended to bask in it, but
that was how it felt to me, and it might as well have snowed, could have
snowed, did snow.

JOAN DIDION[9]

Should we try to tell the truth in memoir? And if so, what kind of
truth, how much of it, and why? Let's start narrowing in on this
question by setting aside moral considerations for the moment and
asking what relationship truth has to the purely literary aims of
memoir.

Writers often suggest that the status of memoir as literature means
that memoirists should aim for a special kind of truth in their writing. The goal, this idea goes, isn't the "literal" truth, but the "literary"
truth. That's a nice phrase, but what could it mean?

It'll help to start by discussing what "literary truth" might look like
in the case of fiction rather than literary nonfiction. One of the major
ongoing debates in philosophy of literature is over how, if at all, fiction
can express truth.[10] It's very common to claim that fiction does have
this power. To take one example, the critic Malcolm Bowie writes in
his book on Proust:

Fiction has . . . assumed a responsibility which in earlier dispensations might have
fallen to theology, or philosophy, or mathematics: to make sense of the world. Fiction, especially novel-writing, is an improbable candidate for this role, for it brings
with it such a lumber of pseudo-fact and gratuitous fantasy. But the novelist . . . is
a heroic discoverer of order in chaos, and of beauty in the bric-a-brac of daily life.
Even as he fibs, fiddles, and fabulates he is bringing a new sense of structure and
a new truthfulness into being. Even as he loses himself in the trifling particulars
of social life or the byways of introspective thought he is finding a lost key to the
nature of things.[11]

Bowie is suggesting here that literary fiction is a source of truth,
knowledge, and understanding—as much as nonliterary disciplines
like science and philosophy (and maybe even more so). But, as Bowie
himself notes, that claim is puzzling on its face. Fiction is, after all,
made up. How, then, could a novel or short story contain truth?

One answer here focuses on what's known as "propositional
truth."[12] A proposition is a claim, of the kind you can assert in a sentence. The proposition that Keanu Reeves is a nice guy can be as-

serted in the sentence "Keanu Reeves is a nice guy," and that sentence is true if (and only if) Keanu Reeves is in fact a nice guy. Fiction is made up of a bunch of sentences that assert propositions, and some of those sentences are undoubtedly true. For instance, a novel can refer to real places (San Francisco), people (Cary Grant), and things (octopuses) and describe those places, people, and things accurately. People can, and do, learn from fiction as a result of this: they glean, say, travel advice, scientific information, historical facts, or cooking instructions in the course of following the story.

But these sorts of propositions clearly aren't the kind of thing that Bowie and other defenders of "literary truth" have in mind. Accessing the truth, via a novel, that Diosdado P. Macapagal was president of the Philippines in 1963 hardly involves finding what Bowie calls "a lost key to the nature of things." When people claim that fiction is a route to truth they're usually envisaging something grander than factual descriptions of this kind. So a common move here is to narrow the category of literary truth from *all* true propositions expressed in a literary work to just those true propositions that have "deep" or "far-reaching" content.

When people make this move, they usually mean propositions that express universal generalizations about human nature or the human condition. These propositions aren't likely to be stated directly in the work, in a simple sentence or two, but they might plausibly be said to be implied by it when it's taken as a whole. In a short piece on a single scene in *Anna Karenina*, for instance, the fiction writer Mary Gaitskill extracts what she takes to be four truths about human nature across the board.[13] People don't have consistent, defined personalities: they act unpredictably and erratically. That's because they contain multitudes: "there may be two, or more, different people inside of us." Some of these internal people are hidden: "the truest parts of people can be buried." And our hidden selves may appear only briefly and never appear again afterward.

Tolstoy may well be saying all of those things in this scene, and they may well all be true. Again, though, it doesn't seem that, if fiction does express truth, this is the main or most important kind of truth that it's expressing. Readers do seem to go to fiction for insight into human psychology, but if they were in search of true universal generalizations about human nature, it'd make more sense for them to read books written by psychologists instead. Psychologists state their claims about human nature directly and clearly; they back them up with well-established methodology, empirical data, and careful argumentation; and they aren't doing several other things in their papers at once that might distract them or us from their observations. Fiction writers, on the other hand, often work by implication and association; they have no distinctive method; they don't amass large amounts of data, perform controlled experiments, or undergo academic peer review; and they're generally as or more invested in telling compelling stories and producing well-crafted language than they are in proving a point. As a result, literary truth would look pretty shabby and unreliable if "true propositions expressing universal generalizations" were all it amounted to.

Some give up at this point and claim that the aim of fiction isn't to express truth at all. But there's another option here. We can argue that literary truth isn't (mainly) a matter of propositional truth, but instead of what we might call "experiential truth." On this line, the truth-related value of fiction isn't that it gives us access to true claims about the world, but rather that it helps us *see what it's like* to have certain experiences of the world (many of which may be unfamiliar to us).

You read *Wuthering Heights*, say, and suddenly you have a real grip on what it feels like to be possessed by a fervent, uncontrollable passion for someone you see as your soul mate, though you yourself have been a cold fish since birth. Here the experience you're having is emotional, but you might experience a more intellectual epiphany instead. Say you read Sartre's *Nausea* and suddenly you *get*, at a deep level, what it would be like to view the world as existentialists do, though you yourself have always been (and after reading Sartre, remain) a committed theist who believes that the world operates rationally according to a beneficent plan.

In these cases, the best explanation for what's going on isn't that you've learned the true propositions that soul mates are real or that with great freedom comes great responsibility (let alone the more prosaic facts that heather grows on moors or that Paris is in France—who knew?). Your new knowledge isn't propositional at all. It's not "knowledge that," as philosophers sometimes put it, but "knowledge how." As a result of reading the work, you know, from the inside, how it feels, emotionally or intellectually, to undergo a certain kind of experience or have a certain kind of worldview. As Hilary Putnam puts it:

I do not *learn* [from reading Celine] that love does not exist, that all human beings are hateful and hating (even if–and I am sure this is not the case–those proposi- tions should be true). What I learn is to see the world as it looks to someone who is sure that hypothesis is correct. I see what plausibility that hypothesis has; what it would be like if it *were* true; how someone could possibly think that it *is* true.[14]

The result may not be a gain in propositional knowledge, but it's a genuine and valuable cognitive advance, anyway.[15] It can help you understand particular other humans and situations in the real world by analogy ("Ah, Jayla's doing a Heathcliff right now!"). And it may also illuminate your understanding of more general ethical, psycho- logical, and philosophical matters—say, the costs of certain choices, the relationships between social values, the springs of human action, the nature of personal identity or consciousness, the limits on free action, and so on. By imagining what it's like for fictional characters to go through experiences or to adopt views unlike your own, you can entertain interesting hypotheses about all these and other top- ics, and note your own reactions to them, which you can then reflect on and test in other ways. The fictional work you read may not itself directly contain psychological or philosophical truths, but the experi- ences you have while reading it may lead you to such truths via inde- pendent means.

I think this experiential truth is the best answer to the question of what kind of truth fiction provides. Fiction may also provide proposi- tional truths, but they're less important because, as I've said, they're not mainly what we go to fiction for, and they're not distinctive of it. I also think that experiential truth is the best answer to the question of what kind of truth literature in general provides: including literary nonfiction, which includes memoir. As in the case of fiction, we *can* go to memoir to learn true propositions about real people, places, and things. ("Huh! Opossums have the lowest brain to body ratio of any mammal!") But we mainly go to it (in the truth department, anyway) to get a grip on what it might feel like to undergo certain experiences or have certain values or views, and, often, to use that reflection to get clearer on our own. ("After reading this essay, I get what it's like to be a refugee/Mormon/deep-sea diver in a way I really didn't before.")

The important difference, of course, is that in the case of memoir, a reader is learning not what it *would* have felt like for a fictional character to undergo an experience *if* they had been alive, but (ideally) what it *did* feel like for the *real* memoirist to undergo a *genuine* experience in the *actual* past. We go to memoir, in large part, to discover what it was like for this particular real person to grow up in that family, live in that place, undergo that ordeal, participate in that event, work in that profession, have that relationship, and so on. This semimagical ability to transmit an experience from mind to mind, or heart to heart, is one of memoir's peculiar charms. The writer is whispering in our ear "this is how I lived: see and feel and understand it through me," and, if they've done their job well, we do, somehow, see, feel, and understand it. We gain an imaginative, empathetic grasp of the experience of another real human, perhaps quite different from us, who we usually never have and never will meet.

It's worth emphasizing here that merely transmitting the experience isn't enough: readers also expect to see the memoirist reflecting on their experience. We want not only to inhabit the author's past, but also to watch the author drawing out their understanding of its significance, of what it meant. Often this involves the author meditating on what happened from the perspective of their later and current self, a meditation that can open up fissures between past and present points of view. But even when this doesn't happen (explicitly), and we get a more univocal take, it's watching the author's mind turning over the past till it glints with insight that's the other distinctive charm of the genre.

When memoirists succeed in capturing their inner experience of the past and its significance, they attain what I'll call "nonfictional experiential truth." It's sometimes called the "subjective truth" instead, but that risks being misleading. That's because, though it's natural to contrast subjective things with objective things, the experiential truth as I understand it here is actually objective, in one popular sense of that slippery term. Experiential truths are true regardless of your views or desires about their subject matter, and you can therefore be mistaken about them, even when it's your own experiences that they pertain to. There are real, objective facts about how you felt at your tenth birthday party, for instance, and if it's the experiential truth you're after, not just anything you say now about those feelings will do.

The more useful distinction isn't between experiential truth and

objective truth, but between experiential truth and what we can call
the "historical truth." The historical truth is what happened in the
past, whereas the experiential truth is how what happened felt to you
and how you interpreted it, then and later. (What I'm calling the historical truth is sometimes called the "literal truth," but that sets up
another misleading false contrast: there can be a literal truth about
how you felt at your birthday party.)

I've suggested so far that experiential truth is the sort of truth that
memoirists should be after. But what does that goal (roughly, what
the past felt and feels like) have to do with the historical truth (how
the past really was)? At first glance, not a lot. Experiential and historical truth can obviously come apart: you can, for instance, experience
your birthday party as a wrongful injury at the time and come to see
later that it wasn't one at all. If experiential truth is the kind of truth
memoirists should be after, then, it can seem like a good idea to just
dispense with concern for historical truth. If the two line up, great; if
they don't, experiential truth should prevail.

Using different terms than me, Vivian Gornick makes just such a
suggestion. A memoir or personal essay doesn't need to get "the lit-
eralness of the situation" right, she tells us, but only to capture "the
emotional truth of the story . . . the bottom of the tale at hand."[16]
Didion suggests something similar before the passage about August
snow in Vermont quoted above. She writes that "how it felt to me"
is her goal as a writer, and says "not only have I always had trouble
distinguishing between what happened and what merely might have
happened, but I remain unconvinced that the distinction, for my purposes, matters."[17]

Some writers make the stronger claim that a commitment to historical truth isn't just irrelevant to capturing the experiential truth,
but actually *obstructs* it. There's a more plausible and a less plausible
version of this claim. The more plausible version says that the experiential truth can sometimes best be expressed by leaving certain historical facts out of a memoir. Henry James's nephew complained to
him that, in James's memoir about his brother William, Henry had
deleted a phrase in one of William's letters. Henry admitted it, but replied that the phrase he'd removed wasn't representative of William's
real self. He'd wanted to "do his best" for William, "that is, do with
him everything I seemed to feel him like."[18]

Tracy Kidder offers a similar example from the writing of his book *Among Schoolchildren*, which narrates the year he spent observing a fifth-grade classroom in Massachusetts. At one point the teacher, Mrs. Zajac, lost her cool, criticized a troubled student's mother in front of the class, and deeply regretted it afterward. The episode happened, undoubtedly, but Kidder decided not to include it, because the drama of the scene would have given it a significance in the book that was out of proportion to its significance in real life. Seen in the context of the entire year, the teacher's indiscretion was clearly anomalous, but the entire year couldn't be reproduced in the book. Kidder's aim, like James's, was to "do with" Mrs. Zajac "everything [he] seemed to feel [her] like," and in this case, as in the case of William's letter, that required leaving something out. In commenting on this choice, Kidder's editor, Richard Todd, writes:

Although the truth must always be found in facts, some facts, sometimes, obscure the truth. Sometimes that essential effort of writing, making some things small and others big, includes making something invisible.[19]

This seems right to me. Though editing people's letters adds ethical complications (James himself felt bad about it and wrote to his nephew "never again shall I stray from my proper work," i.e., novel writing), the general point is persuasive. It reflects the point made in chapter 2 that narratives are necessarily selective, and that such selectivity needn't involve distortion or falsehood, but can be helpfully clarifying, in part by removing distracting and misleading information.

But there's another version of the claim that historical truth can conflict with experiential truth that I find much less plausible. This is the idea that the experiential truth can sometimes best be expressed not by *omitting* genuine historical facts, but by *adding* fake ones: in short, by making stuff up. The narrator of John Barth's "Anonymiad" says: "I found by pretending that things had happened which in fact had not, and that people existed who didn't, I could achieve a lovely truth which actuality obscures."[20] Pam Houston was presumably following this kind of advice when she concocted three of the six people she "interviewed" for a magazine article, and when she claimed to have kayaked rather than hiked the Ardèche river canyon in a "nonfiction" essay for another magazine. "To spice things up," she writes of the latter, "I added a water fight with three Italian kayakers. There was some good-natured flirting across the language barrier."

"It is hard," Houston muses in an essay on these actions, "[...] to stand here and say the scene with the three Italian kayakers is the truest thing in the entire essay (though, of course it is) even though it never really happened."[21]

This kind of claim is really regrettable. It involves a misleading equivocation between two different kinds of experiential truth: the kind we get in fiction and the kind we get in nonfiction. I don't disagree with Houston that, if she were writing fiction, the scene with the kayakers might have expressed a truth. As I said above, fiction can capture a genuine truth about what it feels like to, say, kayak down a river with some hot Italians. But what the scene definitely *doesn't* express is nonfictional experiential truth, of the kind that memoir is after. It's just false to say that the scene with the kayakers is "the truest thing in the entire essay" if it's that kind of truth we're talking about. By playing on our background belief that fiction can express experiential truth, Houston is illegitimately shoring up a much less plausible claim about the nature of truth in nonfiction.

It's much less plausible because a memoirist is quite unlikely to get to the nonfictional experiential truth by making things up. Just inventing what happened at that life-altering birthday party rather than trying hard to remember what it was really like won't allow the author to capture the truth about how it really felt back then or what it means to them now. As Phillip Lopate attests: "making things up, bending the facts, throws off my attempt to get as close as possible to the shape underlying experience or to the psychology that flows from the precisely real."[22]

It might be said here that for the goal of nonfictional experiential truth to be achieved, all the writer needs to do is commit to historical accuracy about the *core* facts of their experience. But it's not always easy to tell which facts about your past are core and which aren't. Lopate suggests persuasively that "the whole plausibility of a nonfiction narrative may be undermined by altering or evading crucial details."[23] There's also a slippery-slope worry here: if the writer gives themself regular license to fiddle with the historical truth about small matters, they may be increasingly tempted to fiddle with it about larger matters, again at the expense of experiential truth.

I think there's a strong argument, based on these reasons, in favor of memoirists adopting a general policy of respecting the historical truth: where that doesn't mean including everything that happened in the past, but does mean not making things up. The chief goal of memoir, when it comes to truth, is to capture nonfictional experiential truth. But achieving that goal requires memoirists to attempt to get a real grip on the historical truth too, and to indicate when and where the two diverge, if they do.

Importantly, while this position rules out Houston-style fictionalizing, it doesn't mean that each particular *sentence* (or paragraph, or section) in a memoir needs to be true. This follows from some important features of literary writing.

In nonliterary writing—such as we get in science and much of history and philosophy—we can usually assess the truth of a piece of work simply by assessing the truth of the individual sentences it contains. In a medical report, for instance, we might get "the patient awoke at midnight on January 16, 1967, overcome by itching" and "the patient presented at the clinic eight hours later covered in hives." We expect each sentence in the report to be "truth-apt" (that is, capable of being either true or false), and we assume that the truth expressed by the report reduces atomistically and without remainder to the truths of the individual sentences it includes. In the standard case, there's no extra truth to be found in the report as a whole beyond that.

Literature, including literary nonfiction, isn't like that. For one thing, not all sentences in a memoir or essay are truth-apt. Some may best be read as proposing a certain vision of the world rather than attempting to make a factual statement. As Peter Lamarque suggests, such a vision "might be uninteresting, incoherent, undeveloped, uninspired, clichéd, far-fetched or generally unappealing ... but it is hard to see how it could be *mistaken*."[24] Similarly, some sentences include metaphors that may be apt or not apt, but not *truth*-apt: not true or false in the way we usually use those terms. Think of Shakespeare's "Juliet is the sun" or Robert Burns's "my love is like a red, red rose." The women described aren't stars or plants, but the statements about them are right in a way that, say, "Juliet is a cockroach" isn't.

Metaphors don't only appear in literary works in a single phrase or sentence, but can also take the form of extended passages or motifs. Carmen Maria Machado's memoir, *In the Dream House*, is made up of a collection of independently titled sections, most under two pages in length. Many of these sections approach the subject of the memoir (the author's relationship with her abusive ex-girlfriend) obliquely and figuratively, using elements of folklore and fiction. One of these sections, *"Dream House as* the Queen and the Squid," is written entirely as a fable. Nothing in that section is strictly true, but the exchange of letters described in it tracks the content of the emails that Machado and her ex sent after their breakup.[25] The metaphorical fairy-tale frame isn't just a handy legal dodge (emails are private property): set alongside the other elements of the book, it adds genuine depth and resonance—nonfictional experiential truth—to the overall story being told, despite itself being fiction.

This example leads into a further point. It's generally the case in literary writing that the meaning of a work doesn't reduce in a straightforward way to the meaning of the set of individual sentences contained in it. The connections between those sentences, their means of expression, their arrangement, the allusions they make to other literary works, and so on, can result in resonances and thematic elements that go beyond the propositions the sentences express. This is especially clear in poetry, maybe, but it's true of fiction and memoir too, and it's part of the mystery and allure of literature in general. In one sense, *Anna Karenina* is just a set of sentences reporting a series of fictional events set in nineteenth-century Russia. But through that set of sentences the novel manages to express a complex set of much larger ideas, none of which are directly stated in the text.

It's those larger truths that literary writers are primarily shooting for, and as a result they may be uninterested in the truth of individual sentences within their work. What matters is the meaning of the work as a whole, not the meaning of parts of it considered in isolation. Fiction writers can be wholly unconcerned with the truth of their individual sentences. But the same is true, to a lesser extent, of memoirists. Timothy Dow Adams says of Gertrude Stein's highly unconventional memoir, *The Autobiography of Alice B. Toklas,* "nearly everything in the autobiography is slightly false, but the whole becomes true."[26] The overall frame of Stein's memoir—the mask of Toklas as narrator, the ironic tone throughout—makes it obvious that calling her to task about the historical accuracy of her sentences would be a giant missing of the point.

A final relevant feature of literary writing is that it's highly imaginative: it involves intense speculation, wondering, exploration of non-existent possibilities. Again, this is clearest in the case of fiction, but it applies to nonfiction too. Memoirists and essayists often reflect on the page about how things *could* have gone, about what might have happened instead, about how they or others could have responded differently than they did, and the implications of all that for understanding the personal past. In real life we do often engage in these kinds of counterfactual reflections and find them illuminating. So it's both realistic and useful for memoirists to engage in them on the page too. For this reason, a commitment to experiential truth doesn't mean that memoirists have to narrowly "stick to the facts." They can also include the counterfacts, provided they're careful to indicate their nature as such.[27]

Sometimes people use a different distinction than the ones I've mentioned so far. They contrast the "truth" with the "deeper truth" (or the "capital *T* Truth") and say that the memoirist's proper aim is the second of those. It's not totally clear what this means. If the "deeper truth" just refers to a truth not visible on the surface of a work's individual sentences, I agree that it's the proper goal (for the reasons I've just mentioned). But if, as it sometimes seems, the deeper truth is meant in a more value-oriented way—as a truth peculiar to literature that's superior to the truth we get from "mere *facts*"—I can't say I'm a fan of this suggestion. The facts or truths attained in history, philosophy, and science can be both profound and highly valuable. Why not just say that literature offers a different set of insights, or a set of insights achieved differently? Truth is of value wherever, and however, we find it: there's no need to make it a competition.

Let's say that all of the above captures the appropriate goal for memoir, where truth is concerned. How do memoirists succeed in achieving it? It's sometimes suggested that all a memoirist needs to do is be *sincere*. If the author has made an honest and sustained effort to recreate their past experience and interrogate its meaning—working hard to plumb the depths of memory and push beyond easy conclusions, rooting out all obfuscation, pretense, or deceit—they've done their job.

This can't be right, though. If a memoirist is to capture the experiential truth, they need to not just intend to get the past right, but *actually get it right*, at least to some significant extent. A memoir-

ist might be totally sincere and truthful, but due to pervasive ignorance or self-deception, provide a substantially false characterization
of their past experience, and most of us would consider this a defect
in their work.

There's a wrinkle here, however. Sometimes a mistaken picture of
the author's experience, even one that results from insincerity, can
give us a true (truer) picture of the author's character. Mark Doty's
sister told him that he made mistakes in his memoir *Firebird*, but that
"the things you got wrong just make it that much more you."[28] Similarly, Timothy Dow Adams writes:

> Sherwood Anderson's cavalier way with facts, his predilection for story over his-
> tory, his manipulation in print of people's characters, and his insistence that if some
> of the people who appear in his books did not actually say the words ascribed to
> them, then they should have—all of these combine to present a truer picture of
> Anderson than a straightforward, factual biography could. The picture is made
> truer when we consider that he was as unreliable with factual truth in his actual
> life.[29]

Given that a large part of the point of memoir is to give a true picture
of one's self, alongside one's experience, this seems like a success of
sorts. Maybe thinking of such cases, the Victorian biographer Leslie
Stephen suggested that "an autobiography, alone of all books, may
be more valuable in proportion to the amount of misrepresentation
which it contains."[30] I wouldn't want to go that far, but I'd like to leave
open the possibility that not all failures to capture the truth about
one's past are demerits. That said, in standard cases, if such failures
are pervasive, they're highly likely to downgrade our assessment of
the value of the work, and for good reason.

Does what I've argued for here commit memoirists to Fingal-
style obsession over getting tiny details right? No, because memoirists have various strategies available to them for dealing with gaps in
their memory and knowledge other than making things up. They can,
for instance, indicate to their readers that they're uncertain about the
matter, signal clearly that they're engaging in counterfactual speculation or speaking figuratively, or decline to describe in high-def terms
material that's fuzzy. (I'll return to such strategies in more detail
below.) A commitment to veracity in memoir is also consistent with a

range of literary devices—such as selection, compression, and meta-phor—that are used regularly in personal narrative. That's because (as I argued in chapter 2) none of these things necessarily converts a story into fiction.

Respect for historical truth in literary nonfiction doesn't turn it into nonliterary journalism, then, as D'Agata seems to fear. It turns it into not lying. That said, it remains very important to remember that memoir isn't journalism, and that fact raises the possibility of a genu-ine conflict for memoirists where truth is concerned.

The goal of capturing the experiential truth of the author's actual life is what distinguishes memoir from other forms of literature. But memoir also shares distinct aims with other literary genres—including, say, the aims of making something beautiful, original, com-plex, shocking, or profound. There's no guarantee at all that a book or essay that captures the experiential truth about your life will have those qualities (because, for better or worse, your life may not have them). As a result, to put it grandly, Art may come into conflict with Truth. We'll address this worry toward the end of the chapter.

Truth-Telling and Ethics

Writers of memoirs might worry about slips in historical truth under-mining their relationship to the literary goal of nonfictional experien-tial truth. But many readers of memoirs are primarily worried about slips in historical truth undermining the writer's relationship to *them*. Certain forms of evasion, dissimulation, or deception on the page, they argue, are morally, not just aesthetically, problematic. So to get a fuller understanding of why truth-telling in memoir might matter, we need to turn to ethical considerations. What are memoirists' moral responsibilities, if any, when it comes to telling the truth, and what do they rest on? We'll start, in this section, with a general discussion of the ethics of truth-telling and apply it to the case of memoir in the next.

A couple of clarifications first. For one, I'm interested here in ethics rather than the law. Writers have legal obligations within particular jurisdictions not to commit specified forms of fraud and libel. I won't be discussing those, but rather writers' moral obligations with respect to truth-telling. Not every moral obligation has a corresponding legal obligation. (I might be morally obliged to call my lovely mother on her birthday, but it would be tyrannical and counterproductive to make that the law.) Relatedly, my aim here isn't to throw anyone into writer jail. To say that someone has a moral duty to do something isn't to say that they should be forced to do it or punished for not doing it. There are good reasons for giving artists wide berth to write and publish, free of either legal coercion or social pressure. That doesn't get them totally off the hook, though. Most of us, writers included, don't care only about what our rights are or about what we can be legally or socially compelled to do. We also want, independently, to do the right thing: to act decently, especially when the interests of others and our relationships to them are at stake.

Second, many forms of falsehood are possible in memoir. Montaigne wrote: "If falsehood, like truth, had only one face, we would be in better shape. For we would take as certain the opposite of what the liar said. But the reverse of truth has a hundred thousand shapes and a limitless field."[31] Even within the general domain of lying, as Dow Adams notes, we find multiple subspecies, including "quibbling, misleading, disinforming, duping, withholding, dissembling, disguising, glossing over, simulating, counterfeiting, embroidering, inventing, fudging, doctoring, and being mendacious."[32] But on top of that, as David Lazar notes, a writer can exhibit falsehood without outright lying, via "forms of psychological manipulation, the drawing of conclusions, and epiphanies that seem labored, unworthy, unbelievable, false."[33] As Lazar remarks, these latter faults can be as or more important to our assessment of the work than lies. That said, it'll make sense to focus here on the more straightforward instance of outright lying. If we can get clear on what makes that simpler case disturbing, we can hopefully extend our conclusions, at least in part, to the subtler variants.

So, lying. What is it, anyway? It'll work well enough here to use the traditional definition of a lie as "making a statement believed to be false, with the intention of getting another to accept it as true."[34] If we go with this, there are a variety of acts that may seem like lying, by virtue of sharing several of its features, but that won't count as lies proper.

Because lying requires *asserting* that something is true, you're not lying if you merely *state* that something is true, while, say, winking, crossing your fingers, acting in a play, telling a joke, or singing a song.

For the same reason, you're not lying if you merely stay silent. In addition, because lying requires an intention to deceive, you're not lying if you state something in the context of a fictional work. Novelists don't intend to deceive their readers, and readers who know they're reading a novel aren't deceived. For the same reason, you're not lying if you state something ironically. Ironists don't intend their audience to take their falsehoods at face value, but to interpret them in a larger context that makes their falsity or the speaker's lack of belief in them clear.

Crossing your fingers, staying silent, writing a novel, and speaking ironically are in some ways like lies, but aren't lies, and aren't morally troubling. Other acts are in some ways like lies, but aren't lies, and *are* morally troubling. One example is withholding information, that is, omitting to provide facts that someone needs if they're to gain true beliefs or correct false ones. Some cases of withholding information are morally permissible (your neighbor doesn't need to know you ate kale salad for lunch yesterday). But if there's a shared expectation that the information in question will be provided (maybe a promise has been made or there's a professional obligation to offer it), keeping someone in the dark about it can be wrong. Other examples of troubling lie-like acts are various forms of deception. Lying may aim at deception, but it's not the same thing, because you can lie but fail to deceive. Deception, for its part, may involve lying, but not necessarily: you can deceive by actions, gestures, facial expressions, exclamations, questions, requests, symbols, or remaining silent, whereas lying involves an actual assertion. All deception requires is that you intentionally cause someone—somehow—to have a false belief that you believe is false.

Finally, hyperbole lies somewhere in between novel writing and deception on the moral spectrum of lie-like acts. It doesn't involve stating or implying something totally contrary to the facts, but it does involve magnifying them. In some cases, it can be outright deceptive; in others, it can be a form of irony or joking.

What makes lying—just straight-up lying, as distinct from all these related things—morally troubling? Almost everyone thinks it is: the condemnation of liars may be one of the few true universals in human moral codes. Some suggest that this is no coincidence: we don't come across societies indifferent to lying, they say, because a society can't survive if its members aren't, at least most of time, committed to telling the truth. The philosopher Francis Hutcheson wrote in 1755: "Suppose men imagined there was no obligation to veracity, and acted accordingly; speaking as often against their own opinion as according to it; would not all pleasure of conversation be destroyed, and all confidence in narration?"[35] The suggestion is that widespread lying pervasively undermines people's confidence in each other's word, and we can expect that in turn to undermine the various projects and relationships that hold society together and enable it to flourish. If we think that the survival of humanity is a morally worthwhile goal, then, we should proscribe lying.

This argument is intuitive and popular. (To take one recent-ish example, James Stewart's Pulitzer Prize–winning book about the mendaciousness of public figures in the United States is subtitled "How False Statements Are Undermining America."[36]) There's surely something right about it, but it can't be the whole story about the wrongness of lying. To begin with, it's unclear that widespread lying *does* destroy social trust. After all, we see plenty of it going on around us, without the social fabric fully shredding to pieces. This might be because we can trust people for reasons other than their truthfulness: even if we can't rely on their word, we can rely on their benevolence or self-interest. Or it might be because it's not the fact of a lie, but the intention behind it that matters most: in some cases, our trust in others can actually increase when they lie to us, if we see the lie as motivated by concern for our welfare.

Another reason the social trust argument can't be the whole story is that it doesn't capture the heart of the anger that most of us feel when we're lied to. When you find out that your family member, friend, or colleague has told you a lie, your first response is unlikely to be "You're undermining America!" (or New Zealand, or Bangladesh). Instead, the injury is likely to feel a whole lot more local than that. The liar hasn't (just) wronged society, you feel, they've wronged *you*—and not merely in your capacity as a citizen.

One way to accommodate this is to stick with the general idea that diminished credibility undermines trust, but apply that idea to trust within individual personal relationships, rather than trust across society as a whole. The moral problem with lying to your friend, then, is that it undermines the trust that's essential to the survival of that particular friendship, a friendship that she (and you) may highly value.

Again, this is clearly part of the story, but also again, not all of it, and for the same two reasons. Personal relationships can survive a significant amount of lying: in some cases, their survival might actually depend on it. And this consideration still seems too distant from the core of what bothers us about being lied to. "You're undermining our friendship!" is certainly closer to that core than "You're undermining America!" but still not close enough. When you find out you've been lied to you don't (primarily) feel you've been deprived of a valuable good. Instead, you feel you've been some potent combination of betrayed and disrespected.

Why do you feel betrayed? One reason might be that, as W. D. Ross suggested, every lie involves the breaking of a promise.[37] Built into each act of assertion, Ross said, is an implicit promise to be truthful. When I say to you "I didn't eat the rest of the cherry pie," you automatically hear me as also saying "I promise I believe that's true." This might explain why lying is usually considered worse than merely deceiving. If I lie to you that I didn't eat the rest of the pie, I'm deceiving you *and* breaking a promise to you, whereas if I just put cherry juice on Fido's face to frame him but remain silent, I'm merely deceiving.

Another way of putting this is to say that a lie actively *invites* trust in a way that mere deception doesn't. When someone accepts the relevant invitation and gives that trust, but then finds out it was unwarranted, they feel not just disappointed or resentful but the distinctive sensation of betrayal.[38] Colin O'Neill makes the interesting suggestion here that to trust someone is to honor them: to regard them as the sort of person who will act with goodwill toward you.[39] Honoring them in this way benefits them, partly by paying them a moral compliment, partly by opening up opportunities for them that put you in a vulnerable position. Since the appropriate response to receiving such a benefit is to be grateful, when someone abuses your trust, they don't merely break a (perhaps implicit) promise to you, but also violate a requirement of gratitude toward you. Rather than being grateful for the honor of your trust, they decide to use it against you. The characteristic element of surprise in betrayal springs from the fact that while you believed the liar had integrity, and also would be disinclined to use that belief of yours against you, neither of those things turned out to be true.

That's the betrayal part of lying, then. What about the disrespect part? Probably the most common argument against lying, other than the argument that it undermines or betrays trust, is that it violates the autonomy, or freedom, of the person lied to. While the trust argument is common among utilitarians, given their overriding concern with social welfare, the autonomy argument was most famously advanced by their chief adversary, Immanuel Kant.[40] Kant argued that morality is centrally concerned with respecting the agency of others: their right to choose and pursue their own goals in life. One way we can fail to respect others' agency is to use violence against them: by physically attacking them or locking them up. But another way we can do it is by lying to them. People need accurate information about the world if they're to identify their options, assess them for desirability and feasibility, and then enact their choices. Lying to someone involves messing with their access to that information and thereby interfering with their decisions. In a certain respect, lying can be seen as worse than physical coercion. It involves controlling someone via their beliefs: reaching, if you like, into their very minds. Because, for Kant, the dignity and worth of every human is grounded in their rational capacities, lying is a direct assault on the core of their personhood.

Lying tends to interfere with people's idiosyncratic aims. But it also interferes, by its very nature, with an aim that almost everyone has. That's the aim of having an accurate grip on how the world really is. Most of us wouldn't want to be deceived even if it had no effect whatsoever on our experiences. When asked to make a hypothetical choice between marriage to a faithful partner and marriage to an unfaithful and deceiving partner—partners who are otherwise identical and treat us in precisely the same way—no one chooses the second over the first, and very few of us claim to be indifferent between the two. This suggests that we value access to the truth just in itself, for its own sake. Harry Frankfurt writes, in this vein:

The most irreducibly bad thing about lies is that they contrive to interfere with, and to impair, our natural effort to apprehend the real state of affairs . . . Insofar as [the liar] succeeds in this, we acquire a view of the world that has its source in his imagination rather than being directly and reliably grounded in the relevant facts. The world we live in, insofar as our understanding of it is fashioned by the lie, is an imaginary world . . . a world that others cannot enter, and in which even the liar himself does not fully reside.[41]

These violations of people's autonomous choices are bad enough— but it gets worse! Liars don't usually aim to distort other people's beliefs just for the fun of it. Normally they're advancing a substantial agenda of their own, and this is another characteristically Kantian way in which they fail to respect the people they lie to. Kant argued that we should never use other people purely as a means to our own ends. But that's what liars generally do: they manipulate their listeners by inducing them to do or not do things in accordance with the liar's own goals. Paul Faulkner notes that one way liars manipulate their hearers is to implicitly threaten them with resentment if they fail to believe the liar.[42] People don't want to insult others by questioning their commitment to veracity, so they're inclined to take liars at their word rather than interrogate them further or seek additional evidence for their claims. In this way, the liar manipulates the lied-to's moral commitments—another core source of their dignity, for Kant— as well as their rational capacities.

A final Kantian argument against lying is that it's unfair. According to the first formulation of Kant's categorical imperative, it's morally wrong to act on principles that you're unwilling to have everyone comply with. You shouldn't single yourself out for special treatment, according yourself moral permissions, and accompanying advantages, that you don't extend to others. But that's precisely what liars do. They can only lie successfully if others don't generally lie, because if there's no norm of truth-telling in place, no one will be inclined to believe what they say. Lying is a kind of free-riding on the integrity of others: liars gain an advantage over their hearers with respect to the information they lie about, and fail to play their part in keeping the institution of veracity that thus benefits them running.

All of these are ways in which lying wrongs other humans. But there's also a strand in Kant that focuses on the wrong that lying does to liars themselves, as well as to rationality, period. Kant notes that lying is stressful for the liar: "truthfulness, if adopted as a principle, spares us the anxiety of maintaining agreement among our lies and not becoming entangled ourselves in their serpentine coils."[43] It can also lead to guilt, and to loneliness, and to the risk of being found out and mistrusted. But, for Kant, the worst part of lying for the liar is that it violates their own dignity as a rational being. As such, lying is also an offense against reason itself. We get something like this last line in the Christian tradition too. Saint Thomas Aquinas argued that intentionally asserting a falsehood is wrong even if you don't thereby intentionally deceive someone.[44] It's simply morally wrong to assert false things, regardless of the consequences for you or anyone else. God, or Reason, I guess, is listening.

Due to the combined weight of all these reasons, Kant is history's most famous opponent of lying. He regarded the prohibition on deception as an unconditional duty that holds without exception, regardless of the consequences—and if you're wondering whether he really meant that, well, he did. He notoriously claimed that if a murderer comes to the door asking whether your friend is hiding inside the house (and he is), you're not permitted to lie about it, even if the result is that your friend is savagely killed right in front of you.

Most people find this kind of absolutism impossible to stomach. They're more inclined to the moderate position that although lying is very often wrong, for some or all of the reasons canvassed above, it can nonetheless be justified in certain limited cases. This line is common among utilitarians. Given that the utilitarian prohibition on lying derives from its bad social consequences, that prohibition can sometimes be overridden when the consequences of lying are either not very bad or are very good. Sometimes lying might be the best or only way to protect or promote other rights, obligations, and interests that utilitarians also care about. But Kantians can take the moderate position too, if they're willing to adjust or reinterpret their founder's theory somewhat. Some lies are only very minor incursions on people's autonomy, and if they're necessarily disrespectful, that disrespect might nonetheless be counterbalanced by the respect motivating the lie. In the case of the murderer at the door, a Kantian can argue that a lie is necessary to preserve the autonomy of the intended victim, and that the murderer has forfeited their own rights to freedom and respect in this situation.

In her classic study, *Lying*, Sissela Bok identifies three main types of excuses offered for lying.[45] The first is to claim that the alleged lie isn't really a lie, because no attempt at deception was involved. This might be because the statement was intended as a joke, ironic comment, or piece of hyperbole, or because the context is one where strict truthfulness isn't generally expected. Unlike in science, journalism, or scholarship, we don't take all statements made in advertising, commercial negotiations, or polite society at face value, and both speakers and listeners are assumed to be aware of this. When you enter a restaurant in a decrepit mini-mall that brands itself as serving "Gourmet Food," you don't tend to scream "Liars!" when your noodles turn out to be pretty average. (On the other hand, you probably would think it inappropriate for the same restaurant to label its food as vegetarian, kosher, or halal when it wasn't.)

The second of Bok's excuses for lying is to claim that, while the statement in question did result in deception, the speaker isn't responsible for the lie. They weren't in full control of their faculties at the time—they were drunk, say, or in a fit of passion, or hallucinating, or being forced to lie by someone else.

The third excuse, the most common and the most interesting, is the claim that, although the lie was a lie, and the speaker was responsible for it, they aren't to blame for it, because certain moral considerations made it permissible in the circumstances. This excuse is really a set of excuses, some of which are more compelling than others. The most compelling focus on the prevention of *harm* and (relatedly) protection of *rights*, either of yourself or others. The case of the murderer at the door obviously falls into this category, and so does lying in self-defense. Most of us think it's permissible to defend an innocent victim or ourselves from unjust aggression through the use of physical force. So it would be odd to think that a lie, which is likely to be less harmful for both parties, is ruled out in these cases. Lying to prevent physical aggression is the clearest instance, but lies to protect a person's privacy might also be justified. We each have a right to control access to a certain zone of mental, social, and physical space. When someone demands access to information within that intimate zone that we or others are unwilling to give, a lie can be the appropriate response. We're especially likely to condone lying to prevent harm when it occurs in the context of an acute and urgent crisis where serious interests are at stake and time is of the essence. But lying to protect privacy might be justified in nonemergency cases too. We don't have a duty to provide true information to someone who doesn't have a right to have it.

Another of these excuses focuses on the production of *benefit*. Some beneficial lies are paternalistic: they aim to benefit the person lied to, rather than someone else (or society at large). I might lie to you that I'm driving you to a quiet dinner, for instance, when actually I'm delivering you to your surprise birthday party, which you're going to love. Or a doctor might argue that telling certain lies to her patients is permissible—or even required—because it will help them get well. These lies are harder to excuse than lies based on harm avoidance, partly because it's harder to know whether the person lied to would actually consent to the lie if they had all the relevant information about their situation. (Some people hate surprise parties.) Norms have shifted in this area in the medical case: doctors used to think themselves permitted to deceive their patients, or at least withhold information from them, in ways that we now consider seriously problematic. So if a paternalistic lie is committed, the liar is likely to skew the justification toward harm avoidance instead. (Not "I lied to you to calm you down and accelerate your recovery," but "I lied to you because if I'd told you the truth, you might have had a heart attack.")

Other beneficial lies aren't paternalistic, but are mutually beneficial: aimed at the good of society more generally. Everyday social harmony depends on a substantial flow of what are known as "white lies": lies that aren't intended to hurt anyone and that cause little if any immediate harm. Instead they grease the wheels of social interaction, tamp down conflict, and prevent awkwardness. White lies can also serve to entertain people, start a friendship, or support someone having a rough time. Almost everyone thinks such lies are fine, provided they don't take over the whole party, or the whole relationship.

Another excuse focuses on *fairness*. This one works especially well in a situation where you've already been lied to by the person you're about to tell a lie to. A lie in such a case can be seen as a form of reciprocity, just punishment, or a righting of an unfair distribution of advantages. As noted earlier, the original liar has acted unfairly in gaining advantage over others while free-riding on the social convention of veracity. So lying back to them might be thought to restore the more just status quo ante, as well as giving them their just deserts. Similarly, a liar might argue that, even if the particular person she lies to hasn't lied to her, given that everyone else around her is generally lying, it would be unfair to herself for her to hold back.

Finally, there's the excuse of *veracity* itself. Liars sometimes argue that a lie is permissible when it's necessary to further the cause of the truth in a broader sense, to counteract the distortion produced by earlier lies, or to maintain the (true) belief in others that the liar is usually truthful.

These considerations do seem capable of grounding permissions to lie, at least in some cases. The challenge is to accommodate the resulting permissions without them running away with us, causing us to lose sight of the force of the many reasons against lying. Bok is very concerned about this prospect. She worries that, while a lie might seem excusable when viewed in isolation, it's likely to prove less so when seen as an instance of a broader practice of ongoing deception. A doctor, journalist, soldier, or politician who permits themself to lie, for good reasons, in a crisis, may find themself lying repeatedly, due the crisis-heavy nature of their profession. The more they lie, and the more others around them lie, the more the practice of truth-telling in their profession will erode, till it becomes both tempting and socially acceptable to lie even in inexcusable cases. Bok isn't even sure that the white lies of polite society are safe. If they multiply, they can create an atmosphere of superficiality, repression, and anxiety that's just as oppressive as the atmosphere of totally free disclosure they aim to prevent.

A society of liars, in which practices of lying in distinct contexts proliferate and reinforce each other till no one's word is reliable, isn't a society most of us would want to inhabit. But we also seem to have genuinely compelling reasons to lie sometimes. Can we settle on any general principles to guide us here? Bok recommends what she calls "the principle of veracity." It states that when deciding whether to lie or tell the truth, we should always give an "initial negative weight" to the lie.[46] This means searching carefully for truthful alternatives, selecting one of those if all other things are equal, and treating the lie—even a white lie—not as inexcusable in principle, but as a truly last resort.

Taking this position means putting the burden of proof on the liar: it's lying, not truth-telling that needs to be justified. But you might wonder whether that's appropriate, given the weight of the reasons on both sides. In his paper "Self, Deception, and Self-Deception in Philosophy," Robert Solomon entertains the idea that it's telling the truth, not telling lies, that mainly needs defense.[47] Deception makes up a large amount of the self-image of every person, Solomon argues, and of every relationship, society, religion, and professional community (including science and philosophy). In pursuit of our educations and careers, in the early stages of romantic love, when becoming parents, or when embarking on a late-in-life change of direction, we're often uncertain about who we are, what our feelings are, what we're doing, exactly. We can tell lies in those contexts not out of malice or greed, but to gain a temporary footing, clarify our doubts, and make an imaginative, experimental leap that we'll later live ourselves fully into. Not only does the abstract notion of the Truth not matter much to us in these cases, but it can also be actively harmful. However much falsehood they may contain, we can't live without our personal and public myths, and tearing them away from us can destroy us and our relationships.[48] Things don't go well for the protagonists of Dostoyevsky's *The Idiot* and Camus's *The Stranger*, who are unable or unwilling to lie. And most of us know from personal experience that, as William Blake put it, "A truth that's told with bad intent, Beats all the lies you can invent."[49] If all this is so, why should we accept the principle of veracity and prioritize truth at, if not all, at least most, costs?

It's clearly hard to get to a stable point on this terrain. If Solomon is right that falsehood sustains human relationships, it can also obviously corrupt and deform them. I think the best argument for handing the burden of proof to the liar isn't that the reasons in favor of truth will generally win out in this contest, but rather the strong likelihood that personal bias will enter into our weighing up of those reasons. We may tell ourselves we're lying only to prevent harm, produce benefits for others, or advance the cause of fairness or veracity, but self-deception, not just other-deception, is a thing. It arguably makes sense to apply a standing negative weight to lying as a useful corrective to our documented tendency to deceive number one.

The Ethics of Truth-Telling in Memoir

I embellish stories all the time . . . Things happen, and I realize that what actually happens is only partly a story, and I have to make the story. So I lie. I mean, essentially—others would think I'm lying. But you understand. It's irresistible to tell the story. And I don't owe anybody the actuality. What is the actuality? I mean, whose business is it?

VIVIAN GORNICK[50]

How do the general arguments for and against lying apply to memoir in particular? Aquinas might argue that lying on the page is impermissible even if you do it in private and store it in the attic: the offense is against Truth itself. But our main concern here is with writing that's published or in some other way shared with others. Is lying about yourself and your life to an actual (or at least intended) readership morally wrong?

Several of the considerations discussed above suggest that it is. Take the *loss of social trust* argument. One writer and teacher of creative nonfiction writes:

> To confuse the reader about the facts in nonfiction is to disorient the reader, unmoor him or her and thus the culture—we lose the ability to meaningfully respond to actual facts if we begin to doubt their veracity. It seems to me no coincidence that this preference for blurring those lines attends the rise of American empire and facts about our democracy that perhaps we'd rather not consider too closely (torture in the name of democracy, for instance).[51]

That might be true of memoirs that incorporate large amounts of "public" material—say, hybrids that weave personal narrative together with history, politics, or social criticism—and have a very large audience. But it's implausible when applied to memoirs that focus more exclusively on the author's personal relationships or inner life, and have a small, often elite, readership (as many literary memoirs do). Lying about your complex relationship with your brother or your youthful attitude toward abstract expressionism, to a very small audience, is highly unlikely to take down the country.

There's a more persuasive version of the social trust argument applied to memoir, though: one that focuses on the way that lying undermines trust in the genre, rather than trust in society at large. If memoirists lie often and are known to, readers of memoirs will be increasingly disinclined to believe what they write. This loss of trust is a real threat to the survival of the genre, in that it threatens to turn memoir, in the reader's mind, into fiction. Truth isn't just a useful means in memoir to other worthy goals. As in the case of science or philosophy, it's a *constitutive* aim of memoir: part of its very point. A violation of truthfulness in memoir is a violation of a central internal good of the genre: it injures it at its core.

We should only be morally concerned about this if the survival of the genre matters, but that case isn't hard to make. We'll go into the value of memoir in greater depth in chapter 5. For now it's enough to note that the existence of memoir is of great personal value to writers and readers of memoirs, that it can be of high aesthetic value, and that it often has broader moral and political value too.

As in the more general case, this loss-of-trust argument has weight, but doesn't capture the sense of personal injury that readers of memoirs often feel when they find out they've been lied to. A lover of memoir might run up to a disgraced liar-memoirist and exclaim "You've undermined my favorite literary genre!" but they're more likely to be thinking "You've *betrayed me*." It's easy to be dismissive of this kind of complaint. The relationship between a writer and a reader isn't personal, in the way an intimate friendship is. Readers can be ridiculed for overidentifying with their favorite writers and treating a work diffusely directed at an indefinitely large number of people as if it were written directly to them. But, though the more attenuated nature of the relationship does attenuate the seriousness of the wrongs that can be done within it, it doesn't deprive the relationship of all moral significance or make it incapable of producing betrayal. In response to Gornick's question above about "whose business" the actuality behind her memoirs is, Mary Karr writes: "If I forked over a cover price for nonfiction, I consider it my business ... inventing stuff breaks a contract with the reader."[52] This phrasing might suggest, misleadingly, that the fault is just a matter of commercial injury or legal fraud. But readers aren't usually concerned merely with the fact that they spent money on a fake memoir. They also spent time and intellectual and emotional energy reading it, and they extended their trust to the author. As O'Neill would characterize it, they honored the memoirist by believing in their goodwill, and rather than responding to the honor with gratitude and integrity, the memoirist abused that trust.

The resulting emotions can be intense. In 2002 the literary journal *TriQuarterly* published a personal essay, "The Facts of the Matter," written from the perspective of an unrepentant rapist, that exposes itself, at the very end, as packed with lies.[53] One reader responded:

I left my first reading of this essay very angry. I felt that I had to constantly extend myself to the author in order to accept that the work was a work of nonfiction because I found the narrator difficult to believe. When it was eventually revealed that I should not have been so generous, I felt betrayed. To quote from the essay, "A lie can be a violation, a forced entry, a kind of rape." While it would be a gross exaggeration to say that I felt raped, I did most certainly feel that my trust had been violated.[54]

Another reader—Sonja Huber, herself a memoirist—felt manipulated alongside betrayed. The aim of the *TriQuarterly* essay was to stir up a debate about the importance of truth in creative nonfiction: a cause that its author strongly believes in. But, Huber argued, it used illegitimate means to that goal. It equated to "literary propaganda," which "robs [people] of their dignity through stirring up emotions and then using the power of those emotions as a stand-in for rational thought."[55] Other, less unusual, deployments of lying in memoir are likely to be viewed as similarly manipulative. In messing with their readers' beliefs to achieve their literary or career goals, lying memoirists use other humans' rational capacities purely as a means to their own ends.

The remaining two distinctively Kantian arguments against lying have some bite in memoir too. Lying doesn't just manipulate readers; it might also, in some cases, disrupt their *autonomy*, by distorting their beliefs in areas that matter to their choices and actions in the real world. Lies in memoir can skew access to the historical record about particular facts, in ways that impact on readers' future experiences. But, independently of that, they undermine readers' more general interest as rational agents in having an accurate grip on reality.

When a liar-memoirist's betrayal and manipulation of their readers is revealed, it can cause real *harm*. Sarah Einstein writes that her mother read James Frey's fraudulent *A Million Little Pieces* (discussed further below) precisely because she thought that his allegedly true story of recovery from addiction would give her hope for her own son's recovery.[56] When Einstein's mother learned that Frey had fabricated large parts of his story, her resentment and distrust toward Frey (as she put it, "Well, I guess he's just another junkie lying to get my money") transferred to her son, and she found herself less able to offer him financial and emotional support in his efforts to recover than she had before reading the book. Einstein argues that in this way Frey's lies "did violence" to both her mother and her brother.

Finally, lying in memoir can be seen as *unfair* to fellow memoirists. Memoirists gain readers in part by giving the impression that their stories are true. That impression is only present because of general respect for the norm of truth-telling on the part of other memoirists. The liar-memoirist free-rides on the integrity of others on her team: taking the fruits of their conscientiousness without playing her part, and maybe even gaining advantages over them in the literary marketplace via her liberties with the truth.

These considerations, taken together, suggest that lying in memoir is morally troubling as a general matter. But can memoirists offer legitimate excuses for lying in particular cases? The second of Bok's three general types of excuses—that the liar isn't responsible for their actions—won't hold here. Memoirists might well write while drunk, but that (as Hemingway is falsely said to have said) is what editing is for. So memoirists are likely to go for Bok's first and third types of excuses, claiming either that they weren't really lying or that they had morally defensible reasons for not telling the truth.

As noted earlier, there are certain contexts or relationships— advertising, negotiation, polite society—where strict truthfulness isn't expected. The conventions in play mean that a certain amount of falsity, or falsity about particular things, is commonly accepted, with the result that false statements of those kinds aren't intended to deceive and therefore don't count as lies. It's sometimes argued that the literary conventions of memoir have this character. Readers expect a certain degree of laxity about the truth in memoir across the board, the line goes, so when memoirists deliver on that expectation no one is duped.

The problem with this excuse is that, unlike in the more ritualized examples of advertising jingles, bargaining sessions, and norms of etiquette, there's a lot of disagreement over what the reigning truthfulness conventions in memoir are. Theorists of memoir often refer to Philippe Lejeune's idea that autobiography involves a tacit "pact" between reader and writer. But beyond the basic promise on the part of the autobiographer that the narrator-protagonist has the same identity as the author, the terms of that pact are vague. In which areas do readers expect memoirists to tell the strict truth, and in which do they not? There's likely huge variation in opinion across readers on this question. Given this, it's very difficult for a writer to be sure that she won't deceive at least someone when writing something she knows to be false.

Gornick tries to place the blame on the naive and uneducated reader here: she diagnoses complaints about the liberties she takes with the truth as evidence that the genre is "still in need of an informed readership."[57] This implies that there's some consensus among memoirists about what the relevant conventions are and that readers just need to get wise about it. But memoirists are plausibly just as divided on the question as their readers. Gornick writes that "what is owed the reader of a memoir is the ability to persuade that the narrator is trying, as honestly as possible, to get to the bottom of the tale at hand,"[58] with the implication that nothing *more* than that is owed. Karr, on the other hand, states that her own practice "wholly opposes making stuff up."[59] Sonja Huber writes, still more demandingly, "I believe in having every sentence aim for a truth that is a communication between the reader and the writer. That might be a high standard to hold, but it is mine."[60] If the solution is to inform the reader, then, what exactly are we informing them of?

Couser suggests that there are certain subgenres of memoir where the terms of the truthfulness convention are clearer than this. Take autobiographical humor writing, for instance. Some readers criticize David Sedaris for the documented and acknowledged untruths he tells. But most of them feel adequately keyed in from the outset by his tone that, as a humorist, he'll be engaging in comic tactics like irony, hyperbole, and narrative compression: that's a large part of what they come to his work for. This is a case of a subgenre where laxity with the truth is genuinely expected. By contrast, in the well-established subgenre of substance abuse recovery memoirs, readers arguably have especially restrictive standards. Couser writes:

People who seek out narratives of rehabilitation invest in them heavily, and may take them quite literally . . . in the ethics of recovery, the candid acknowledgment of one's failings is considered a crucial step . . . Too many readers have suffered too much torment as a result of substance abuse to tolerate those . . . who hype their stories for dramatic effect.[61]

One complicating factor here is that a memoir can have multiple audiences, and some of those audiences may be unfamiliar with the subgenre the memoir falls into (and therefore with its reigning truth conventions), while others may be adequately keyed in. An interesting but controversial example of this might be found in the scandal that erupted in 1998 over Rigoberta Menchú's celebrated book *I, Rigoberta Menchú*.[62] Menchú, a Guatemalan human rights activist, was charged with making multiple false claims in her book, which was first published in 1983 during her country's terrible civil war. Some defended Menchú by appealing to the Latin American subgenre of *testimonio*, which allows writers to speak from the experience of a community rather than merely that of an individual. Among other apparent misrepresentations, the narrator of the book claimed to have personally witnessed the torture and execution of one brother and the death by starvation of another, which Menchú herself was found not to have done. But many similar deaths did in fact occur in Menchú's community, and the *testimonio* form permits authors to narrate in the first person significant events that other community members witnessed or participated in. While the terms of the *testimonio* truth contract were arguably clear to Guatemalan readers, they weren't to Menchú's many North American readers, who were unfamiliar with the narrative tradition she was working in. The result was a major uproar up north, with some calling (unsuccessfully) for the revocation of Menchú's Nobel Peace Prize. (The example is controversial, because Menchú herself gave a number of different and conflicting defenses of the historical inaccuracies in her book, some of which had nothing to do with the *testimonio* genre. Some continue to argue that she was simply lying.)

The nature of the relationship between reader and writer—the fact that it's highly limited, takes place only at a great interpersonal distance, and results in a semipermanent written record—may mean that our expectations of truthfulness are generally stricter for writers than personal associates, even if their violation is less ethically momentous. In personal conversation it'd be crazy to believe everything the other party tells you about their life. But that's partly because the context allows for cues other than verbal ones, opportunities to ask clarifying questions, evidence that the listener is becoming confused, and a chance to correct for errors later. Writers generally lack these resources with respect to readers, and everyone might expect more careful attention to the truthfulness of what's said as a result.

Given all this, it's usually more straightforward and plausible for liar-memoirists to argue that, though they did indeed intend to de-

ceive, they had good moral reasons for doing so. The most persuasive arguments here are those of *harm avoidance* and *the cause of
veracity*. One reason a memoirist might have for not telling the truth
in their work is that doing so would hurt the people they describe.
Usually the concern is with harming others, but a memoirist might
also lie to avoid harming themself. They might consider certain truths
too private to reveal or too distressing to write about. Though this
doesn't count as a lie, exactly, Bernard Cooper explains his decision to
leave his three deceased brothers out of his memoir about the AIDS
crisis, *Truth Serum*, as follows:

> To be blunt, I decided to limit the body count in this book in order to prevent it from
> collapsing under the threat of death. For the most part, however, this decision was
> personal rather than literary: there is only so much loss I can stand to place at the
> center of the daily rumination that writing requires . . . Only when the infinite has
> edges am I capable of making art.[63]

These considerations raise a larger set of issues about duties to those
depicted in a memoir that I'll save for detailed treatment in the following chapters, but they're clearly highly relevant to the current
question.

As for veracity, it's always open to memoirists to claim that they
lied to advance the cause of truth. This was the justification offered by
the anonymous author of the *TriQuarterly* essay mentioned above. As
a meta-essay on the genre itself, that was a special case. But the same
excuse is also present whenever a memoirist argues that they're lying
about particular facts "to express a deeper truth": usually the experiential truth at the heart of the genre.

It's also possible to give a more general *benefit*-based argument
for lying in memoir. A rip-roaring first-person tale of a fight against
social injustice or recovery from personal trauma might be thought to
have morally valuable consequences that outweigh the moral wrong
of any lies incorporated into it. Whether or not you're comfortable
with this type of justification will depend partly on your general
view about whether morally valuable ends can sanctify morally suspect means and partly on your estimate of the risks involved. Many
have argued that part of what's wrong with fake social justice memoirs—some characterized Rigoberta Menchú's book this way—is that,

once they're exposed as fake, they undermine trust in the credibility of genuine social justice memoirs, thereby undercutting the benefits they were designed to produce.

Someone could, finally, attempt to excuse lying in memoir on *fairness* grounds. A memoirist could write a lying countermemoir with the purportedly excusable aim of undoing the wrong of an earlier lying memoir on the same subject. Or they could claim that the people they're lying about acted immorally themselves in the past and deserve everything that's coming to them. Or they could argue that the whole genre is so shot through with lies that they'd be putting themself at a disadvantage by sticking to the truth. I take the weakness of these arguments to be apparent in the mere stating of them, but maybe, in some rare cases, they might work.

Given the force of some of these excuses, an absolutist position prohibiting all lying in memoir is unappealing. But the force of the reasons against lying—mainly the importance of truth-telling for the survival of a valuable literary genre, and the badness of betraying, manipulating, and distorting the agency of readers—means that a broad permission to lie is unappealing too. If we're focusing exclusively on *moral* reasons, then (I'll return to this caveat below), it makes sense to apply a version of Bok's principle of veracity to memoir. That means that, before including a known untruth in their work, memoirists should consider carefully whether a truthful alternative would do just as well, and, if so, use that instead. If the lie would have significant moral advantages over the truthful alternatives—most likely because it protects the rights or morally defensible interests of others or the writer or because it advances veracity more broadly— the memoirist can permissibly make it. But the lie should always be given an initial negative weight in the calculation and be chosen only as a last resort. This is largely because, though there will often be arguments on both sides, the memoirist needs to guard against the very real possibility that their personal incentives will skew their assessment of those arguments in their own favor. Memoirists who are very confident that the widely acknowledged conventions of the subgenre they're working in allow for undeceitful untruths can be more relaxed about all this. But memoirists can't plausibly claim across the board that readers don't expect them to tell the truth: appealing to that alleged fact is a bogus excuse for lying.

Even if all lies should be given an initial negative weight, some should be given a much heavier negative weight than others. We plausibly have a moral spectrum of truth-twisting in memoir, with some forms of deceit being so problematic that they're effectively inexcusable and other forms being more easily justified. At the fully inexcusable extreme, there's impersonation: an author claiming to be another person (whether real or imagined). In the early 1970s, Clifford Irving wrote a fake "as-told-to" "autobiography" "on behalf of" the millionaire recluse Howard Hughes, which he sold to McGraw Hill for $765,000.[64] In 1995, Bruno Dössekker wrote a memoir under the pseudonym Binjamin Wilkomirski, in which he claimed to be a Polish Jewish Holocaust survivor, when in fact he was born to Christian parents and spent his whole life in Switzerland.[65] These and similar hoaxes are direct violations of Lejeune's autobiographical pact, in that they sever the identity of author and narrator-protagonist that's the fundamental literary convention of memoir. They represent an existential threat to the genre.

Slightly further along the spectrum toward permissibility we have the act of making up events or episodes out of whole cloth. There are enough fake occurrences and major exaggerations in Frey's *A Million Little Pieces* (most impressively, he converted a few hours at a police station into a three-month prison stay) that he originally tried to sell the book as a novel, before rebranding it as a memoir. Random House accepted the memoir with zero fact-checking after having rejected the same manuscript when submitted as fiction. In what turned into a national scandal, the book was championed by Oprah, exposed as lie-ridden, savaged by Oprah, and then partially pardoned by Oprah. Frey and his defenders tried several of the excuses outlined above. Some argued that Frey had just done on a large scale what all memoirists do: implying either that he wasn't really aiming to deceive anyone or that his deceits were only fair in a game where no one's playing by the rules. Frey's own note to readers, included in later editions of the book, implied that his past trauma made him not fully responsible for his lies: "People cope with adversity in many different ways … My mistake … is writing about the person I created in my mind to help me cope, and not the person who went through the experience." He also went for the veracity-based excuse, claiming that he "stands by the book as being the essential truth of my life." Prison minister

Marty Angelo, on the other hand, opted for a benefit-based rationale in defense of Frey: "In terms of the benefit to readers as a self-help book, the message is the key issue, not the minor story details. One needs to stay focused on what the real message is—overcoming addiction."[66] The majority of the public weren't satisfied with any of these excuses, though the book continued to sell in the thousands and was later made into a movie.

At the other end of the spectrum, edging closer to full permissibility, are a varied set of lesser untruths. In an article for the *American Scholar*, Andrew Hudgins catalogs eight types of "lies" he told in his book of autobiographical poetry, *The Glass Hammer*.[67] The first three—"the lie of narrative cogency" (omission, compression), "the lie of texture" (adding fake details), "the lie of fictional convention" (framing your life in mythological terms)—he's not overly concerned about. The next five cause him more guilt: "the lie of emotional evasion" (leaving out things you're ashamed of), "the lie of the recreated self" (writing to make yourself look good), "the lie of extended consciousness" (appropriating the experiences of others or knowledge of your later self), "the lie of interpretation" (squeezing your life into a narrative arc), and "the lie of impressionism" (exaggerating your feelings for aesthetic effect.)

The moral terrain is murkier here, partly because it's unclear that some of these are lies. For one thing, as I argued in the previous chapter, presenting an experience via selectivity and compression, or framing your life via a mythic or narrative arc, isn't necessarily to *mis*represent it. For another, some of the types of falsehood that Hudgins lists may not be intended, or likely, to deceive. Readers don't expect writers to remember dialogue in word-for-word detail, and they're aware that names, physical appearances, and places may need to be changed for confidentiality. When Harry Crews narrates a long talk he "had" with his dog Sam,[68] when Lia Purpura slips in and out of the voice of a buzzard,[69] when Machado tells us about a letter-writing squid, or when Frank McCourt narrates his own birth, everyone involved is perfectly aware that there's some fictionalizing going on. Other items on Hudgins's list, though lies, may be about matters so trivial that they're unlikely to undermine the credibility of memoir, period, or cause serious injuries to readers in terms of betrayal or disrespect. In this category we can arguably include the creation of composite (minor) characters and events, using a single episode to stand in for a longer period or experience, and breaking up dramatic scenes to provide descriptive material or information for the reader that the author didn't have at the time. (Mary Karr includes all of these on a list of fudges she does regularly and doesn't feel bad about.)

Where a particular lie ends up on this moral spectrum depends on a mixture of factors. Our assessment of the moral gravity of a lie increases the larger its *scope*, the more self-interested its *motivations*, the more harmful its *consequences*, the more vulnerable its *victims*, and the more easily *avoidable* it is. Cases of impersonation and major fabrication tend to score high on all these dimensions. James Frey lied large, for apparently self-interested reasons, thereby undermining the credibility of a morally valuable subgenre, directed at an especially vulnerable readership, despite the ready availability of continuing to present his book as fiction. Similarly, "Wilkomirski's" large-scope fakery exploited the experiences of some of history's most oppressed people, risked enabling the cause of Holocaust deniers, and may have edged genuine Holocaust survivor memoirists out of the market, gaining an unfair advantage over them and depriving readers of accurate and valuable information about the historical record. Rigoberta Menchú, on the other hand, engaged in misrepresentations of smaller scope, out of apparently altruistic motivations, and arguably made a genuine, sustained effort to accurately present the complex history of her unjustly oppressed community. As a result, she scores low on the five dimensions listed, and her lies, if lies they are, are therefore more excusable.

A few defenders of hoaxers aside, I suspect that almost all memoirists would agree with these assessments. Very few in the field condone full-scale imposture and large-scale deception. But thinking about the moral arguments against these extreme cases can help us assess the more minor cases that Hudgins describes too, given that the same ethical considerations for and against truthfulness are at work there, albeit to a lesser degree.

What can memoirists do, other than make a sincere effort to transmit their experiences and other information accurately, to support the baseline norm of truthfulness the genre depends on? One practice is to make clear upfront in each work what the author takes the "truth contract" to be. As Sarah Einstein notes, "The tradition makes room for the inclusion of imagined or even blatantly false narratives, but it is an expectation of the genre that when the author does this, she will also signal the reader that this is the case."[70] So, if extensive fictionalizing is taking place, the author can make a general disclaimer ("based on a true story") at the beginning of the book, or identify and explain the rationale for particular fictional elements in a preface, appendix, or notes. David Sedaris's author note for *When You Are Engulfed in Flames* states, "The events described in these stories are realish." The first chapter of Lauren Slater's experimental memoir *Lying* consists of the single sentence: "I exaggerate," and she repeatedly draws attention to the possibility that she may be departing from the factual truth via a preface written by someone else, throughout the book and in the final chapter.

If an author is uncertain about the truth of what they relate, they can again signal that uncertainty in the work. They might do this incrementally as they go ("It might have happened this way...," "I imagine ...," "Maybe I said ...") or by a general reminder to the reader of the fallibility of memory. Henry Adams (who wrote his memoir in the third person) included the passage: "This was the journey he remembers. The actual journey may have been quite different, but the actual journey has no interest for education. The memory was all that mattered."[71] Stendhal wrote: "I don't at all claim to be writing a history, but quite simply to be recording my memories so as to work out what sort of man I may have been [...]."[72] Montaigne wrote: "In the examples that I bring in here of what I have heard, done, or said, I have forbidden myself to dare to alter even the slightest and most inconsequential circumstances. My conscience does not falsify one iota; my knowledge, I don't know."[73] In the case of controversial material that the author is confident about, they can make an effort to transparently disclose their sources, again either in appendixes or in the text itself.

Mary McCarthy went for several of these strategies, belatedly, in the postscripts she attached to each chapter of *Memories of a Catholic Girlhood* (which had been published as separate stories in magazines several years previously). She repeatedly calls herself out for taking previously undisclosed liberties with the truth: confessing doubts, noting where her memories differ from those of other family members, and highlighting the places where her other gig as a fiction writer led her into temptation. ("There are several dubious points in this memoir," "the story is true in substance, but the details have been invented or guessed at," "this was the kind of answer I might have made," "The most likely thing, I fear, is that I fused two memories. *Mea culpa*," etc.[74])

If an author doesn't want to go for explicit disclaimers and clarifications, which can be clumsy or clog up the text, they can give clues to readers about the intended truth contract via formal, structural, or tonal features instead. In *Woman Warrior*, Maxine Hong Kingston switches to the third-person omniscient point of view to signal that she's moving from memory to myth. Beth Kephart recommends dropping quotation marks or using nontraditional ones, to indicate that dialogue is being only approximately reported.[75] And discontinuous essays or essayistic memoirs that circle around their subject, cycling back to earlier claims and questioning or contradicting them, can intentionally transmit a general attitude of skepticism throughout toward the truth of the author's individual statements.

Another practice is simply to avoid writing about—or writing in detail about—material that you don't feel sure of. Kephart tries to "kee[p] most dialogue exchanges tight," and Thomas Couser counsels against the employment of "high density and specificity of detail" in description.[76]

Literary Truth, Ethics, and Art

Lying, the telling of beautiful untrue things, is the proper aim of Art.

OSCAR WILDE[77]

The upshot of the discussion so far is that both the goal of capturing your past experience on the page and the goal of acting ethically toward others support a strong, though not exceptionless, commitment to truth-telling in memoir. Memoirists may inadvertently fail to tell the truth, due to all the cognitive limitations discussed in the previous chapter, and they may sometimes have morally defensible reasons for concealing or misrepresenting it. But their general practice should be to aim their arrow at it, within these constraints.

Things would be nice and clean if we could leave it at that, but we can't. That's because (literary) memoirists have a third shared aim, beyond experiential truth and moral decency, and that aim can send the arrow in a very different direction. Memoirists, as well as being humans and moral agents, are also artists, and the relationship between truth and art is complex and controversial.

Some, like Wilde above, argue that truth has nothing to do with art or is even hostile to it. The main reason for thinking this is that truth can be aesthetically constraining. As philosopher John Gibson puts it: "Of all the uses of language we have developed, the literary has some claim to being the most liberated. It speaks in freedom from the truth and the facts, and it is largely unconstrained by the very world that our other, less elevated uses of language struggle to represent."[78] Nietzsche went further, arguing that lying has positive aesthetic value in itself: it's an imaginative achievement, and the results are invigorating and inspiring. John D'Agata suggests something similar when he reminds us that subversion is one of the traditional functions of art: "Don't we expect the artist to test limits, to challenge the rules, to break taboos?"[79] Lying is a doubly subversive act, in that it both transgresses against a core moral principle and is premised on distortion and confusion: by its very nature it messes with expectations, throws people off, keeps them unsure and guessing.

Others argue, in contrast, that real art is always aimed at truth with a capital *T*. As Emily Dickinson put it:

> I died for beauty, but was scarce
> Adjusted in the tomb,
> When one who died for truth was lain
> In an adjoining room.
>
> He questioned softly why I failed?
> "For beauty," I replied.
> "And I for truth,—the two are one;
> We brethren are," he said.[80]

Dickinson's suggestion has contemporary adherents in philosophers like Noël Carroll and Martha Nussbaum, who argue that the cognitive value of literary works is closely bound up with their aesthetic value.[81] For such theorists, a central part of what makes literature valuable *as literature* is the truth it allows us to access. Nussbaum argues, for instance, that the realist novels of James, Dickens, and Proust are literary masterpieces in large part because of the complex ethical knowledge they communicate. The truths that *À la recherche du temps perdu* conveys aren't just of incidental intellectual value, but part and parcel of the work's artistic merit. Even those who accept this (controversial) view as a general matter, though, are likely going to have to agree that untruths will *sometimes* serve aesthetic purposes better than truths.

There are a couple of different ways of thinking about what to do when distinct goals, values, or principles come into conflict. One is to establish a hierarchy between the distinct items, so that one principle always overrides another or one goal always has to be satisfied before another is addressed. Philosophers have often argued, along these lines, that in a conflict between morality and other values, morality always wins. In the case we're considering, if the moral principle of veracity requires you, the memoirist, to tell the truth, but the value of beauty tells you to lie, there's really no contest: you have to go with the truth. (The situation is complicated by the fact that morality itself contains a variety of different principles and goals.)

Nietzsche vigorously rejected the priority of morality, including veracity, over all other values: "A great man ... What is such a man? ... He would rather lie than tell the truth, because lying requires more spirit and *will*. There is a loneliness within his heart which neither praise nor blame can reach, because he is his own judge from whom is no appeal."[82] Nietzsche can often be read as arguing in favor of a value hierarchy with art at or near the top. But another option is to deny that any such general hierarchy exists. On this approach, we're simply faced with a plurality of independent and irreducible domains of value—morality, aesthetics, truth, personal well-being, maybe religion, and so on—none of which takes any general priority over the others. Bernard Williams is famous among philosophers for pressing the position that morality shouldn't always win out over other values, even if it sometimes should.[83]

This no-hierarchy position doesn't always land you in a deliberative standstill. It might be that a course of action produces so much of one value, or lines up so well with one principle, that its minor encroachment on other values or principles becomes insignificant. But that can't be guaranteed. So if you take this pluralistic line, you set yourself up for the possibility of genuine, lasting, and troubling dilemmas between incompatible values.

Because I think a shorthand for "genuine, lasting and troubling dilemmas between incompatible values" is "life," I'm a pluralist about what philosophers call "practical reason" and don't think there's always one single, clean, authoritative answer to the question of what we ought to do. Nor, relatedly, is there always one single, clean, authoritative answer to the question of whether a memoir is "good" or not. It's possible for the very same memoir to be morally defective and a consummate work of art.

When a work's moral defects are apparent on the page, sure, the result can sometimes be an aesthetic defect.[84] A successful aesthetic experience often requires the audience to be fully immersed in the text, emotionally gripped by it, and moral qualms can jolt us out of that immersion. This is why evidence of racist or sexist attitudes in an artwork can be an aesthetic, not just an ethical, problem. But the thing about lying, as opposed to overt discrimination or hostility, is that it can often be invisibly executed. The fact that we can't tell a memoirist is lying doesn't diminish the immorality of their action, but the lie might have neutral or even positive aesthetic value.

When Bruno Dössekker's faux Holocaust memoir was revealed as a hoax, many critics argued that it no longer had any literary value. The historian and anti-Semitism scholar Stefan Maechler wrote: "Once the professed interrelationship between the first-person narrator, the death-camp story he narrates, and historical reality are proved palpably false, what was a masterpiece becomes kitsch."[85] According to another critic, on the other hand, the book's aesthetic merits survive the revelation: "Those merits reside in a ferocious vision, a powerful narrative, an accumulation of indelible images, and the unforgettable way in which a small child's voice is deployed in an unfeeling adult world, during the war and thereafter."[86] For many of us, this is likely to be an instance where knowing that the book is a hoax would deprive it of much of its aesthetic value. But if you *didn't* know …?

James Frey defended his major lies on aesthetic grounds by saying "I wanted the stories in the book to ebb and flow, to have dramatic arcs, to have the tension that all great stories require."[87] And the lesser lies that less deceitful memoirists engage in are often committed for similar aesthetic reasons. Hudgins's "lie of interpretation" and "lie of impressionism" are motivated this way. Hudgins writes that adding retrospectively felt emotion to a narrative or molding it to fit a satisfying arc are "inescapable for a writer attempting to create an artistically coherent work." Hudgins doesn't see aesthetics as fully justifying his misrepresentations: he thinks they're ethically problematic, and he feels "uneasy" committing them. So, for him, this isn't an instance of the general position that art trumps morality. Nonetheless, morality isn't trumping art either: "I accept, however uneasily, the lies I had to tell."

I think, on the basis of the pluralist position, that memoirists are sometimes permitted on aesthetic grounds to tell lies (where that "permitted" doesn't refer to a specifically moral permission, but just an assessment of what they have overall best reason to do in the circumstances). But because moral values matter alongside aesthetic values, and because lies are only sometimes aesthetically valuable, this permission is limited. The extreme disvalue of the most morally troubling lies will almost certainly trump their aesthetic value. So it's only the more minor lies that are likely to survive this contest, and even they will struggle to justify themselves in light of the value of the independent goal of capturing experiential truth.

While we should stay attuned to the possibility of conflicts between morality, art, and truth, and not try to artificially resolve them out of existence, we should also be careful not to exaggerate them. There are definitely cases where optimal capturing of the truth does seem to require a certain amount of ugliness in one's prose. Roy Pascal writes of eighteenth-century scholar K. P. Moritz's autobiography, *Anton Reiser*:

> It lacks on the surface some of the qualities of a work of art. It is written awkwardly, without ease of style, and the narrative is often interrupted by analytical reflection and pedagogic comment. There is little evocative description, and where it is attempted, it easily becomes sentimental, crude. Feelings are in general drily and abstractly delineated, not presented, and the characterizations of other persons tend to the caricature ... Yet are these faults? His analytical method belongs intimately to this man ... so that he cannot even get absorbed in his own story.[88]

But in other cases, it's not expressing but *messing* with the truth that's an aesthetic liability. Judith Barrington suggests that "tampering with the truth will lead you to writing a bit too carefully—which in turn will rob your style of the ease that goes with honesty."[89] And it'd be a mortal sin against life to suggest that the historically accurate facts, free from your tampering, can't be beautiful. Finally, the formal constraints imposed by the truth can be aesthetically productive. The furniture designer Charles Eames said that "design depends largely on constraints."[90] If writing memoir without regard for the truth is like Frost's description of free verse as "playing tennis without a net,"[91] we might wonder if veracity and art are the sworn enemies that Nietzsche and Wilde claim they are.

In all likelihood, quite a bit of lying goes on in memoir. Memoirists are people, and studies suggest that in everyday life people lie in about one out of every four of their social interactions.[92] James Patterson and Peter Kim have estimated that 91 percent of Americans regularly tell lies and that only 45 percent of them occasionally avoid lying because they think it's morally wrong.[93]

But there's some reason to think that memoirists might lie below the species average on the page. Memoirists write about their values on paper, and experimental studies have shown that people lie less in paper messages than by email,[94] and when they're given an opportunity to first affirm their core values by writing about them.[95] More importantly, the aim to tell the truth is built into the activity of memoir. Mary Karr writes that an obsession with the truth is the quality she finds most consistently in the memoirists she knows: "Truth is not their *enemy*. It's the bannister they grab for when feeling around on the dark cellar stairs. It's the solution."[96] They don't always find it, of course—it's dark down there! But they keep trying, and if what I've written in this chapter is right, they have many good reasons for that.

If the temptation to lie in memoir is sometimes strong, the desire to tell the truth is probably usually stronger. It's a noble aim, and pursuit of it has its own rewards whether or not it's achieved. Memoirists might take heart from psychiatrist Marcel Eck's claim that "we will be judged not on whether we possess or do not possess the truth but on whether or not we sought and loved it."[97] And on whether or not we made a good story out of it too.

FOUR

What Do Memoirists Owe the People They Write About?

A few summers ago I attended a writing conference panel on memoirists' obligations to the family, friends, associates, and acquaintances they represent in their memoirs. A writer on the panel mentioned that he'd attended another panel, featuring a famous autobiographical novelist and personal essayist, where the same question had come up. When asked what we owe to those we write about, the novelist-essayist had summarized what US law requires in this area and then abruptly stopped. After telling this anecdote, the writer laughed approvingly, and everyone in the audience joined in.

Well, almost everyone. No one wants to be the stern moralist in a room full of gleeful writers, so I kept my mouth shut. But this little story and its reception bothered me, for a couple of reasons. One suggestion the novelist-essayist seemed to be making is that our responsibilities to those we write about are very minimal. US law imposes only two requirements on memoirists: first, not to engage in defamation, and second, not to violate privacy, narrowly understood. Defamation involves publishing something false about someone and thereby damaging their reputation ("lower(ing) them in the estimation of the community or deter(ring) third persons from dealing with them"). Invasion of privacy involves publishing material about someone that isn't of public concern (that doesn't "further the public interest") and that a reasonable person would consider offensive if made public.

It's relatively easy for a memoirist to avoid breaking the law in these two ways. You can avoid defamation by not lying, by researching thoroughly and supporting your claims adequately, and by adding caveats for material you're unsure about, that is disputed by others, or that you've embellished. You can avoid a legal violation of privacy by removing identifying characteristics, having your memoir published by a respected publisher to demonstrate that it's of public concern, and carefully considering whether any highly sensitive material is truly essential to your story. If the person you're writing about is dead, you're even safer: only living persons can sue for defamation or privacy violations. Beyond that, the First Amendment allows writers unlimited free speech.

These legal restrictions are ethically defensible and important, but do they really exhaust our responsibilities to others when writing memoir? Memoir can cause serious injuries to innocent (and not-so-innocent) people and permanently damage or destroy valuable relationships, even when it tells nothing but the truth and is published by a big-name publisher to general public acclaim. It's funny until you do it, or until someone does it to you or to someone you love. Most of us, I suspect, at least when pressed, think there are moral limits on what you can justifiably write about others that go beyond what the law requires.

Another suggestion the novelist-essayist seemed to be making is that the only reason for caring about how you treat loved (or hated) ones in your work is that you might get sued. That's equivalent to saying that, although you might have a self-interested reason to consider how you treat others when writing about them, you can—and maybe should?—set *moral* reasons aside.

That vision of freewheeling artistic license is certainly invigorating, and if you need it to get the first draft of your memoir written without being crippled by guilt, I guess you should indulge in it. But I suspected while observing the free spirits around me at that panel that if you'd pinned them down, one on one, to the position that anything goes morally in memoir, they'd exhibit signs of unease. To judge by their conversation and writing about their craft, many memoirists spend a significant amount of time agonizing over their own treatment of intimates in their work, and the agony isn't focused on a fear of getting fined or thrown into jail. Instead they're worried, directly, about harming others, or invading their personal space, or betraying their trust, or exploiting them, or stealing their stories. Many writers claim to avoid writing memoir precisely because the moral burdens it imposes are too crippling to make the endeavor worthwhile.

When encouraged by his nephew to do it, Sigmund Freud replied: "A psychologically complete and honest confession of life ... would require so much indiscretion (on my part as well as on that of others) about family, friends, and enemies, most of them still alive, that it is simply out of the question."[1] Other writers start writing memoir and then stop, for the same reason.

Such anxieties aren't peculiar to the genre of memoir. Novelists often base their characters on real people and biographers always do; in both cases, the individuals described may claim to have been wronged by the author. Similarly, outside the literary realm, journalists, ethnographers, and doctors or therapists who publish case studies face many of the same dilemmas that memoirists do about what to reveal about others in their writing, and how. But the ethical terrain may be murkiest in the case of memoir, for several reasons.

First, authors in other life-writing fields have available a pair of easy forms of moral insurance that are less accessible to memoirists. One is disguise. Novelists have much more leeway than memoirists to conceal the identity of the people they base their characters on. If a memoirist goes too far in the direction of concealment, they'll violate the truth-telling commitment built into their vocation. And certain identities simply can't be concealed: your mother is your mother, and everyone knows (or can find out) who she is, whether you change her name, eye color, and hometown or not. Another form of moral insurance is the securing of consent from subjects. This tactic is relatively unconstraining for ethnographers and clinicians, because they generally have a large and steady stream of subjects to choose from. If Ada doesn't want to be written about, Dr. Freud can write about the more-than-willing Edith instead. But most people's intimate circles are pretty small and fixed. If a memoirist's ex-wife or father or best friend doesn't want to be written about, the price of respecting consent may be not writing the memoir at all. Is that a price the memoirist is morally obliged to pay? It's unclear.

Second, it's harder for memoirists than other life writers to convincingly offer a widely used excuse for harm: benefit to third parties. In the case of narrative-based social science or medical research, the benefits for those other than the author of publishing the narrative may be uncontroversial. Ethnographic research can advance our scholarly understanding of others and ourselves, and therapeutic case studies can improve treatment for mental or physical illness. In contrast, it's much less obvious, to the average person, that the writing of a memoir will help others in these or other concrete ways. As a result, it can seem that the only one benefiting from throwing the near and dear under the bus is the person doing the throwing. This forcefully raises the difficult question of how to weigh self-interest against the interests of others.

Third, life writers in several of these other fields are members of organized and recognized professions. Professions usually develop at least rudimentary codes of practice, laying out special standards their members are collectively committed to. In academia, journalism, medicine, and psychotherapy, those standards include rules concerning how to responsibly write about others in public. Journalists, for instance, commit themselves to respecting anonymity of sources when requested, clarifying the conditions of promises made in exchange for information, and seeking out subjects of news stories to give them the opportunity to respond to allegations of wrongdoing. Scholars or clinicians who write narrative case studies commit to securing consent and concealing identities when private or potentially harmful material is revealed. These codes don't plausibly cover the entire terrain of ethically responsible journalism, scholarship, or medicine, but they're something. Memoir, on the other hand, isn't a profession. Memoirists may attend classes, conferences, writing groups, and readings together; they may subscribe to the same literary magazines, buy the same books, and follow each other on social media. But they generally see themselves as individual artists or craftspeople working independently, not members of an organized group cooperatively pursuing a common goal, and they don't subscribe to a set of collectively binding moral standards. As a result, there are no generally recognized, public conventions among memoirists about how to treat real people on the page, even standards of the minimal variety used by the life-writing professions.

Relatedly, the professionalized forms of life writing have a more formal and well-defined structure than memoir. They tend to arise within the context of a research project, limited in time and scope, that begins with an explicit contract between all parties involved. In contrast, the material of memoir usually arises in an unorganized manner, across the everyday course of a life, where written contracts in advance of interaction are either impossible or undesirable. (Try to get someone you've just started dating to sign a contract about their privacy rights in your future memoir and see how that goes for you.) The result, once again, is that there's much more ongoing disagreement among memoirists (and their subjects and readers) than among journalists, academics, and clinicians about what it is and isn't OK to tell the world about others.

I think memoirists could do with more guidance in this murky terrain than they currently have and the aim of this chapter is to provide it, but my ambitions are limited. I won't presume to definitively answer every question memoirists might have about their duties to those they write about. The moral issues here are complex and delicate, involving the intersection of a diverse set of important values. The question of how best to respond to those values in any particular case is likely to depend on the details of the situation or relationship involved, making sweeping generalizations implausible and unhelpful.

My goal here, then, is the more modest one of clarifying the types of moral considerations that individual memoirists would do well to keep in mind when coming to their own, no doubt uneasy, compromises in this department. It's always helpful when making ethical decisions to have a clear grip on what's at stake, so that, if some values or interests need to be sacrificed, you're at least doing it clear-eyed, in the least costly way you can manage, and for reasons you and others can understand. So I'll start by distinguishing between five different forms of moral wrong that memoirists might do to others in the course of writing about them: harm, privacy violation, exploitation, betrayal, and unjust appropriation. I'll then draw from that discussion some general guidelines for how to minimize injuries to others when writing about them, while retaining the artistic freedom on which good memoir relies.[2]

Harm

The most obvious way you might wrong someone in memoir is by harming them. In fact, many people assume that harming someone and wronging them are equivalent, so that the popular injunction "first, do no harm" isn't just the beginning but also the end of the story: harm covers the whole moral ground. But that's not so, for a pair of reasons. First, harming someone doesn't always involve wronging them. And second, some wrongs don't involve harm. Harm is less central to the ethics of memoir than you might at first think. That said, it remains pretty central. So it makes sense to start here with a brief discussion of what harm is, exactly, and what role it plays in ethics.

On the classic account given by Joel Feinberg, to harm someone is to set back one or more of their interests.[3] You have an interest in something when you stand to gain or lose depending on how it goes. For instance, most of us have an interest in our mental and physical health. We stand to lose—things go worse for us, our well-being is reduced—when our health deteriorates. When someone causes that to happen, they harm us, by putting us into a worse condition than we would have been in, were it not for their act.

Although all harms involve setbacks to interests, not all setbacks to interest qualify as harm on Feinberg's account. Harm requires a setback that's both significant and lasting. Trivial or passing incursions on our happiness or comfort—"unpleasant sensations (evil smells, grating noises), transitory disappointments and disillusionments, wounded pride, hurt feelings, aroused anger, shocked sensibility, alarm, disgust, frustration, impatient restlessness, acute boredom, irritation, embarrassment, feelings of guilt and shame, physical pain (at a readily tolerable level), bodily discomfort"[4]—don't count. They may be unpleasant and distressing, and we may dislike, resent, and want to avoid them. But—as long as they're low in intensity and don't last long or insistently recur—in themselves, they don't genuinely harm us.

Within the category of genuine harms, we can further distinguish between setbacks to a person's ultimate goals in life and setbacks to a person's "welfare interests." Feinberg defines welfare interests as the necessary means to ultimate goals, whatever those goals are. They include interests

in the continuance for a foreseeable interval of one's life, and the interests in one's own health and vigor, the integrity and normal functioning of one's body, the absence of absorbing pain and suffering or grotesque disfigurement, minimal intellectual acuity, emotional stability, the absence of groundless anxieties and resentments, the capacity to engage normally in social intercourse and to enjoy and maintain friendships, at least minimal income and financial security, a tolerable social and physical environment, and a certain amount of freedom from interference and coercion.[5]

Such welfare interests by no means capture everything we value in life—they establish a pretty minimal threshold—but the other things that we do value, including the things we value most deeply, depend crucially on them. A memoirist, for instance, may care most about writing a good book, advancing social justice, and raising her children to be happy and healthy. A serious setback to her welfare interests may make achieving all of those ultimate goals very difficult, if not impossible. But a setback to one of her three ultimate goals might leave the other two intact. For this reason, harm to your welfare interests, even if you don't care much about them directly, is the most serious form of harm a person can suffer.

If you accept Feinberg's account of what harm is, it becomes pretty clear that harming people isn't the only way to wrong them. That's because we can wrong people even if we don't set back their interests. One way we can do this is by hostilely or negligently exposing them to *risk* of harm, even if no actual harm results. Another way is by violating their rights, or lying to them, or breaking a promise to them, or betraying their trust, or speaking viciously about them, without them ever finding out about it. (Many, though not all, philosophers impose an "experience requirement" on well-being: something can't make your life go better or worse if you're unaware of it.) A further way is by subjecting them to mutually beneficial exploitation, a type of wrong we'll discuss more below. Although exploiting someone often involves lowering their well-being, it doesn't always. If you demand that I pay you $10,000 to save me from drowning in a freezing lake, you've exploited my vulnerability, but you've also increased my well-being over the status quo, in which I faced a certain and horrible death.

Not only are some wrongs not harms in this way, but some harms are not wrongs. This follows from some important points about the moral significance of harm (rather than the nature of harm), which we'll turn to now. There are a number of ways of setting back someone's interests without acting immorally toward them (several of which parallel the excuses or justifications for lying that we discussed in the previous chapter). For one, you might harm someone by accident or as a result of coercion (someone else might physically compel you to pull the trigger) in which case you can plausibly argue that the harm wasn't really *your* action. For another, you might harm someone as a necessary and proportionate means of protecting yourself or others from their attempt to violate your rights (say they're coming at your child with a machete and you grab it and slice off their hand). These two defenses are unlikely to apply to the writing of memoir, so we'll set them aside.

Another couple of defenses are more relevant. Harming someone is wrong only when they have a *right* to remain at the level of wellbeing you find them at. Setting back people's minimal welfare interests (listed above) usually involves violating their rights in this way. If I intentionally make it that the case that your social or physical environment becomes intolerable or that you suffer grotesque disfigurement, for instance, I've pretty clearly violated your rights and wronged you. But setting back a person's interests above that basic level needn't involve a rights violation. Say you meet a billionaire, and give them well-intentioned investment advice that causes them to become a mere millionaire. This might count as a genuine harm rather than a mere hurt: maybe their most cherished ultimate goal thereby becomes unreachable. But you haven't violated their property rights, by stealing from or defrauding them, and no one has a right to remain a billionaire per se. In large part, that's because giving people rights to what they need to pursue their ultimate goals (as opposed to their basic welfare interests) would impose duties on others that are so burdensome as to unjustifiably limit the duty-bearers' freedom to pursue their own legitimate goals (a freedom that is itself a vital welfare interest).

Another feature of this last example is that the billionaire presumably *consented* to receiving and taking your advice. The presence of consent is a distinct, important way in which a harm can fail to involve a wrong. It's not unusual for a surgeon to cause major setbacks to a patient's interests, including their basic welfare interests, when an operation goes poorly. But we don't consider the resulting harms moral wrongs, provided that the patient validly consented to the surgery in full knowledge of the risks. (If a wayward surgeon surprisescalpeled you while you were peacefully sleeping at home, we'd have a very different reaction.) Some argue that consenting to a harm *always* makes that harm morally permissible. But we have to be careful here, because some alleged instances of consent may be merely apparent: the consenter may have had inadequate information, been mentally incapacitated or been under subtle forms of duress. And maybe there are some rights we simply can't waive. Michael Sandel cites the real-life case of the German man who volunteered to have another man slice off his penis, kill him, carve him up, freeze him, and then consume his body, fried in oil and garlic, over the course of a few months.[6] Most of us want to say that a morally wrong harm was committed here (to understate it), even if the victim gave his full consent. Or, if, understandably, you don't know *what* to think about that case, consider the much less unusual one of domestic abuse. The fact that some victims of abuse might be said to consent to it in no way makes it OK.

Finally, in some cases harms aren't wrongs because they're made permissible or required by the presence of morally significant competing interests. Humans have very different natures, perspectives, aims, and circumstances; resources and knowledge are limited; social life is complicated. Given all this, what's good for me may be very bad for you, and vice versa, for reasons we have no control over — and then multiply that by six billion. We couldn't associate with each other at all, or have adequate individual freedom of action when we did, if we didn't allow ourselves to sometimes set back each other's interests in some ways. As a result, we often get ourselves into situations where it's unavoidable that someone's interests be hindered if others' interests are to be protected or advanced. In those cases, certain harms will be unfortunate, but not immoral.

Decisions about how to appropriately adjudicate between competing interests of, or risks of harm to, distinct individuals are among the hardest and most consequential in ethics, and people disagree over which principles should guide them. One plausible principle is that we should attempt to minimize harm overall. A related principle is that we should prioritize the protection of more important interests over less important interests. A distinct principle is that we should ensure a fair distribution of harm (or risk of harm) across individuals, so that one person or group of people doesn't bear the unjust bulk of the burden. It's difficult to specify what these and other principles recommend in particular cases, and their recommendations can conflict. But each principle acknowledges the point currently at issue, that some harms are morally permissible or even required.

How might we apply these general points about the nature and significance of harm to the specific case of memoir? One thing that's uncontroversial in this debate is that writing about someone in your memoir can set back their interests (usually emotional, social, reputational, or financial). On reading your work, your subject can feel disappointed, angry, embarrassed, or ashamed. And when others read your work, they may form beliefs about your subject that negatively alter their attitudes and future behavior toward them, in ways that undermine matters your subject has a stake in.

The first thing we've seen above is that the presence of these impacts alone doesn't show that harm has been done. If your subject's feelings are injured in minor and/or passing ways, you may have hurt or offended them, but you won't have harmed them. Similarly, if certain others come to distrust or avoid your subject in certain limited areas, you may have lowered your subject's well-being, but not in a way that counts as genuine harm. On the other hand, if reading your work produces a major and lasting negative impact on your subject's emotional life, or if your other readers avoid or harass your subject in a significant, widespread, and continual fashion as a result of what you write, your memoir may cause genuine harm.

The second thing we've seen is that, even if your memoir does harm your subjects in these ways, we can't immediately conclude that you've acted wrongly by publishing it. Your subjects can most plausibly claim to have been wronged if your memoir undermines their basic welfare interests, in a way that you could have readily foreseen. Maybe your subject is an intensely private person who suffers from significant social anxiety, and you had good reason to believe that revealing certain sensitive facts about him in your memoir would plunge him into an extended episode of depression and paranoia. Or maybe your subject is a closet atheist who has lived and worked in an isolated intensely religious community all her life and is certain to be fully ostracized if you out her as an unbeliever. The chance that you'll do a wrong here is much higher than in cases of more minor (although genuine) harms, such as setbacks to a person's ultimate goals rather than their basic welfare interests. Say what you write (truthfully) about your famous ex-wife in your memoir turns public opinion against her in a way that permanently undermines her philanthropic career, but she still has plenty of alternative employment and social opportunities available to her. Other things being equal, this seems like a morally blameless harm.

A third thing we've seen is that even genuine and serious harms can be morally permissible when they're the unavoidable result of others pursuing their own morally legitimate and significant interests. This is the reason we can't be fully confident that a wrong has been committed in the cases of the socially anxious man and the outed atheist: we haven't considered the interests of others involved yet. One key person to consider, of course, is the memoirist, but third parties may be implicated too. A very general consideration that covers both is the interest in the survival and flourishing of memoir as a literary genre. For reasons we'll discuss in more detail in chapter 5, the moral liberty to write and read honest, deep, and wide-ranging books and essays about real-life people and events is one that many people appropriately highly value. If memoir is to do the valuable work it does, it may sometimes need to harm, or risk harm, as part of its baseline commitment to truth-telling. But there may also be other important interests at play in particular cases. Writing a memoir that happens to treat a sensitive topic may be one of the memoirist's ultimate goals. And an honest treatment of the specific subject at issue may be helpful to the memoirist's readers, particularly if the topic written about has typically been neglected or shrouded in secrecy, maybe as a result of social injustice.

When important interests are at stake on both sides, as they often are in memoir, how do we decide which harms to subjects are justified? As suggested above, a plausible general principle to start with is that we should attempt to avoid harm overall, to the extent that we can. This implies that you shouldn't write a memoir with the sole intention of harming someone, and that if you can write your memoir without needless harm, you should. This latter implication suggests that you should ask, of each harmful (or potentially harmful) part of your work, whether that part is truly necessary to the personal, aesthetic, and ethical aims of your project, or whether another non-harmful approach would work just as well. This principle arguably applies not just to genuine harms, but also to more minor hurts. What you write about someone may not severely or permanently set back their interests, but it could still cause them suffering. Inflicting pain on someone wantonly or maliciously—for no defensible reason—is wrong.

The cases where you can costlessly avoid harm while writing memoir are the easy ones, of course. The trickier cases are the ones where taking the nonharmful route would involve significant costs to other interests, values, and principles. Say that what you plan to write (truthfully) about Maxwell is almost certain to harm him, emotionally and socially, given what you have to say about him and your relationship. You *could* leave Maxwell out of your memoir, but doing so would significantly distort your narrative arc, leave several of your central themes underdeveloped, and seriously mess up your tone (readers can tell you're hiding something major!), with the result that your book is aesthetically crippled and also doesn't sell well, permanently stalling your literary career. Assume that leaving Maxwell out would, in addition, deprive you of the opportunity to enlighten and support others who have come across the likes of Maxwell and seriously misrepresent the basic facts of your life to your unwitting and trusting readers. We have Maxwell's interests on one side, and the values of Art, Self-Interest, Social Welfare, and Truth on the other. What should win out?

When interests conflict in the writing of memoir, in these and related ways, much of what Feinberg proposes about how to balance interests in general is plausible. He suggests that we need to attend to four key considerations: *degree, vitality, reinforcement,* and *moral quality.*[7] First, other things being equal, we should prioritize preventing the total thwarting of one interest over preventing a minor incursion of another interest. (Consider the case where Maxwell's social life will be ruined if you include him, whereas the literary quality of your book will improve just a bit.) Second, we should prioritize the protection of more vital interests over less vital interests. One interest is more vital than another when it plays a more central role within the broader network of interests of which it's a part. (Consider the case where Maxwell doesn't care much about his reputation, so damage to it doesn't impact his overall system of interests much, whereas your identity as a successful writer underpins multiple aspects of your self-interest.) Third, we should prioritize the protection of interests that are more strongly reinforced by the interests of others. (Consider how damage to Maxwell may injure only Maxwell, whereas your reticence may setback the interests of your potential readers as well as yourself.) Fourth, we should deprioritize the protection of interests whose inherent moral quality is low. (Let's say that the public interest in your story about Maxwell derives exclusively from a sensationalist and morbid curiosity about his highly unusual sex life, the scandalous actions he performed when drunk, and his spectacularly debilitating terminal disease. The public may have *an* interest in reading about all this, but the satisfaction of that interest has pretty low moral value and shouldn't weigh heavily in the calculus).

Assessments of degree and moral quality are relatively easy to make. (It'd be difficult to rank all interests on a scale of moral quality, but things are clear enough at the extreme lower end where the principle we're using kicks in). It's much harder to assess vitality and reinforcement. It's tempting for a memoirist to simplify this task by appealing to the supposedly overriding value of truth-telling. Telling the truth is so vital, it's sometimes suggested, on both literary and moral grounds, to the whole network of interests of both memoirists and their readers, that it outweighs any degree of harm to any number of subjects. This extreme position is implausible. As discussed in the previous chapter, there's often great value to telling the truth, in memoir as elsewhere, but we shouldn't be absolutists about it, and one of the most plausible justifications for lying or deceiving others is avoiding harm. Memoirists sometimes try to get around this fact by arguing that the truth is ultimately a healing force, so that even those who are superficially harmed by reading about themselves or those they know will benefit from it in the long run. Again, this might be true in some cases, but in others it's just a convenient fantasy. People ignore and repress truths and deceive themselves for good reasons. As Bok notes in her discussion of lying, "the self-appointed removers of false beliefs from those for whom these beliefs may be all that sustains them can be as harmful as the most callous liars."[8]

There are two further factors that memoirists need to consider, in addition to the four key interest-balancing principles of degree, vitality, reinforcement, and moral quality. One is uncertainty. No memoirist can be sure in advance how much harm or benefit their memoir will cause when read. So in making assessments of the vitality of the interests involved, the extent of their reinforcement, and the degree to which they'll be impacted, memoirists have to rely on judgments of probability. One plausible principle here is that, other things being equal, we should prioritize the protection of interests that are certain to be harmed over interests that simply might be harmed. Another plausible principle is that the graver the harm in view, the fewer risks we should be willing to run. Another is that the more valuable a potentially dangerous activity is, the more likely the danger needs to be in order to curtail the activity. (If your memoir is highly valuable, a tiny risk that it will harm Maxwell shouldn't weigh overly heavily.)

A further factor is the moral innocence or guilt of the person being written about. The destruction of a person's reputation is a harm, but a harm that some people have no right not to suffer. If you've performed nasty actions, having others find out about them may be a legitimate price for you to pay. In some cases, the destruction of your reputation might even be required, to protect others from you and your kind in the future. (Let's assume that Maxwell is a selfish jerk who did you wrong. Can you really be required to sacrifice your literary, personal, and social justice goals for the sake of protecting him from the social consequences of his own jerkiness?)

It's sometimes suggested that the past wrongdoing of your subject justifies any harm whatsoever that you do them in writing about them. (People often cite memoirist Anne Lamott's dictum on this point: "If people wanted you to write warmly about them, they should have behaved better.") But I don't think we can derive a carte blanche from this consideration. For one thing, there's a fine line between just recompense and *revenge*. If your treatment of your wrongdoers is mainly motivated by the latter, it may not be justified: vengeance is a morally suspect motivation. For another, we generally think that retaliation for wrongs has to be *proportionate* to be justified. (Maxwell may have injured you, sure, but your publishing a permanent record of the injury may do him much worse harm.) Finally, what at least some (not all) wrongdoers deserve is compassion and forgiveness, especially if they've sincerely acknowledged the badness of their behavior and made a serious attempt to adequately atone for it.

The plausibility of all of the above already shows that there's more to the ethics of memoir than the legal requirements in this area suggest. (I'm not implying that the law should be more stringent than it is: there's an important difference between what it's morally wrong to do and what it's morally OK to coerce us not to do, and the second isn't my topic here.) But there are two limitations in the US legal treatment of memoir that we haven't yet addressed. One is that the law limits itself to only two wrongs you can commit in memoir, libel and violation of privacy, whereas at least another three — exploitation, betrayal, and unjust appropriation — seem worth considering. Another is that, of the two wrongs the law does discuss, the second, violation of privacy, gets an overly narrow and vague treatment. The following sections of this chapter will attempt to fill these gaps by going more deeply into the question of which incursions on privacy are morally justified and which additional wrongs memoirists should be alert to. Many privacy violations and instances of exploitation, betrayal, and unjust appropriation can be understood as forms of harm. But they don't always involve setbacks of interest, and our concern with them isn't always due to their impact on our well-being. (Our foundational concern about them may not be that they cause us to *suffer*, but rather that they *disrespect* us.) So what we're turning to now is related to, but also independent of, what we've already discussed. My strategy in this interconnected terrain will be to treat each wrong individually for now, and draw them back together later in the chapter.

Privacy

Probably the greatest fear that people have when a memoirist appears in the family, romance, or neighborhood is that the writer will reveal information to a public audience that the subjects of that information prefer to have permanently withheld. This is exactly, of course, what many memoirists have done. In *Father and Son*, Edmund Gosse used his mother Emily's "secret notes, in a little locked volume, seen until now, nearly sixty years later, by no eye save her own,"[9] and quoted extensively from his deceased father's letters. Other memoirists have, among other things, revealed their closeted parents as alcoholic, mentally ill, or gay; their ex-lovers as cheaters or abusers; and their hometown as packed with bigots, philistines, or snobs.

Some subjects have reacted poorly. Mark Doty's very reserved father returned to sender a copy of his son's memoir of growing up gay in mid-century Tennessee and permanently cut off all contact with him.[10] Others have seemed less fussed. When his mistress threatened to reveal their affair in her memoirs, the Duke of Wellington reportedly yelled "Publish and be damned!" And Mary Karr's mother replied, when asked by her memoirist daughter if she minded being outed in *The Liars' Club* as a knife-wielding alcoholic who set her children's toys on fire: "Oh hell, the whole town knew about that."[11]

In some cases, whether or not the subjects themselves are bothered, the reading public is outraged on their behalf. Rousseau was roundly criticized for "confessing" Madame de Warens while confessing himself. More recently, Rachel Cusk was savaged in the British media after publishing *A Life's Work* and *Aftermath*, memoirs about her experience of early motherhood and the dissolution of her marriage that included material heavily critical of her ex-husband and many scenes featuring her young daughters.[12] The condemnation was so intense that Cusk claims that after publishing the second she was unable to write for the following two years and has now given up the traditional memoir for good.

While the personal and public consequences of such revelations can be dire, memoirists keep risking them. How could they resist? It's impossible to write a memoir of any substantial length without describing people other than yourself, given how much of each person's identity and history is formed in relationship with other humans. And it's, if not impossible, at least very difficult, to write a *good* memoir without including material about those other people that risks being regarded as inappropriate for public consumption. The central aim of memoir, after all, is to provide a searching, honest, vivid account of the author's inner life and outer experience, one that doesn't avoid the more fraught and painful aspects of the past and that brings its characters to life on the page, in all their weirdness and wonder. A common motivation for reading memoir is precisely to see up close what other people's relationships are like, and therefore to probe what the memoirist's family members, friends, ex-lovers, and acquaintances may forcefully want to keep hidden.

Most of us accept the above points and agree that memoir, by its nature, has to enter into the intimate lives of others to some significant extent. If we believe that memoir isn't an inherently reprehensible project, as most of us also do, we'll therefore regard many of these intimate revelations as ethically defensible: a necessary cost of doing morally legitimate business. That said, most of us also regard some such incursions as beyond the ethical pale. Some discussions of intimate material involve *privacy violations*, and we think memoirists should avoid those, to the extent that they can. How is a memoirist to decide which of these categories their work falls into? To get clearer on that question, we need to think about what privacy is.

The concept of privacy covers a very wide and diverse category of things, which makes coming to a fully general definition of it difficult. But the particular form of privacy that's centrally at issue in memoir is relatively narrow. What the subjects of memoir are concerned about is informational privacy: control over others' acquisition and distribution of information about oneself. We each have a rough sense that certain facts about us shouldn't be sought or obtained without our authorization, and that, if they do get disseminated to others, it's us, not others, who should determine the timing, manner, and extent of their communication.

The sense is rough because it's unclear what makes a given piece of information private in this way. It can't just be a matter of its content. Information about subject matters that some consider highly sensitive—sexuality or health status, say—others are fine with having broadcast near and far. We could simplify matters here by suggesting that which forms of information are private should be determined by what each individual *wants* to be private. But this is both too permissive in some cases and too restrictive in others. You might want to keep the fact that you've just been on a killing spree private, but it's pretty clearly legitimate public info. And you might be totally fine with your government tracking your every movement, but many of us will consider this an appalling privacy violation regardless, and for good reason.

Another reason that subject matter alone can't demarcate the bounds of privacy is that the scope of the private zone is plausibly context sensitive. What should count as private in a given case depends partly on which agent is seeking or revealing the information in question, and for what purpose. It's never appropriate for your employer to seek information about your romantic or sexual activity, for instance, but it might be appropriate for certain branches of the government to be interested in it, for certain limited purposes (when determining your eligibility for citizenship or your tax status, say, or while investigating you in relation to a sex crime). Or—to return to our focus

here—compare the case of a journalist who has no personal relationship with his subject and is publishing material about her family life
for a sensationalist tabloid article, with the case of a writer who was
married to the subject for thirty years, and is using the very same material within a well-rounded and empathetic memoir. The first case is
much more likely to be viewed as a privacy violation than the second.

These examples suggest that whether a piece of information is appropriately regarded as private depends on whether access to that
piece of information is *warranted* in the case in question: whether
it's backed by morally defensible reasons. If so, the concept of privacy isn't just a descriptive term, but an essentially normative one: its
boundaries depend on ethical considerations. This suggests that we
need to work out why privacy is important to us in order to see more
clearly what it is.

Why, then, do we value control over others' access to information
about us? One obvious answer is that we're worried that others will
use certain pieces of information, advertently or not, to set back our
interests in some way. A subject of memoir might be concerned, for
instance, that public knowledge of her health condition or sexual history would make it harder for her to get a job or cause her crippling
embarrassment in her judgmental social circle. This answer makes
our concern with privacy a subset of our more general concern with
harm.

Worries about the consequences of personal revelations for our
well-being are doubtless part of the story here, but they're not usually
all, or even most, of it. People are frequently disturbed by incursions
into what they regard as their private affairs even if no harm seems
likely to result (maybe because the information revealed is quite ordinary and doesn't set them up for mistreatment or discrimination of
any kind). Edmund Gosse's mother might well have been annoyed
with her son for reading her diary even if he never told anyone else
about it and his behavior toward her remained unchanged afterward.
"My secret diary," she might well have said, "is none of your business, Ed!"

It's easy to associate that kind of claim with a hyperindividualist
attempt to keep others at bay. But several philosophers have argued
that privacy is actually a deeply social value: on balance, it serves to
draw us together rather than keep us apart. Privacy matters to us,

they suggest, because it's necessary for the flourishing of a rich array of valuable relationships with our fellow humans.

Charles Fried argues, along these lines, that it'd be impossible for us to have intimate relationships of love, friendship, and trust with other people if we had no control over the information about us that others have access to.[13] It's essential to love and friendship that the people involved share with each other information that they don't share with others. If you discover that your alleged friend doesn't tell you any details about their inner life or activities that they don't also tell everyone else, you have good reason to doubt that you're friends after all. Fried suggests that it doesn't actually matter much what the content of the shared information is, provided that it has some degree of exclusivity: that it singles out the knower as special in some way. But the content does seem to matter, too. If you discover that your alleged friend has kept from you the fact that they're in the midst of a divorce, a cancer diagnosis, and a mental breakdown, their sharing their holiday menu plan only with you wouldn't do much to reassure you that your friendship is real. Intimate relationships depend not just on exclusivity but also on vulnerability, and an extension of information that embodies both is a kind of gift. Informational privacy—control over what to share, when, and to whom—creates what Fried calls the "moral capital" we need to make these gifts, and therefore to build and maintain the intimate relationships that rely on them.

James Rachels argues for a broader version of this thesis, according to which privacy is essential not just for romance, family, and friendship, but for a diverse array of other relationships too.[14] He suggests that all relationships are partly structured by the type and degree of information that the parties reveal to each other. You share a certain kind of information about yourself with your doctor, another kind with your professor, another with your mother. We couldn't have these, and the many other varied relationships that make up our lives, if we didn't have the ability to select what we disclosed to particular others. Informational privacy functions as a kind of valve we can open and close as we choose, thereby adapting our interactions with others to the kind of relationship we want to have with each other.

These arguments underscore the importance of privacy for sustaining fulfilling and varied relationships with others. But privacy is important for nonsocial reasons too. Probably all of us value retaining

space in our lives that's accessible to no one else, not even our intimates. We want a realm of our own, set apart, that others can't enter.
Keeping certain information secret is one means of creating and
protecting this realm. Secrecy may be especially valued when other
means—anonymity (when no one pays attention to you) and solitude
(when no one has physical access to you)[15]—are hard to come by.

People have different reasons for valuing this secret realm. One
is the importance of what we might call "inner solitude" for retaining a sense of your own identity. If you're like the average modern
human, your flourishing depends on seeing yourself as a distinct individual with a definable identity, made up of unique qualities and value
commitments that are uniquely your own. This is tied up with seeing
yourself as an autonomous agent, with control over your thoughts, actions, and projects, and relatedly, as not just a biological being, but a
person, in the more expansive philosophical sense of that term. Maintaining this sense of identity requires the maintenance of some degree
of inner separateness from other humans, an inward domain where
you're immune to the scrutiny of others. If your every thought and
feeling were constantly on display, it'd be hard to maintain a clear grip
on where your mind and life ended and those of others began, and to
plan and carry out your own projects without self-consciousness, dis-
traction, and obstruction.

For some of us, the demarcation of an inner realm has further spiritual or religious significance: it's seen as essential for contact with the
good, the meaningful, the transcendent, or the divine. Theists and
mystics characteristically see themselves and others not only as distinctive but as infinitely layered: as possessing depths and possibilities that are unfathomable and ineffable. As Sissela Bok expresses this
idea, "human beings can be subjected to every scrutiny, and reveal
much about themselves; but they can never be entirely understood,
simultaneously exposed from every perspective, completely transparent either to themselves or to other persons."[16] For supernaturalists,
although much of human life occurs on the surface of these depths,
humans can't flourish without dipping below them at least some of
the time. And accessing the deeper layers of our personhood is, again,
felt to depend on a degree of informational separation from others.
Prayer and meditation often occur in silence and solitude; what happens during them is generally left undiscussed. And the ability to re-

treat to a place of inner solitude, even in the physical company of others, is viewed as an everyday means of elevation from the mundane to the exalted.

Whether our reasons are philosophical-moral or spiritual in this way, many of us see the inner realm as having a precious or sacred quality, as both an embodiment and protector of our dignity and value. Simply having this space available is deeply important to us, independently of the content of what we place in it. Our commitment to informational privacy is a means of fostering it and the highly valued experiences it provides.

Informational privacy matters for additional reasons in other contexts. It's an essential safeguard of political freedom, for instance, and of personal property. (If you couldn't conceal the location of your keys, or the relation between those keys and the house, car, office, and storage unit they open, you might have trouble retaining every material thing you own.) But I think the three reasons just described are the crucial ones in the case of memoir. I suspect that if we quizzed them about it, we'd find that when subjects of memoir object to a memoirist revealing information about them on grounds of privacy, it's because they view the revelation as a threat to one or more of their well-being, their ability to control the shape and extent of their social relationships, and the survival of a precious inner realm they view as theirs alone.

I take these to be legitimate fears, worthy of respect, and therefore of serious consideration on the memoirist's part. But whether or not they establish a conclusive argument against revealing the information in question depends, of course, on the interests and values on the other side. Privacy has positive value as a protection against harm, an enabler of relationships, and a guardian of the inner realm. But it can also be used for ill. Feminists have persuasively pressed this line.[17] Claims that the domestic realm is private, and therefore immune to scrutiny, have historically served as a shield for the domination and abuse of women and children. The resulting suggestion on the part of some that we should fully eliminate the public/private distinction risks inviting equally alarming forms of oppression on the part of the state or society. But the more moderate point that claims of informational privacy can sometimes be unjustified and dangerous is totally persuasive.

Memoirists who write about intimate relationships are often motivated by a desire to reveal and explore matters that others have illegitimately kept private. "Trauma memoirs" published by writers raised
by alcoholic parents or married to abusive spouses frequently have this
character; "social justice memoirs" chronicling histories of discrimination and harassment do too. The writers in question may have spent
many years shrouded in oppressive secrecy and are likely to view their
subjects' accusations of privacy violations as illegitimate attempts to
maintain their domination or avoid the just consequences of their actions. The writer generally sees the idea of privacy as a major contrib-
uting cause of their past suffering and certainly not as something to
be respected now.

The general argument has force in nonabusive situations, too.
Many secrets are kept out of embarrassment or self-criticism, much
of which may be unmerited. The keeping of such secrets over a long
period of time can entrench the shame, undermining the secret
keeper's mental health and stunting and corrupting their relationships with others. A memoirist may see the exposing of this sort of fes-
tering secret as a gift to the secret holder, a means of draining it of its
destructive power. The secret holder is likely to see things differently.

Claims to privacy, then, generate counterclaims, and some of those
counterclaims may be justified. The difficulty is working out which.
Patricia Hampl's essay "Other People's Secrets" is a complex and moving evocation of the memoirist's challenges here, not least of which
is the elusiveness of their own true motivations.[18] As a young writer,
Hampl published an autobiographical poem that revealed her mother
as having epilepsy. In Hampl's view at the time, her mother's lifelong unwillingness to let others know of her epilepsy was baseless
and harmful:

I did not approve of the secrecy in which for years she had wrapped the dark jewel
of her condition. I did not feel she *deserved* to be so upset about something that
should be seen in purely practical terms. I hated–feared, really–the freight she
loaded on the idea of epilepsy . . . It was all, as I told her, no big deal. Couldn't she
see that?[19]

The young Hampl believed that her writing of the poem was justified, despite her mother's determined reticence on its subject, partly

due to the intrinsic value of art, and partly due to a conviction that the airing of the secret would be healing for her mother: "for doesn't the truth, as John, the beloved apostle promised, set you free?"[20] She showed the poem to her mother, who consented to its publication. Later in life, Hampl had doubts about whether or not she'd done the right thing, and asked her mother how she'd felt at the time. It became clear, then, that her mother had actually been deeply grieved by the revelation and had only agreed to it to support her daughter's writing career. In retrospect, Hampl sees that it wasn't her mother's well-being, but her own needs and wishes, that mainly drove her decision to publish the poem: her desire to defuse the fear her mother's secret had caused her as a child and her desire for public recognition of her work. She also recognizes that she'd misread, or refused to see, the significance that her mother's medical condition had for her mother, regardless of how unimportant it seemed to Hampl, and that both the publication and the content of her poem hadn't respected that significance:

I can see now that she was standing up for the truth of her experience, the literal fact of it, how it jerked and twisted not only her body but her life, how it truly *seized* her. My poem and I–we merely fingered the thing, casually displaying it for the idle passerby. What she knows and how she knows it must not be taken from her.[21]

We can arguably see in this story several of the ideas discussed in the previous few pages. Without asking Hampl's mother, we can't really know what exactly it was about the poem's revelation that distressed her, but we can make some guesses. She might well have been concerned that others' knowledge of her epilepsy would harm her, by adversely affecting her social relationships. But it seems likely that she was also troubled, independently, by a perceived lack of control over the scope and nature of those relationships. Before the poem's publication, she'd chosen to reveal her condition to only a small circle of intimates and, presumably, her doctors. But her daughter's act had made it accessible to an audience indeterminate in shape and size. Even a single incursion of this kind can destabilize a person's sense of autonomy across the board, by revealing the fragility of the convention of informational privacy on which all our social relationships depend. There's a clue, too, in that characterization of the secret as a "dark jewel," that Hampl's mother had come to regard her concealed condition as a valuable part of her inner realm, an instance and symbol of her partial inaccessibility to other humans. Her epilepsy was a crucial part of her, and its concealment a crucial way of preserving some part of herself from the scrutiny of others. In the act of concealing it, the condition she'd found shameful had become, in its own way, precious. In face of these subtle psychological facts, the youthful Hampl's countervailing bald claims about the value of truth and art are revealed as flat-footed and self-serving.

It's better to come to this kind of realization late rather than never, but it'd be nice to have some guidance memoirists could use at the time to work out when truth, art, self-interest, and social value *should* prevail, and when a subject's privacy should instead. What can we say about that?

I suggest we start by looking at what life writers in an adjacent field have had to say about a similar issue. In the everyday course of their work, journalists are frequently faced with the question of what type and degree of personal material it's appropriate to reveal in their articles. A body of writing and set of conventions about the ethics of journalism has built up as a result, from which we can extract the following widely accepted principles.[22]

First, *certain means of obtaining information from others are either ruled out or face a heavy burden of justification.* Journalists shouldn't deceive, trick, surprise, threaten, bribe, or seduce people into revealing information they'd otherwise have kept secret. They shouldn't trespass, steal, eavesdrop, or record conversations without prior consent. They should be careful when dealing with young, mentally disabled, inexperienced, or otherwise vulnerable sources who may be incapable of giving meaningful consent to interviews. They shouldn't pay for access or material or threaten to harm those who fail to cooperate with their requests. They must maintain careful and transparent boundaries regarding personal relationships with their sources. They should generally identify themselves as journalists, be clear about the subject matter and aims of their work at the outset of interviews, and not pose as members of other professions. Undercover investigations are permitted in only the rarest of circumstances and should be reserved for topics of the utmost public importance. The underlying principles at work here are the general moral prohibitions on lying, deception, and coercion.

Second, *information offered to a journalist in confidence, in the course of an interview or other communication, should not be publicly disclosed.* This follows from the general moral prohibition on the breaking of promises.

Third, *the importance of gaining a subject's consent to publish information about them varies with the value to the broader public of the information in question.* A blanket norm requiring journalists to obtain consent for every piece of personal information they publish would be inappropriate. Journalists have a professional duty to publish stories that protect and further public welfare and democratic citizenship. Giving all individuals a veto over what journalists can and can't publish would make this core mission of journalism impossible. But the lower the social value of the information at issue, the more important consent to its revelation becomes. If the public interest in a given piece of information about someone is based merely on curiosity or desire for entertainment, and if the person objects to its disclosure, their request for privacy should be respected. If, on the other hand, revelation of the information promises overwhelming benefit to the public, either by serving genuine needs or (somewhat less persuasively) by satisfying widely shared desires, overriding the person's consent may be justified. The underlying principles at work here are those of promoting the general welfare while at the same time attempting to minimize harm and respect autonomy.

Fourth, *the importance of gaining a subject's consent to publish varies with the innocence of the subject.* Criminals may well object to public exposure of their crimes, but journalists needn't respect such wishes in their work. The justification here may rely on the principle at play in the previous case: information about crime is likely to be highly newsworthy. But it may also rely on the independent idea that people forfeit some of their rights when they violate the rights of others.

Fifth, *there should be a presumption against publishing revealing material about (innocent) victims of crime or tragedy.* Clifford G. Christians writes: "Families of firemen killed on duty should not be covered unless at their request. Reporters at a burning home leave the sufferers alone; they tell the story without interviewing or filming the victims."[23] Victims of sex crimes should be treated with special sensitivity and discretion. Vulnerable people in the grip of shock, grief, and trauma may suffer further from public exposure of their distress and may also not be in the right state of mind to give genuine, well-informed, and reflective consent to public disclosure. The risk of harm, then, is high, and the countervailing benefit—"the fact that readers and viewers are attracted to the intimate details of human misery"—isn't important enough to outweigh it.

Sixth, *the form and degree of appropriate scrutiny varies with the type of individual scrutinized.* Reporting that would be objectionably intrusive in the case of private citizens can be acceptable in the case of public figures.[24] Personal information about holders of, and candidates for, government positions can count as newsworthy when it's relevant to their job performance or eligibility for office. Personal information about other celebrities can count as newsworthy when it's the object of widespread public desire. The social value of the information, combined with the fact that the people in question have voluntarily entered the public arena in search of power or attention, means that the subjects' resistance to its disclosure may sometimes permissibly be overridden. (It's not always easy, of course, to work out what personal information *is* relevant to office or which public desires are worthy of respect.) Personal information about private citizens, on the other hand, is much less likely to offer significant public benefits of the kind journalism is designed to serve.

We can helpfully draw on these principles when turning to the case of memoir, though they need elaboration and adaptation in light of the important differences between journalism and personal writing.

The first two principles—the prohibitions on underhanded means of gaining information and on violating confidentiality—transfer straightforwardly. Lying, deception, and promise-breaking are generally wrong, whether you're writing an article for the *New York Times*, a personal essay for the *Kenyon Review*, or a self-published memoir. As a result, as a general rule, memoirists shouldn't try to gain information for their work in any of these ways, and they shouldn't use information in their work that they've gained in such ways in the past. This obligation isn't absolute, because the prohibitions against lying, deception, and promise-breaking can sometimes be overridden. I made this point about lying and deception in the previous chapter, so let's focus on promise-breaking here. A convincing case is that of Karen Thompson, who in 1991 had to out her life partner Sharon Kowalski as gay, to secure guardianship of her after Kowalski was seriously brain damaged.[25] Thompson's respecting her prior promise to keep Kowalski's sexual orientation secret would have imperiled a relationship that both women highly valued and possibly deprived Kowalski of care she urgently needed. Breaking a promise to keep a secret can be permissible when the revelation is of great value, as it was in this case. It's also permissible when the promise was made under duress or in ignorance, or when the promisee later releases the promiser from their obligation. But, as with lying and deception, the reasons for promise-breaking have to be highly compelling, and it seems safe to say that the average memoir won't be able to generate them.

The fourth principle transfers relatively straightforwardly, too, with the caveats mentioned in the earlier section on harm. Just as it's easier to justify harms to wrongdoers than innocent people in memoir, it's easier to justify unwanted personal disclosures about the guilty than about the innocent. But memoirists should take care here to examine their motives (revenge and vindictiveness don't offer much in the way of justification), to keep any intrusions proportionate to the severity of the subject's wrongdoing, and to consider whether the subject deserves forgiveness rather than retaliation.

The third, fifth, and sixth principles of journalistic ethics are harder to translate to memoir without strain. Together they establish a strong presumption against publishing information about the personal lives of (innocent) private citizens. The presumption can be overridden, but only when doing so would provide overwhelming benefit, most likely by promoting the general welfare and democracy or by satisfying desires widely held by the general public.

This presumption is doubly problematic for memoirists. First, in most cases, the bulk of the subject matter of memoir is precisely the personal lives of private citizens (including victims of crime or tragedy). And, second, memoirists will only rarely be able to point to the reasons for overriding privacy intrusions that journalists use. Much of what's written in most memoir seems unlikely to generate significant benefits for public welfare and democratic citizenship and, as far as curiosity and entertainment go, the expected readership may be rather small. Journalistic principles would allow for memoirists to publish some personal material about private citizens, but only if they obtained consent from their subjects first. But that would effectively require giving the subjects of memoir a veto over the matters that make up the heart and bulk of the memoirist's work, a veto that many subjects may be highly determined to exercise. The result of respecting these principles would be to make much memoir impossible.

The key issue here is that the aims and value of memoir are distinct from the aims and value of journalism, and the principles applying to each activity therefore appropriately differ. I'm reserving a fuller discussion of the value of memoir for chapter 5, but we can at least say this here. Memoir is centrally valuable for the window it provides into the intimate lives of others. It's memoir we go to, not journalism, or even biography, when we want to understand at a deep level what is was like, how it felt, to go through the sorts of experiences that make up the heart of human life. That understanding may not generate sociopolitical benefits such as public health, safety, and democracy, the way journalism does (though it might sometimes), but it does provide more personal benefits, in giving us the kind of insight, sense of solidarity, and succor we need to conduct our own lives well.

Because the revelation of intimate information lies at the very heart of memoirists' work (and because that work is highly valuable), the burden of proof when justifying intimate revelations is lighter than in the case of journalism. Many revelations that would count as impermissible privacy violations in a newspaper article won't count as such in a personal essay or memoir. That's because in the latter case, unlike the former, they aren't gratuitous, but a necessary, non-incidental means of achieving the legitimate and valuable aims of the enterprise.

This argument doesn't establish a free-for-all, however. When subjects object, or would be likely to object, to the inclusion of information about themselves, memoirists need to carefully consider whether their work really will advance the values just mentioned, or whether it merely serves interests of low moral quality (say, idle curiosity, desire for entertainment, or malice). If inclusion will advance less frivolous interests, memoirists also need to consider whether less intrusive writing would work just as well (in which case they have strong reason to take that alternative route). They should also avoid highly sensitive unwanted intimate revelations that are likely to strongly injure the subject while only *slightly* increasing the benefits produced by the work, either because the revelations are of minor value in themselves or because the work that includes them will have a very small circulation. (These are variants of the considerations of *moral quality, degree*, and *reinforcement* that Feinberg recommends for the weighing of competing interests.)

A distinct difference between memoir and journalism is that the memoirist is personally involved in the material discussed. (Immersive journalism is an intermediate case here, which is why it's hard to categorize the work of, say, Joan Didion, as clearly one or the other.) This matters because privacy claims can sometimes be presented as property claims: "you can't tell people about what went down, because it's *my* business!" That line might work to ward off some journalistic intrusions. But it doesn't work so well when what went down went down between you two, so that it's clearly also your business. By their nature, relationships don't belong to a single person, and therefore, to some extent, the incidents that occur within them are common property. (I don't like this property language, as will become clear later in the chapter, but we'll go with it here.) As Bill Roorbach puts this point, "Listen, it's your story, too. If ... you had a parent who drank, that drinking happened to *you*."[26] US courts have proved receptive to this point. They're more lenient to memoirists who reveal personal information about others when the memoirist has been intimately involved with the subject, on the ground that the writer is telling their own story and is "more than a disinterested party."

Again, this argument doesn't set up a moral free-for-all. As noted above, intimate relationships depend on a generally respected convention that not everything that happens within them is up for public consumption. Memoirists depend on that convention when they enter into relationships with others, so it's unfair for them to simply ditch it when it pleases them to. (This is why people don't simply waive all their claims to informational privacy when knowingly associating with, befriending, dating, or marrying a memoirist.) Some experiences shouldn't be written about, out of respect for the interests and wishes of others, even if you partly "own" them.

It should be clear by now that in the case of privacy, like the case of harm, memoirists' ethical obligations to their subjects exceed what the law requires. As we saw earlier, the position of the US legal system on privacy is that it's permissible to publish material about others that "furthers the public interest" and that a "reasonable person" wouldn't consider offensive if made public. But individuals can have legitimate privacy claims over that sort of material that ought to be respected. People are under no general moral duty to offer up material about themselves and their lives that promotes the public welfare, and reserving some information exclusively for themselves or their intimates may be important to them even if others would consider its content innocuous (remember Hampl's mother). It makes sense for the law to be relatively lenient here, given the difficulty of coming to a definition of the proper bounds of privacy that covers all people subject to the law and takes into account each of the complex values and interests at work in particular cases. (Attempts on the part of the state to adjudicate these issues more finely would themselves produce serious privacy violations.) But this doesn't get memoirists off the hook. They have not a legal but a moral duty to think more deeply than lawyers do about the ethical reasons for and against personal disclosures about the people they discuss in their work.

Exploitation

"You can use me," a friend once said, "just don't abuse me." But who, exactly, makes that distinction?

PATRICIA HAMPL[27]

Some complaints from subjects of memoir have a different flavor than the ones discussed so far: they focus not so much on the state of being harmed or exposed, but on the state of being *used*. If the memoirist makes a lot of money out of publication, the accusation might center on that: the subject may feel that their experiences, including possibly their misfortunes, have been trafficked in for the writer's financial gain. But even if the book or essay sells badly or not at all, the subject can complain of being used as fodder for the author's art or career.

Subjects (or their advocates) are especially likely to object to being used in these ways if the memoirist enjoys significantly greater power than the person they're writing about. Those who are disabled, mentally ill, very young, very old, relatively uneducated, or socioeconomically disadvantaged may end up inadvertently exposing themselves within an intimate or professional relationship with a memoirist who then goes on to use that material in a public sphere that the subject has reduced or no access to. There can be a strong sense in such cases (though not only in them) that the subject isn't merely being used, but being used *unfairly*: in a word, that they're being exploited.[28]

To exploit someone is to take unfair advantage of them: to use their vulnerability—whether a standing condition or temporary misfortune—for your own benefit. The wrong of exploitation differs from the wrong of harm or privacy violation because it always involves benefit to the agent. Even if the exploitation backfires later, the exploiter necessarily gains something from the exploitee in the moment. In contrast, it's possible to harm someone or violate their privacy while getting nothing out of it yourself.

Exploitation also differs from harm in that it doesn't have to involve any setback to the exploitee's interests (though it often does). The exploitee may gain alongside the exploiter, by comparison with the preexploitation baseline: both walk away better off. For that reason, exploitation is also much more likely to be consensual than harm is. But acts of mutually beneficial and consensual exploitation still remain exploitative, because the interaction at issue, whatever the shared gains, remains in some way unfair.

In what way, exactly? Exploitation usually involves two forms of unfairness: both "substantive" and "procedural." It results in a state of affairs—often a distribution of goods—that favors the exploiter in some morally problematic way. But it also involves a form of interaction, on the way to that state of affairs, that's itself morally troubling: say, coercion, deception, manipulation, domination, or disrespect. The kind of exploitation that Marx focused on involves both of these things. The proletariat certainly get a meagre share of the profits from their work. But they're also coerced, harassed, duped, and despised by their capitalist overlords. Neither the state of affairs produced nor the process alone fully captures the phenomenon. The same can be said of canonical cases of exploitation that don't involve material goods. A therapist who seduces a client is likely to gain sexual gratification without much emotional cost, while putting the mental health of the client at significant risk. That's a substantive inequality. But the way that the therapist gets to that uneven outcome rightly bothers us too: the seduction is likely to be dubiously consensual and exhibit rash disregard for a vulnerable person's basic welfare. (The details of the relationship matter, of course, but in this kind of scenario, I'm inclined to say not much.)

Exploitation happens in multiple spheres of human interaction: the workplace, the classroom, the home, the doctor's office, the international order. By comparison to some of these instances, the injury of being exploited in memoir may seem small-fry, but it's no less real for that. Life writing in general is actually a very fertile field for exploitation, given the power imbalances it often involves. Anthropologists and other social scientists who conduct narrative research, doctors and therapists who publish case studies, and investigative journalists who engage in long-term projects enter into intimate relationships with their subjects that involve unequal levels of exposure, knowledge, stakes, and voice. The subjects of such studies generally reveal much about themselves, while learning little about the writer in return. The writer is often higher in status and authority, by virtue of their professional expertise. The piece may be just one among many projects for the writer, but of unique and deep significance to the subject. (Dan Bar-On, who interviewed the children of Holocaust perpetrators and survivors for a book, writes that he and his colleagues "hold the meaning of people's lives in our hands."[29]) Finally, if the subjects don't like how they're portrayed, they often don't have the ability to defend themselves in print with the same degree of eloquence and breadth of audience that the writer possesses. All of this would be less morally fraught if the interests of life writers and their subjects were always perfectly aligned, but they're not. Writers are mainly interested in writing a good piece, not in the interests of their subjects. Subjects, for their part, care mainly about how the piece represents them, not about the writer's intellectual or literary achievement or career.

The fact that memoirists are often of the same socioeconomic or professional status as the intimates they write about might seem to even out the power imbalance somewhat. While social science, medicine, and journalism require degrees, anyone can write a memoir, these days, it might be suggested—the subjects can fight back in print, if they want! But this a pretty weak defense. Writing a memoir that people actually want to read is no piece of cake. Few nuclear families are like Tolstoy's, which contained a possible world record of seven successful memoirists (both parents and five of the six children). And even in that case, the wife and kids might have claimed to have been unfairly used: holding your own on the page against Leo Tolstoy is tough.

Memoir almost always involves using people, from a position of (locally) superior power. But not all memoirs are exploitative. The key question, when trying to work out whether a given memoir exploits its subjects, is whether the use in question is unfair.

A popular way of spelling out the idea of fair use of another person appeals to the Kantian notion of respect. Kant is often cited as saying that we should never use others as a means to our own ends, but what he really said is that we should never use them as a means *only*. What he meant by that is that we should continue to respect another's moral status as a free and equal person while we benefit from interacting with them. Russ Shafer-Landau offers a vivid example here.[30] There's an important moral difference, he notes, between employing a plumber to fix a leak and knocking the plumber unconscious and using his head to block the hole in the pipe. The second action simply uses the plumber, whereas the first uses him while also respecting his dignity as a rational agent with his own goals and agency.

The rule that you ought to respect someone while using them plausibly rules out the procedural violations that characterize canonical examples of exploitation. It's hard to respect a person while coercing, deceiving, manipulating, or oppressing them. So memoirists who engage in those sort of actions in the course of their work are taking unfair advantage of their subjects. Getting subjects to provide information about themselves, or otherwise cooperate in the writing of the memoir, under duress or via subterfuge will count as exploitative. It's this sort of wrong that Janet Malcolm criticized in her classic *The Journalist and the Murderer*, which describes the impressive lengths to which writer Joe McGinniss went to extract intimate information from the convicted murder, Jeffrey MacDonald, about whom he was writing a book. (McGinniss lived with MacDonald for six weeks prior to his conviction, accompanied him to his murder trial, corresponded with him for three years while he was imprisoned and visited him twice, all the while professing friendship, sympathizing with and advising him, and giving him the clear impression that the book he was writing would exonerate rather than condemn him.) Malcolm writes that getting the story requires journalists like MacDonald to create a "deliberately induced delusion" in their subjects, "followed by a moment of shattering revelation" when the subject reads the book or article.[31] The result is the subtype of exploitation we call *swindling*: using deception to deprive someone of something they value.

But those are the easy cases, at least where ethical evaluation is concerned. The harder and more common cases are those in which memoirists write about their subjects without asking for their assistance. In those cases, if you like, the memoirist risks exploiting the past relationship rather than the present one.

What would that look like, though? Let's stick to the case of friends, for simplicity (the point will carry). It's tempting to think that it's only ever permissible to seek gains from your friends that are internal to the friendship. While there's nothing wrong with seeking companionship and love from them—those goods are built into the nature of the relationship—it'd be wrong to treat your friends as, say, a route to social or career advancement. But that's overly restrictive. Friends do often provide external goods and opportunities to each other, and we don't generally have a problem with that. As long as the receiving friend isn't treating their friend *only* as a means to those goods, nothing seems out of line.

Claudia Mills argues on this basis that there's nothing wrong per se with a memoirist gaining financial or literary benefits from writing about their friends and other intimates.[32] Doing so is only exploitative when the motivation to get those benefits is driving the relationship (which won't generally be the case, especially when memoirists write about their more distant past) or when the memoirist fails to value their friend appropriately while writing about them. She suggests that the most likely failure in the latter case is that of violating the friend's privacy, but we could point to non-privacy-related harms too. In such cases, the wrong of exploitation ultimately reduces to the wrongs of unjustified harm and exposure, with the added twist that the memoirist gains disproportionately from the act. You can avoid exploiting someone in memoir in these ways, then, if you avoid coercing, deceiving, manipulating, or oppressing them, and also engage in only the sorts of warranted harms and intimate revelations discussed in the previous sections.

There's a further form of exploitative memoir writing, though, that fails to value subjects appropriately in a different way. The chief complaint here isn't that the subject is being harmed or exposed to advance the author's finances or career, but instead that they're being used to make a *point*, in a way that disrespects them. Maybe the memoirist is using the subject's actions or experiences to illustrate an argument or worldview the subject disagrees with or finds repulsive. Or maybe the subject feels they're being reduced in print to nothing *but* a point, even if it's one they too endorse.

Michael Dorris's memoir *The Broken Cord* is a particularly depressing example of this.[33] The book recounts Dorris's adoption of a three-year-old Native American son, Adam, who turned out to have serious cognitive impairments as a result of fetal alcohol syndrome. In his narration of this experience, Dorris reacts to the diagnosis with dismay and rage, from which he never recovers. He then goes on to use Adam in the book as a type and a lesson, setting his son's individuality aside in support of his own (ableist and racist) crusade.

This type of exploitation is distinctively objectifying. As in the case of the plumber mentioned above, Dorris is treating his son not as a valuable human being, but as a mere *thing*, someone whose worth, dignity, and agency are nonexistent or irrelevant. Dorris was quite explicit about this in an essay published after his son's death, in which he wrote: "When at last I accepted that I could not affect my by now grown son's life, I elected, instead, to document it. If he could not contribute to society by his actions, then, I reasoned, let him act as an example, as a flesh and blood object lesson against the dangers of drinking alcohol during pregnancy."[34] Such objectification usually involves an at least implicit denial of the full humanity of the subject. Dorris did it openly: "By all evidence, [Adam] had been deprived of the miracle of transcendent imagination, a complex grace that was the quintessence of being human."[35] This is egregious, but less egregious examples can still exhibit significant objectification, whether acknowledged by the author or not.

The best way to avoid exploiting someone like this is to aim for a subtle, sensitive, and expansive treatment of those you write about. As Leslie Jamison puts it in an interview: "I owe [my subjects] most importantly the dignity of complexity on the page. I owe them the chance to contradict themselves, the chance to be more than evidence supporting a thesis statement I devised for them to serve."[36]

It's worth noting, finally, that the moral nature of your past relationship with someone may also be relevant to whether or not it's OK for you to gain by writing about them. Kiese Laymon says in an interview about his memoir, *Heavy*: "there were people in my life that I'd harmed—I tried to write about that harm, because I thought that was the right thing to do. And some of those people were just like, 'Naw, you don't get to harm me and then ultimately get paid for harming me.'"[37] Just as wrongdoing subjects of memoir may deserve less protection from their victims, wrongdoing *writers* of memoir may deserve less freedom with respect to theirs.

Let's say you do end up exploiting someone in your memoir: using your superior power to illegitimately press for an outcome that you don't deserve to enjoy. That's wrong, but how *bad* a wrong is it? There's disagreement over this. Most people agree that nonconsensual and harmful exploitation lies somewhere in the range from bad to atrocious. You might try to justify it via benefit to third parties, but the bar of success there will be very high. The moral status of consensual and mutually advantageous exploitation, on the other hand, is controversial. Some theorists claim that mutually beneficial, consensual exploitation isn't morally problematic, period. Others claim that, although it is, it isn't a serious wrong, and is therefore easily outweighed by other considerations.

If you're lucky to have a subject who's willing to be exploited, then, and whom you can benefit (albeit not as much as you benefit yourself) by exploiting, it may not be much of an ethical problem to go ahead and do it. Some people are delighted to be used in memoir, even if the material revealed about them takes advantage of an intimate relationship and violates their privacy. It makes them feel significant, it might make them famous, and it saves them the bother of writing a memoir themselves. Such people, provided they're also interesting, are a true gift to the memoirist: why not, so to speak, exploit the opportunity?

Betrayal

"You must not tell anyone," my mother said, "what I am about to tell you."

MAXINE HONG KINGSTON[38]

The celebrated 1976 memoir *Woman Warrior* begins with the arresting line above: arresting, because telling everyone is exactly what Hong Kingston goes on to do. Any unease we feel about this act might be diagnosed as a worry about harm, privacy, or exploitation. But the act also has an additional whiff: the distinctive scent of betrayal.

All relationships are built on and depend on trust, of at least a minimal kind. Even my tenuous and highly limited relationship with my dry cleaner depends on my trusting that he won't shred my shirt when I hand it over or come at me with a knife when I enter his store. Intimate relationships, of course, depend on trust of a much more sweeping and consequential kind. We trust our friends (and our family, if we're lucky) to provide some of the things that matter most to us in life, both intrinsically and instrumentally: love, companionship, encouragement, and emotional and material support. And we trust them to deal delicately with sensitive information about ourselves and our lives that we necessarily reveal when relating to them, information that might become dangerous to us if found in the wrong hands.

Annette Baier argues that trust isn't just a matter of relying on others.[39] You can rely on your very punctual neighbor to leave his house for work each morning at seven without *trusting* him to do it. What's distinctive about trust, Baier suggests, is the additional element of belief in the trustee's goodwill toward you. You trust your friend (or dry cleaner) to fulfill your expectations not just out of self-interest, habit, or indifference, but out of some degree of genuine concern for you. Or, Carolyn McLeod suggests, it may not be their goodwill toward you that you believe in, but their moral integrity: their commitment to acting decently toward others across the board.[40]

Trusting someone necessarily involves making yourself vulnerable to betrayal: the other person's act of unjustly failing to live up to your trust. Just as trusting is more than relying, a sense of betrayal is more than a sense of disappointment. Feeling betrayed is a *moral* emotion, a sense not only that your expectations haven't been unmet, but that you've been wronged as a result.

It's not always wrong to let down someone who has trusted you. For one thing, you might have overriding moral obligations that point in the other direction. But also—to lump a lot of extenuating factors together—people can trust you for very weird reasons, without your assent or even knowledge, to do immoral things you're incapable of doing. If Otto, a mere acquaintance with a strange fixation on me, trusts me to support his bigoted proposal at a meeting of the Faculty Senate, of which I'm not in fact a voting member, he can hardly accuse me of betraying him if I don't turn up. (Or rather, he could, but that would just be Otto being very odd again.) In general, you can't be held morally responsible for instances of uninvited, unwelcome, immoral, or unwarranted trust.

But some failures to live up to another's trust are wrong. If you induce in someone a reasonable belief that you can, wish to, and will act with competence and goodwill toward them in some domain, and there are no countervailing moral reasons against your so acting, your failure to act that way is bad. If you don't act as expected, you won't have just let them down, but let them down unjustly; you won't have merely "betrayed their trust," as we sometimes say: you'll have betrayed *them*.

We usually reserve the word "betrayal" for unjust trust violations that are particularly consequential and distressing. It would be strange for me to say that my dry cleaner had "betrayed" me by shredding my shirt. On the other hand, it wouldn't be at all strange for me to say that my memoirist ex–best friend had betrayed me by publishing that devastating personal essay she wrote about me.

Betrayal is painful not just because being wronged always hurts to some extent, but also because it represents a serious threat to the relationship it occurs in. Betrayal usually causes the person betrayed to reassess the nature of the relationship and its future viability. This is because trust involves a belief that another will look after what one cares about, and, as Baier writes, "the best reason for confidence in another's good care of what one cares about is that it is a common good, and the best reason for thinking that one's own good is also a common good is being loved."[41] Being betrayed can therefore cause a friend to wonder if the love they imagined they enjoyed was illusory.

Alongside being hurtful in these two ways, betrayal within intimate relationships is often experienced as what we might call a "double-whammy wrong." First, there's the immediate wrong of the betrayer's unjustified failure to do the specific thing that was reasonably expected of them. This is somewhat like the breaking of a promise, and anyone, even a non-intimate, could feel wronged by that. Second, though, there's the fact that the betrayer did this generic wrong specifically *to her friend*. ("How could you do that—to me, of all people?") The fact that the wrong was committed within an intimate relationship is felt, somehow, to magnify its wrongness. This might be because of the heightened degree of trust we generally accord to friends: we expect them to take extraspecial care not to wrong us in particular. That heightened degree of trust increases our vulnerability to them, and we generally take wronging hypervulnerable people to be especially wrong.

The double-whammy nature of betrayal helps to explain why the wrongs of harm, privacy violation, and exploitation in memoir are each often experienced, simultaneously, as serious acts of betrayal. There's the immediate wrong ("you *harmed* me!") and also the secondary wrong ("you harmed *me!*"): you harmed me, that is, in a context where I trusted you not to, as my friend.

Claims of betrayal are more common and more fervent in memoir than in several other forms of life writing precisely because that secondary kind of wrong—"you wronged *me!*"—is more likely to appear in the course of autobiographical writing. Memoirists are often writing about people with whom they have extended intimate relationships, whereas biographers, social scientists, and journalists generally aren't. (Biographers often have no relationship at all with their subjects, so the possibility of trust and betrayal is conceptually ruled out.) In the case of more lengthy and collaborative writing projects—say, a piece of authorized biography, immersive journalism or extended narrative research, or a therapeutic case study—the subject might well feel let down and wronged by the writer. Janet Malcolm writes of the immersive journalism case:

> The catastrophe suffered by the subject is no simple matter of an unflattering likeness or a misrepresentation of his views; what pains him, what rankles and sometimes drives him to extremes of vengefulness, is the deception that has been practiced on him. On reading the article or book in question, he has to face the fact that the journalist—who seemed so friendly and sympathetic, so keen to understand him fully, so remarkably attuned to his vision of things—never had the slightest intention of collaborating with him on his story but always intended to write a story of his own. The disparity between what seems to be the intention of an interview as it is taking place and what it actually turns out to have been in aid of always comes as a shock to the subject.[42]

But the sense of betrayal that a subject feels here is still unlikely to reach anything like the same extent as that felt by a memoirist's injured close friend, parent, or spouse. Memoir is constitutionally set up for the worst kinds of betrayal.

Claims of betrayal in memoir aren't always persuasive, though, for three key reasons. First, because trust is often implicit, and because relationships are complex and evolving things, the precise nature of what the trustee is expected to do will often be vague and disputed. The writer's friend may believe it was common knowledge between them that the friend trusted the writer never to discuss parts of their relationship in print, but the writer may not have known that at all (and it may not have been reasonable to expect them to). This doesn't look like betrayal.

Second, part of trusting someone is according them significant discretion over how to execute whatever performance by them is expected. You don't trust someone if you spell out in extreme detail what they need to do and check up on them repeatedly while they're doing it. This means that, even when what the truster expects is clear at a general level, the trustee may inadvertently make mistakes when exercising their discretion over how best to fulfill their responsibility. In writing their book, a memoirist might, then, genuinely think they're doing right by their friend, albeit mistakenly. Again, that's an unfortunate situation, but not a betrayal.

Finally, the memoirist might have defensible reasons, whether moral, intellectual, or aesthetic, for violating their friend's trust in some instances. As Claudia Mills writes, "To be a friend is to stand to another in a relationship of trust, for the sake of one's friend; to be a writer is to stand ready to violate that trust for the sake of one's story."[43] Working out when the writer role should win out over the friend role is very tough, but it'd be implausible to claim that it *never* should.

Mark Doty makes the radical suggestion that all memoir betrays all its subjects all the time. The problem, he suggests, is that the mere act of describing an intimate friend on the page is necessarily a violation of trust:

To represent is to maim . . . I must create [my mother] as a character in my book, and I am making decisions about how that person . . . will be presented. I simply can't write a book in which she remains inscrutable . . . I sift through what I know and I choose emblematic moments, emphasize one strand over another . . . my picturing will distort its subject . . . This particular form of distortion–the inevitable rewriting of those we love we do in the mere act of describing them–is the betrayal built into memoir, into the telling of memories.[44]

Doty is making three claims here: first, that we can only ever write distorted descriptions of our intimates; second, that such distortions wrong the subject; and third, that the wrong in question is betrayal, in particular. The first two claims crop up elsewhere, too. Patricia Hampl writes:

> The truth is: The constraining suit of words rarely fits. Writer—and readers—believe in the fiction of telling a true story. But the living subject knows it as the work of a culprit.[45]

And the narrative researcher Ruthellen Josselson writes: "Language can never contain a whole person, so every act of writing a person's life is inevitably a violation."[46]

I'll buy the first claim, but the second is dubious as a general matter. If you *can't* write a truly nature-identical description of someone, how can they complain if you fail to do it? As philosophers like to put it, "'ought' implies 'can.'" You can only have a moral obligation to, say, rescue a drowning child, if you're actually able to swim out and save them. Doty's idea might be that if he can't get his description of his mother perfect, he shouldn't even try. But why think that? If we followed this kind of rule across the board in life, we'd give up on almost everything that matters.

The third claim, that there's such a thing as "betrayal-by-description," is more interesting. Doty, Hampl, and Josselson are right to suggest that the mere act of being written about is often discomfiting to a memoirist's subjects. But I don't think the discomfort really reduces to the distorted nature of the description. Instead, I suspect, subjects are fundamentally troubled by the attitude that a writer necessarily takes up when setting out to describe them, even when the description is apt.

The attempt to capture a friend in words involves stepping back from the relationship, detaching, to see the friend as other, non-intimates, might. It involves substituting the attitude of friendship for the attitude of writership, and usually doing so without the friend knowing, in real time, that it's happening. Thomas Mann wrote in an essay:

> The look that one directs at things, both outward and inward, as an artist, is not the same as that with which one would regard the same as a man, but at once colder

and more passionate. As a man, you might be well-disposed, patient, loving, positive, and have a wholly uncritical inclination to look upon everything as all right,
but as artist your daemon constrains you to "observe," to take note, lightning fast
and with hurtful malice, of every detail that in the literary sense would be characteristic, distinctive, significant, opening insights, typifying the race, the social or
the psychological mode, recording all as mercilessly as though you had no human
relationship to the observed object whatever.[47]

It's alienating to have a friend do this to you, even if what they say
is true. It can be experienced as a violation of the spirit of friendship,
a rejection, alongside a deception. The taking on of the attitude may
be temporary, but it reminds the subject that their friend always has
available to them this kind of external perspective on them (and that
in fact all of the subject's friends do, writers or not).

That experience can certainly feel like betrayal, but does it really
count? That depends on whether or not it's reasonable for us to expect our friends to always maintain the friend attitude to us and never
take on the more external one. (They can't accuse us of betrayal if the
expectation we're failing to fulfill wasn't warranted to begin with.)
I don't think that it is reasonable, partly for the "ought implies can"
reason. We're friends, but humans too, and it's arguably impossible
to never see our loved ones from a more detached perspective at
least some of the time. There's also, I think, value—for ourselves, our
friends, and others—in our taking up that perspective sometimes. It
involves a move in the direction of greater objectivity (though we can
never fully get there), and objectivity has its uses within relationships
as well as outside them. For both of these reasons, then, I disagree
with Doty's claim that every act of description is a betrayal. But if
you're a memoirist, it's worth thinking about how your subjects might
experience your descriptions as such and about what you might do to
lessen the blow. Feeling betrayed hurts, even if the hurt isn't itself a
betrayal.

Appropriation

Let's say your memoirist friend hasn't significantly set back your interests, hasn't revealed private information about you, hasn't unfairly
used your vulnerability for their own gain, and hasn't betrayed you.

Might you still have a justified complaint about what they've written about you? One remaining possibility here is that they've *stolen* from you: they've taken a story that was yours and treated it as their own.

This complaint is most plausible when the story doesn't centrally involve the memoirist themself. As I noted earlier, what happens within a relationship, if it belongs to anyone, surely belongs to both people involved, not just one of them. This doesn't mean that either person can do what they like with the shared story—some actions may violate privacy or cause unwarranted harm or exploit a vulnerable person—but it does mean that claims of *stealing* are hard to support.

On the other hand, if the story is about an experience that the memoirist didn't personally share, but only heard about from her subject, the claim of theft is, on its face, more persuasive. Matters are tricky here, though, because it's not always easy to draw the line between someone else's story and one's own. The sharing of stories about each person's experiences is a key part of intimate relationships. Those stories can come to deeply affect how the teller and listener relate to each other and, sometimes, how they relate to third parties. In such cases, the story may start as one person's, but become another's (or start as one story and expand into another). Think of the stories about their own earlier lives that parents tell their children. These stories, especially if they involve intense or traumatic experiences, can become part of their children's understanding of who they themselves are and where they come from. Whose story is it, at that point?

These "relay stories" that originate in the life of one person and are passed on to someone else are a common subject of memoir. Memoirists are often fascinated by the stories their parents, siblings, spouses, and other intimates did or didn't tell them at crucial moments, and the way those disclosures or secrets affected their own lives. Again, if the stories in question are genuinely significant to the writer's life, it seems inappropriate for the originator of the story to claim exclusive ownership over it.

Let's say we're not talking about shared relationship stories or relay stories, though: just stories heard from someone else. Is it OK for writers to use those in their memoirs? (I'm not referring here to a writer falsely claiming to have experienced the events in the story: that's covered by the distinct topic of the ethics of lying. I'm thinking of cases where the writer relates the story in the course of describing a subject who claims to have experienced it.) Here we get to a deeper debate about the very idea of ownership over a story.

On the modern understanding of property, to own something is to have a bundle of rights over it: rights to, among other things, use, exploit, abuse, control access to, and alienate that thing. Our most ready examples of property are tangible goods. If you own a house, for instance, you have rights to live in it, gain rent from it, burn it to the ground, lock people out of it, and sell it. But we can also own more abstract items: for instance, we can have intellectual property rights to a work of art or a piece of technology. In those cases, our bundle of rights includes rights to perform or use the thing, make money from it, sell it, and prohibit others from doing the same things, for a speci-fied amount of time. Property rights are generally legal rights, whose content is articulated and enforced by the legal system. But some ar-gue that these legal rights are grounded in moral property rights: in fact, they say, it's the prelegal moral rights that make the case for establishing the legal ones.

Do we have intellectual property rights over our stories about our lives? Let's dispense quickly of the legal issue first, since it's not our key question. We don't have any sort of legal property right over our life stories unless we've put them into tangible form: by writ-ing them down (on paper or electronically) or by recording or film-ing them. If we have done this, we can sue others for plagiarism or copyright violation if they reproduce (some of) the text verbatim or paraphrase a phrase or summarize an idea without citing us, with-out our permission. But what's really being protected here is a par-ticular expression of the story, not the basic shape of the story itself. People can't sue others for writing stories similar to their own. Shake-speare couldn't have sued the makers of *West Side Story* for stealing his *Romeo and Juliet* plot, were he still alive, though he could have sued them if they'd quoted directly from his play without attribution. So, technically, the law doesn't recognize legal property rights over stories per se, even if they're written down.

Do we have *moral* property rights over our stories, though? It might be that, even though the law doesn't (and shouldn't) protect them, we should recognize others' ethical entitlement to the stories they tell about their own lives. A version of this suggestion has become popular recently in the context of a broader debate over what's known as "cultural appropriation."[48] It's common now to argue that outsiders to a social group (usually a racial, ethnic, or religious minority) shouldn't represent the experiences or adopt the traditional aesthetic resources of insiders of that group when making art. This position comes in different forms, but includes the claims that outsiders shouldn't "speak in the voice of" insiders (by attempting to represent what it's like to live their lives) or use the distinctive narrative conventions of insiders (say, plot lines, symbols, themes, or motifs). White writers shouldn't, for example, write novels with Black narrators or protagonists or structure them as riffs on Native American folktales.

A variety of different arguments are offered to support these prohibitions. One focuses on the risk of misrepresentation. Outsiders are likely to (some say necessarily will) represent insiders in distorted or stereotypical ways that may be slanderous, offensive, or harmful. Another argument focuses on the danger that outsiders will violate the privacy of insiders when conducting research for their projects. And a further argument centers on the way that outsiders use their greater cultural power to siphon off disproportionate material benefits from insiders' intellectual and aesthetic traditions. These arguments deserve serious consideration, but I'll set them aside here, since they relate to questions of harm, privacy, and exploitation that we've already discussed. Instead I want to focus on the arguments against outsider representation of insiders that specifically refer to the idea of *theft*, our current subject.

The theft argument against cultural appropriation comes in two forms, depending on what the maker of the argument claims is being stolen. In the *subject-matter* version, the claim is that outsiders are stealing the aesthetic resources of insiders: the narrative structures, themes, symbols, and suchlike that are distinctive of their culture. In the *audience* version, the claim is that outsiders are stealing the attention of a group of readers, hearers, or viewers, attention that insiders are entitled to instead. Lenore Keeshig-Tobias, a Canadian First Nations writer, makes the first of these arguments, approvingly citing Alexander Wolfe, a Saulteaux storyteller, as saying: "Each family handed down its own stories. Other stories belong to other families, could not be told, because to do so would be to steal."[49] But she also writes something that points to the second: "There comes a time when … all white supporters of Native causes, will have to step back in the true spirit of respect for self-determination and equality, and let the real Native voices be heard."[50]

Let's take the audience argument first. The general claim that non-minority writers shouldn't hog the unjustly limited market for litera-ture about the experiences and cultural forms of minorities has a lot going for it. But it's misleading to put this claim in terms of theft. No artist, whether minority or majority, has a property right over the attention of others. You earn the attention of members of the reading public by saying something that interests them: you aren't entitled to that attention in advance. So, though we might well urge that non-minority writers should leave the representation of minority experi-ences to minority writers, at least till greater social justice is achieved, we should do so on grounds other than the claim that minority writers have property rights over the reading public. That particular claim is implausible, even offensive, and does no help for the cause.

The subject-matter argument—that members of cultural groups own the aesthetic resources characteristic of their culture—is simi-larly problematic. Again, there may well be very good reasons for out-siders to avoid using those resources, but the idea that insiders have, specifically, property rights over them is hard to defend. (If you're a Westerner, do you really want to say that you and your Western fel-lows *own* the Oedipus plot? If so, on what basis? And why? I can't think of convincing answers to these questions.) It's sometimes sug-gested that the plot lines, symbols, and themes of the world's cultures are the common property of humankind: that we all own them, as part of our global cultural heritage. But I think it more plausible to say that no one owns them: ownership is just the wrong way to think about such things, whether within a culture or without.

The core wrong of cultural appropriation isn't theft, but unjusti-fied inequality. I suspect that when further examined, most instances of the audience and subject-matter arguments discussed above will really reduce to that distinct and very compelling egalitarian concern. Ijeoma Oluo explains it well:

Cultural appropriation is the product of a society that only respects culture cloaked in whiteness … because we do not live in a society that equally respects all cul-tures, the people of marginalized cultures are still routinely discriminated against for the same cultural practices that white cultures are rewarded for adopting and adapting for the benefit of white people. Until we do live in a society that equally respects all cultures, any attempts of the dominant culture to "borrow" from marginalized cultures will run the risk of being exploitative and insulting.[51]

Although the ownership arguments I've described are standardly given in relation to stories told by groups of people, the points made cross over to the case of stories told by individuals about themselves too. There may be good moral reasons not to include the stories of others in your memoir — reasons of harm, privacy, or exploitation, say. But I'm unconvinced that the moral prohibition on theft is among them, because I don't find the specific idea that people have property rights over their stories persuasive.

Wouldn't we think, though, that if your friend disclosed to you a great and detailed plot for a novel, and you then went away and wrote it up and sold it in secret, you'd be doing something wrong, precisely for the reason that you'd stolen her story? I think we should consider it wrong, but for a different and better reason than that. This case is instructively different from the case of cultural aesthetic resources and real-life stories shared by a memoirist's friend. The novel case involves someone engaging in significant original creative work: using her imagination to make something new. Traditional cultural story forms are, by definition, not created by currently living individuals in this way. And individuals don't engage in creative work when merely talking truthfully about their life experiences to another person. The moral problem with writing up the plot your friend tells you isn't that you're stealing from her, but that you're free-riding on her creative efforts: exploiting her labor without permission or compensation. That's a perfectly good reason not to do it, without bringing in the fuzzier and implausible notion that she has property rights over the story.

Might memoirists be charged with unjustly appropriating something else, other than a subject's story? In her essay "Whose Truth?," Phyllis Rose suggests that what really bothers subjects is that a memoir takes from them "their opportunity for self-representation," which "seems to some people who've been robbed as tangible an asset as their mutual funds."[52] "Everyone has fantasies of themselves that allow them to act in the world," Rose writes, and appearing in a memoir can destroy those fantasies, by revealing to the subject how one (maybe particularly observant, insightful, and articulate) intimate really sees them. The subject may then be unable to maintain their cherished sense of themselves in their relations with the memoirist, with others, and—perhaps worst of all—with themselves. "Robert Burns said it's a gift 'to see ourselves as others see us,'" writes Rose, "but really it's a torture." This kind of outcome isn't just occasional, Rose writes, but endemic to memoir: "You cannot write about someone else, however briefly, however sympathetically, without stealing a little bit of their self-determination."

The general point here seems right, but, again, referring to the act as "stealing" is misleading. (Rose might be speaking metaphorically.) An act of theft isn't just a taking, but an unjust taking: you can only steal something that others have a right to. But no one has a right to maintain a self-image of a certain type—other than the general status we all possess, as human beings worthy of basic concern and respect—or to demand of others that they reflect and support it.

There may be loss in these cases, then, and there may sometimes be good moral reasons not to cause that loss, but the language of unjust appropriation is out of place. I think this conclusion holds across the board: though subjects do accuse memoirists of stealing, as long as they aren't plagiarizing text or ideas without attribution, this is one form of wrong memoirists don't need to worry about.

Taxonomies are helpful in ethics, but they can also make things look overly simple. The wrongs of harm, privacy violation, exploitation, and betrayal that I've distinguished in this chapter are in principle different from each other, but in practice they're often hard to disentangle. And they may not capture everything that matters. A writer may have a legitimate sense that what they're writing is ethically fraught, without being able to formulate the worry in terms of any of these wrongs.

One reason for this might be that the writer isn't violating any *duties* to their subjects, and in that sense isn't technically speaking wronging them, but is instead displaying one or more *vices* in their writing. There are two basic questions we can ask in ethics: "What should I do?" and "What sort of person should I be?" Utilitarians and Kantians focus on the first question, and philosophers known as "virtue ethicists"—most famously, Aristotle—focus on the second.[53]

It's not like people in either camp simply ignore the other question, but they treat it as derivative from the one they favor. Utilitarians think, for instance, that you should be the sort of person *who would do what a utilitarian would do*. Aristotle, on the other hand, thinks that you should do the sort of action *that a good person would favor* (where a good person is one who possesses a set of virtues and lacks a set of vices). We don't need to get into the details of this complex debate here. The pertinent point is that, for a virtue ethicist, ethics isn't just about acting rightly toward others in terms of respecting their entitlements not to be harmed, exploited, betrayed, or robbed, or to have their privacy respected. It's also, and primarily, about displaying virtuous character traits like sensitivity, perceptiveness, emotional intelligence, imagination, maturity, good judgment, and balance. These traits are apparent in a person's inner life and attitudes, not solely in their outward behavior, so focusing exclusively on the impact of a person's actions on others can miss some important moral phenomena.

A memoirist, for instance, might scrupulously respect their subjects' moral entitlements, while nonetheless writing passages (or entire books) about them that are, say, mean-spirited, ungenerous, unempathetic, heavy-handed, vengeful, cruel, spiteful, unkind, unforgiving, condescending, self-centering, self-aggrandizing, self-indulgent, self-righteous, hypocritical, cowardly, disloyal, ungrateful, prejudiced, chauvinistic, reckless ... the list of possible vices goes on. In such a case, we might not say that they've *wronged* their subjects, but they've nonetheless been a *jerk* or morally *oblivious* in their writing about their relationships with others. Their behavior invites the succinct all-purpose admonition for vices: don't be that person.

Another reason you, a memoirist, might feel ethically uncomfortable about your work, even if you can't be charged with any of the wrongs described in this chapter, derives simply from the moral weight that comes with getting up close to another person's deepest vulnerabilities. You may not be doing anything wrong, or displaying any vices either, but the *potential* for perhaps inadvertent, perhaps mysterious, wrongs and insensitivities is great, given the power you wield, the emotionally charged and psychologically complex nature of memoir writing, and your uncertainty about the feelings, beliefs, and motivations of both your subjects and yourself.

Ruthellen Josselson's collection *Ethics and Process in the Narrative Study of Lives* contains a set of illuminating autobiographical

essays about the subtle psychodynamics of writing about others, written by narrative researchers and therapists. Several of the authors
discuss the potency of the experience of being "written down." The
psychoanalyst Pirkko Lauslahti Graves writes, for instance: "No matter how tactfully and respectfully one describes the clinical material,
the written word has a unique power that is different from spoken
statements."[54]

This power is partly to do with the (semi-)permanence of a written record. Psychologist Terri Apter writes of reassuring the subject
of one of her case studies that her identity has been anonymized.
"Roberta" replies:

No. I know. And I'm not worried about that. Not that. It's just the image of me. Sitting there, filled with such awful feelings. They come, and I hate them. But then
they go. Now there's something about them that won't go.[55]

But another aspect of the written word's power is the quasi-
mystical authority that many of us invest in writing. Roberta follows
up the above by saying "and when [the awful feelings] come, they're
real, now, in a different way." Having oneself described in print, having
one's personality, struggles and actions named on the page, carries
existential significance for some people. Josselson writes that writer-
psychologists can "in our pronouncements, seem rather like oracles
or like the angels who might appear at the end of a life to tell a person what it all meant."[56] Relatedly, she suggests, subjects of narrative
case studies may engage in what psychoanalysts call "transference":
they come to view writers as "carriers of core aspects of themselves."

Not all memoirists wield that kind of power, but some, depending
on their status and relationship to those they write about, might. No
memoirist can tell in advance what set of psychic snowballs their act
of writing may set off in their subject, or how hot—to mangle a metaphor—those snowballs may get.

Part of what's called for in this very complex and delicate terrain
isn't a set of moral principles, but (to echo Aristotle) a set of dispositions to respond to others with sensitivity, discretion, and tact, in
ways that are acutely attuned to the specifics of the relationship and
circumstances. That said, it's useful to have a set of principles at hand
too, to provide some general orientation and food for reflection, as
long as you don't attempt to apply them overly rigidly. So here's a list

of the main proposals I've made in this chapter, expressed as succinctly as I can get them:

HARM. Memoirists should avoid exposing their subjects to harm (or risk of harm) without adequate justification.

- They should take very strong care not to undermine subjects' basic welfare interests and should avoid lesser harms and hurts to subjects when there are no morally significant competing interests at stake.
- When there are significant competing interests at stake (either their own or others), memoirists should
  (i)   prioritize preventing the total thwarting of one interest over preventing a minor incursion of another interest,
  (ii)   prioritize the protection of more vital interests over less vital interests,
  (iii) prioritize the protection of interests that are more strongly reinforced by the interests of others, and
  (iv)   deprioritize the protection of interests whose inherent moral quality is low.
- In cases of uncertainty about the impact of their writing, memoirists should prioritize the protection of interests that are certain to be harmed over interests that simply might be harmed. The graver the harm in view, the fewer risks they should be willing to run. The more valuable a potentially harmful piece of writing is, the more likely the harm needs to be in order to curtail the writing.
- In cases where the subject has wrongly injured the memoirist or others, harming them by revealing the wrong in print may be justified, provided that the harm isn't disproportionate or motivated by vengeance.

PRIVACY. Memoirists should avoid unwarranted exposure of information about their subjects that their subjects wish to withhold from a public audience.

- They shouldn't try to gain personal information from their subjects by lying to, deceiving, or manipulating them.
- They shouldn't break any promises they have made to keep information confidential, absent very compelling reasons.
- Exposure against subjects' wishes is more likely to be warranted to the extent that the memoirist's work
  (i)   is very likely to
  (ii)   substantially promote
  (iii) highly valuable interests
  (iv)   for a significant number of people

or

(v)   when the subject is demanding concealment of a wrong they've com-
        mitted.

EXPLOITATION. Memoirists should avoid taking unfair advantage of their sub-
jects for their own benefit.
  • They shouldn't enter into relationships primarily for the literary material
    they're likely to provide.
  • They shouldn't use information about their subjects that they have gained by
    coercion or subterfuge en route to their literary goals.
  • They should take special care not to harm or expose subjects who are in a
    position of significantly weaker power than themselves.
  • They should take care to respect the full and complex humanity of their sub-
    jects, rather than reducing them to stereotypes or object lessons.
  • Exploitation of a subject's vulnerability is more likely to be justified when it's
    (i)   mutually beneficial and consensual
            or
    (ii)   provides *very* substantial benefits to third parties.

BETRAYAL. Memoirists should not unjustifiably violate the trust of their subjects.
  • If a memoirist has induced in their subject a reasonable expectation that they
    will not write about them (at all, or in a certain way), they should comply with
    that expectation, in the absence of strong countervailing reasons.
  • If the trust the subject placed in the memoirist was uninvited and unwelcome,
    the memoirist can permissibly fail to comply with it.

APPROPRIATION. Memoirists should not plagiarize, that is, reproduce other
writers' text or ideas without attribution.

Do these principles apply to writing about the dead as well as the
living? Many memoirists have waited till the deaths of loved or hated
ones before doing a number on them. That might make sense from
the perspective of self-interest, but it doesn't plausibly remove the
moral stakes.

Why not? Due to their endorsement of the "experience requirement" on well-being that I mentioned earlier, many philosophers believe that you can't harm someone after their death. You have to be
aware of being harmed to be harmed, they claim: no one's well-being

goes down if they don't notice it happening, and no one's noticing anything from beyond the grave. But not everyone endorses this requirement. It makes most sense if you believe that well-being is a mental state: a matter of pleasure, say, or happiness. But that isn't the only, or even the most popular, account of what well-being is. Many argue that well-being isn't fundamentally a matter of how you feel, but a matter of a state of affairs obtaining: specifically, that of the world lining up with your desires or preferences. Those people will claim that someone can harm you while you're alive by thwarting one of your desires, even if you never hear about it. So why not say the same after your death? You can have active desires just before you die, so maybe the impeding of those desires after you go can still count as a harm to you, even if your corpse fails to register the fact.[57]

Whether or not you think the harm class of wrongs in memoir applies posthumously, then, depends on whether or not you endorse the experience requirement on well-being. But it's less plausible to impose an experience requirement on the wrongs of privacy, exploitation, plagiarism, and betrayal. It seems perfectly possible to unjustly expose or use someone, or violate their trust, even if they never hear about it. If so, much of what I've suggested above will have posthumous as well as prehumous application, regardless of what your theory of well-being is.

I've argued above that the principles I've offered here provide a reasonable approximation of what it's wrong to do to others while writing about them. But along the way we've also touched on a number of general reasons to resist the idea that such actions are wrongs, all things considered. So let me recap and draw together those objections now, too. They fall into two categories: the radical criticism that we shouldn't be at all concerned about the interests and entitlements of subjects when writing about them and the more moderate criticism that, though we do have moral duties to subjects, the principles I've argued for overcomplicate our obligations.

What I'll call the *Forget Them!* approach claims that, while you may well injure others in all the ways I've discussed while writing about them, you shouldn't worry about that. Some of the reasons for taking this position are themselves moral in nature. It's argued, for instance, that memoirists have an overriding moral duty to tell the truth—for all the reasons discussed in the previous chapter—

whatever the fallout for others. (Rousseau proclaims in his *Confessions*: "There is only one thing that I need fear in this whole undertaking, which is, not that I might say too much or tell lies, but that I might not say everything and so conceal some truths."[58]) It's also sometimes suggested that the practice of memoir in general, or the content of a particular memoir, is of such great benefit to society that memoirists' moral duty to promote the general welfare by publishing their work systematically dominates any lesser duties we might have thought they had to individual subjects. Other times the claim is that memoirists have not an overriding moral duty, but a moral right, to engage in free expression.

Another reason for taking the *Forget Them!* approach is nonmoral. The only thing a (literary) memoirist should care about, the claim goes, is Art. Worrying about the concerns of subjects is likely to undermine that supremely important aim, and the value of achieving it outweighs any harm done in the process. William Faulkner wrote, for instance: "The writer's only responsibility is to his art ... If a writer has to rob his mother, he will not hesitate; the 'Ode on a Grecian Urn' is worth any number of old ladies."[59]

These arguments are certainly on to *something*. As I argued at the end of the previous chapter, practical reason is complex, containing diverse moral as well as nonmoral values. Memoirists should care about all of truth, social welfare, freedom of expression, and art. But the claim that any of these things is so overwhelmingly significant as to trump every concern of all of a memoirist's subjects is extremely implausible. As Felicia Ackerman notes, presumably no one would think that, if Keats had (somehow) had to murder, torture, or rape someone to get "Ode on a Grecian Urn" written, he would have been justified in doing it.[60] And once we admit that aesthetic concerns should give way to those moral concerns, the door is opened to others.

There's also the obvious point here that not every memoirist rises to the level of Keats. In his memoir *Family Man*, Calvin Trillin proposes what he calls "the Dostoyevsky Test":

If you have reason to believe that you're another Dostoyevsky, there is no reason to be concerned about the effect what you write might have on the life of some member of your family . . . you can say anything you need to say. If you don't have reason to believe that you're another Dostoyevsky, you can't.[61]

Maybe Karl Ove Knausgaard believes he's another Dostoyevsky. He writes: "if you want to describe reality as it is, for the individual, and there is no other reality, you have to really go there, you can't be considerate."[62] As Daniel Mendelsohn suggests, Knausgaard was presumably following this principle when he published 150 highly detailed pages in the final volume of *My Struggle* about the mental breakdown his bipolar wife suffered after he minutely dissected their relationship in the earlier volumes.[63] I don't think even Dostoyevsky gets a free pass.

What I've tried to do is incorporate the importance of these other non-subject-related values into the principles I've suggested, both by keeping the principles relatively limited in scope, and by including escape clauses for those (I think unusual) cases where a serious conflict arises. Maybe sometimes a memoirist really should just let it rip, for Truth, Society, or Art, and allow the human casualties to pile up. But I strongly suspect that in the large majority of cases there'll be a less subject-violating alternative available that doesn't leave Truth, Society, or Art bleeding on the tracks instead. As for free expression, to put it succinctly, we're not talking here about censoring writers, but asking them to exercise their right to write with decency and grace.

What I'll call the *Simplify!* approach agrees with me that moral duties to subjects matter, but argues that we can capture those duties via a much shorter set of guidelines. In fact, on a pair of popular versions of this approach, we can reduce them to just one. The first version suggests that all that matters is whether or not a subject *consents* to the fact, content, and manner of their portrayal. Some memoirists go to great efforts to inform or even collaborate with their subjects while writing their books, and commit in advance to respecting any wishes subjects may have about how they're represented. Annie Dillard reports: "I tried to leave out everything that might trouble my family ... I've promised to take out anything that anyone objects to— anything at all."[64]

As I suggested earlier in the chapter, however, reliance on subject consent in memoir both over- and understates the memoirist's moral obligations. Making consent necessary would gut the possibility of writing memoirs about children, severely cognitively disabled people, and others who can't give valid consent to being written about. It's certainly true that memoirists need to exercise special caution when writing about such people—Thomas Couser's book *Vulnerable Subjects* is an excellent discussion of this—but surely some such memoirs are permissible and even desirable. Requiring consent would also aesthetically cripple many memoirs written about less vulnerable subjects, including those written about people who don't deserve to have their past deeds shielded. In other cases, merely obtaining consent wouldn't be demanding enough to satisfy our moral duties to others. Consensual exploitation and consensual rights violations remain morally problematic, even if less so than the nonconsensual kind. The final problem is that, in practice, it can be hard to tell whether a subject is genuinely consenting or not. They may be uninformed about the risks or under hidden pressure; they may even, like Hampl's mother, be lying to the memoirist about their preferences. For all these reasons, it's better moral practice to concentrate directly, at least in part, on the moral merits of what you plan to do to someone, rather than the simple fact of whether or not they said yes to it.

The second version of the *Simplify!* approach argues that our duties to subjects of memoir reduce to the single matter of whether or not we have good *intentions* toward them. Andre Dubus III said in an interview about his memoir *Townie*, which included material about the rape his sister suffered and his brother's attempted suicide:

The hardest part was writing about my family. I had a conversation with the novelist Richard Russo, who's a buddy of mine. I told him I was tortured about writing about my family, and he said, "Look, if this were me, I'd ask myself, Am I trying to hurt anybody with this book? Am I trying to skewer anybody? If the honest answer is no, I'm just trying to capture as honestly as I can what it was like for me, then I'd do it." It was such good advice.[65]

Was it, though? It's certainly morally better to write memoir without malice rather than with it. But, taken alone, this is a very low bar. Writers can intend only the very best for their subjects, while inadvertently (or maybe even advertently) harming, exposing, exploiting, and betraying them all over the show. In Dubus's case, maybe the strategy worked. According to his editor, including his siblings' stories improved the book and his family didn't object (though his sister decided not to read it). Perhaps the demands of art and morality were jointly satisfied here. But as a general rule of thumb, good intentions are a very blunt moral instrument.

Are there other rules of thumb memoirists might use when writing that are more likely to get their work in line with the moral principles I've recommended? A few good suggestions come up repeatedly among writers discussing the craft of memoir. One obvious one, of course, is to do as good a job as you can of anonymizing your subjects when you're presenting sensitive material. Some efforts in this direction won't be possible, and others will run up against the moral demands of truth-telling, but if you can do it, and without overly sacrificing the truth, you should.

A more substantive and demanding strategy is to aim for as much empathy and compassion as you can muster when describing others in your work. This doesn't mean you should only say nice and flattering things about your characters—that way lies the death of art. It just means that you should try to see even your wounders and antagonists as the complex people they are: woven, usually, of both good and bad, and possessed, often, of understandable motivations for their actions. Relatedly, it's important to guard against describing your subjects via stereotypes or caricatures and to try to bring out their individuality instead.

Another good, and maybe even more difficult, piece of advice is to aim for egalitarianism in your treatment of others and yourself: or, if anyone gets treated more harshly, make it you. Cheryl Strayed recommends being ruthless with yourself and gentle with others.[66] It can also help to underscore any similarities between you and your more problematic characters and acknowledge your own role in whatever conflicts with them you describe.

If your subjects are likely to disagree with your interpretation of events, Karr suggests, it helps to "lay out [your] prejudices and gesture there might be another opinion."[67] She also recommends not declaiming with great certainty about other people's inner lives.

Though intentions aren't everything, it's not a bad idea for a memoirist to check in internally, both at the beginning of their project and throughout, about why exactly they're writing the piece. If the motivation starts to seem primarily like anger or revenge, it's advisable to either stop writing it and allow some time to cool off or dial up alertness to any evidence of unfairness and misrepresentation in the writing.

Once the piece is written, it can sometimes be a good idea to invite subjects to read it in advance of publication, so they have the opportunity to alert you to anything they want changed. (As I've noted, I don't believe in offering veto power here, but some of what you've written may be accidentally injurious and changed at low cost.) If that seems unwise, running your piece past other readers instead is definitely a good idea. Most memoirists recommend at least alerting your subjects to the fact that the piece is being published, and giving them a rough idea of how they appear in it, so that the news doesn't come from third parties, or as a violent shock. In some cases, it might make sense to tell major subjects at the outset of the project, especially if you continue to interact with them, to allow them to assist you in not exploiting or betraying them while writing it.

Those are the more minor forms of moral insurance. One of the more substantial is to simply leave certain subjects out of the piece. If you find you can't write about someone in a respectful, balanced, and truthful way, or if they very strongly object to being included, it may be better not to write about them at all. Dan Barry barely mentions his siblings in his memoir *Pull Me Up*, despite the fact that it's all about his childhood, for the simple reason that "they don't want to be written about."[68] Most radically, you could abandon memoir for autobiographical fiction, or just fiction, instead. Phyllis Rose may be right that "some humiliations should only befall fictional characters. Some truths about human nature should be detached from living, particular people and portrayed only in novels."[69]

Memoir is an ethically fraught business. Memoirists are often accused of wronging their readers, usually by not telling the truth, as the previous chapter discussed. But they're also often accused of wronging their subjects, as this chapter has detailed. In some of these cases, once again, the accusation is of lying. On October 3, 2009, the Norwegian newspaper *Klassekampen* published a letter from fourteen members of Karl Ove Knausgaard's family, calling the first volume of his highly autobiographical novel "the literature of Judas," "a book full of insinuations, untruths, false characterizations." In other cases, and probably more frequently, the criticism isn't that the memoirist hasn't told the truth, but rather that they've told too much truth:

they've aired for the reading public matters that their subjects wanted hidden.

All of this may seem dark. So it's worth ending with the reminder that memoir can also have very good consequences for its subjects. The experience of being written about can give someone a valued sense of being understood, prompt in them increased self-awareness or self-forgiveness, and provide them with an avenue for moving on from past injuries they've received from or inflicted on the author. Mary Karr reports that reading *The Liars' Club* was healing for her mother and sister in this way.[70] In other cases, it's a third party who gets helpfully illuminated. Robert Anthony Siegel's mother told him that reading his book about his father gave her new insight into her deceased husband, a man she'd puzzled over alone in the fifteen years since his death.[71]

I've argued against the idea that there's anything inherently wrong with writing about intimates and others in your memoir. But I've suggested that there are ethical constraints on how you should go about doing it and proposed some ways for trying to respect them. If that advice is good, and if you've followed it to the best of your ability, your moral bill of record will be clean. But you might well still feel uneasy, pained, or even agonized about what you've done. Why?

One reason for unease is that you may know you've hurt people, and the fact that doing so was morally justified doesn't mean that you don't regret it. (We arguably *should* regret hurts we cause, even if we also think we should have caused them.) Another reason is that the writing of your memoir may have changed your relationships with your subjects and you may have a sense of loss and grief about that. In writing *Firebird*, Mark Doty came to empathize with his father in a way he hadn't been able to before. He writes:

The great psychological magic act of memoir [is] that the people you've known become your characters, and you cannot hate your characters—if you treat them as evil, one-dimensional, or even merely inscrutable, the form simply collapses into a narcissistic muddle. Thus the work of trying to write a good book becomes, unexpectedly, an empathic adventure, a quest to try to see into the lives of others.[72]

Unfortunately, however, his aged father wasn't able to join him on the journey, and instead permanently cut him off. Doty isn't certain on balance if the insight he gained was worth it: "I have replaced an inauthentic relationship [...] with an authentic silence. Is that better? I can't honestly say that I am sure."[73]

Finally, maybe you feel uneasy about having injured others in your memoir because you're projecting. The real problem might not be that you've revealed too much about others, but that you've revealed too much about yourself. Getting clearer on what that might look like is what we'll turn to next.

FIVE

Why Write a Memoir?

Writing a good memoir is a daunting endeavor. First, there's the difficulty of capturing an authentic interpretation of your past experience in words, in light of the dangers of self-deception, self-ignorance, memory failure, and the distortions of narrative form. Second, there's the difficulty of balancing the commitment to telling your readers the truth with the possibly conflicting aim of producing a work with high literary value. Third, there's the difficulty of working out how to write about your subjects without wronging them in the process and how to weigh those moral requirements against the distinct imperatives of both truth and art.

But that's not all. As well as imposing these cognitive, aesthetic, and ethical demands, there's the fact that writing a memoir is personally costly to the writer. Producing a memoir of any substantial length and seriousness requires expending a huge amount of time and effort, in a pursuit that many of the writer's intimates and associates may not understand or respect. It can be emotionally exhausting during the writing phase and anxiety-inducing after publication and may damage or destroy relationships the memoirist cherishes.

William Bell Scott said in the nineteenth century that "to write one's mental history is too difficult as well as too dreadful": it's "like walking into the street naked, and is only likely to frighten our neighbors."[1] Henry James wrote of his autobiographical writing: "I […] had to turn nothing less than myself inside out."[2] And Melissa Febos suggests, more recently: "If it doesn't feel at some point like peeling off your own skin, you're probably not being honest enough."[3]

Given all that, why would someone do it?

The Memoirist as Narcissist

To have written an autobiography is already to have made yourself a monster.

WILLIAM H. GASS[4]

One common answer, usually from outside the memoirist camp, is that memoirists are narcissists, who get a kick out of contemplating and displaying themselves for a public audience. William H. Gass — fiction writer, essayist, critic, and philosopher — wrote a jeremiad against memoirists on this theme in *Harper's* in 1994, in the early years of today's memoir boom. In the essay, "The Art of Self: Autobiography in an Age of Narcissism," Gass takes a swipe at what he presents as the infantile self-preoccupation of the contemporary personal writer:

Look, Ma, I'm breathing. See me take my initial toddle, use the potty, scratch my sister; win spin the bottle. Gee whiz, my first adultery—what a guy! That surely deserves a commemorative marker on the superhighway of my life. So now I'm writing my own sweet history.

As Gass's title indicates, critiques of this kind often diagnose the problem of memoir as an instance of a broader social problem. Critics disagree over the causes: maybe it's the erosion of communal bonds by urbanization and industrialization, or the destruction of the collective moral compass by atheism and postmodern nihilism, or the mainstreaming of navel-gazing via psychotherapy and self-help, or the look-at-me culture born of talk shows, reality TV, and social media. But whichever it is, the idea goes, all of us are now prone to hyperinflating the significance and interest of our own selves, actions, and experiences. A 2008 study showed that twenty-first-century American college students were getting higher scores on the Narcissistic Personality Inventory than any previous generation.[5] A 2012 study revealed a 42 percent uptick in the use of "I" and "me" by American writers since 1960.[6] Linked? Why not?

The claim that memoir is narcissistic comes in three distinct but compatible forms. One charge is that memoirists are vain. As Gass puts it, the autobiographer thinks of "himself as having led a life so important it needs celebration, and of himself as sufficiently skilled at rendering as to render it rightly." This might be an apt thought for a few people, Gass suggests, but those cases are rare: most lives are "empty of interest." Back in the good old days, it was mainly the eminent who offered the stories of their lives up to the public. But now we're flooded with "nobody memoirs" (as they're sometimes called): personal narratives written by people who attained no kind of fame or great achievement prior to the writing. We also have a glut of what might be christened "baby memoirs": books delivered by under-thirty-five writers with (allegedly) little claim to breadth of experience and depth of insight about life.

Memoirists sometimes try to defend themselves against the charge of vanity by pointing to their detailed dissection of their vices, errors, and misfortunes. ("If I had written to seek the world's favor," Montaigne writes, "I should have bedecked myself better."[7]) But this too can be turned against them. It's possible to take pride both in your thrilling misdeeds and in your willingness to probe and expose them. Similarly, presenting your life as a chronicle of relentless suffering, injustice, and self-destruction can be a way of bragging about your intensity, sensitivity, and profundity. Rousseau's *Confessions* is the archetype here: as well as being awash in self-pity, it is, Barbour notes, "an apology" (in the technical sense of "defense") "disguised as a confession, turning to the author's credit every instance of wrong-doing he performed."[8]

A second variant of the narcissism charge is that memoirists are self-absorbed. Whether or not they think they're wonderful and special, they certainly engage in very sustained self-examination. But the world contains a rich plenitude of things to occupy yourself with: if you're going to write about it, why turn in to the one rather than out to the many? Surely only excessive (and possibly neurotic) self-concern could explain it. C. S. Lewis reports at the end of his memoir *Surprised by Joy* that his conversion to Christianity has undermined his autobiographical impulse. The progression of his inner life no longer interests him much, because his faith has cured him of self-fascination: "For many healthy extroverts self-examination first begins with conversion. For me it was almost the other way round."[9]

The third variant of the charge is that memoirists are attention-seeking exhibitionists, engaged in disclosure for the sake of disclosure. They're so obsessed with gaining an audience that they're willing to sacrifice all discretion, decorum, and grace to get it. This criticism may seem quaint in the age of mass celebrity culture and Twitter, but that's part of the point. Our gleeful consumption of click-bait personal essays like the viral "It Happened to Me: My Gynecologist Found a Ball of Cat Hair in My Vagina" is just an indication of how low we've collectively sunk.[10] Memoirists and essayists of the nineteenth and early twentieth centuries were perfectly comfortable with raising the charge of crass exhibitionism against their fellows. Emerson snarked at Montaigne's overly intimate "grossness,"[11] and Herbert Spencer wrote in his self-restrained autobiography that it would "be out of taste to address the public as though it consisted of personal friends."[12]

If these charges were true, memoir would be an embarrassing occupation. Narcissism is shameful because it involves two kinds of error, one cognitive, one ethical. The cognitive error is the failure to see your talents and accomplishments with the appropriate perspective and distance, as those of just one fairly ordinary human being among others. The ethical error is the unjustified belief that you have greater moral status than others and that you therefore deserve more than them, including more attention and more sympathy.

Narcissism is not only a mistake but also a moral vice, because those who exhibit it tend to ride roughshod over the entitlements of others. If you insist on taking up outsized space in your social relations, someone else is going to have to move over. Narcissism is also unfair, in the Kantian sense of being nonuniversalizable. It's a conceptual impossibility for everyone to get above-average treatment, so narcissists act on a principle they can't possibly endorse for everyone.

Narcissists are like young children: they perceive themselves as the glorious and rightful center of their social scene and, in acute cases, the universe. It's cute in a kid, but part of growing up is to get past this skewed perspective: to move from "I" to "you" and "they," or at least to "we." The narcissist's mind has snagged and stalled at the first person.

So has the memoirist's, but is it for the same reason?

To take the vanity charge first: as the rest of this chapter will show, there are a wide variety of motivations for writing a memoir other than the desire to brag about your talents and accomplishments. And a large number of memoirs out there show little evidence of either straightforward boasting or the slyer "I was appalling!" form of self-aggrandizement mentioned earlier. Most memoirists recognize that gaining the trust and empathy of their readers requires them to engage in genuine self-criticism, involving real vulnerability and discomfort, rather than the kind that only pretends.

It's also worth thinking about what it means to say that most lives are unimportant and "empty of interest" and where that claim may be coming from. The idea that "nobodies" exhibit an absurd vanity in writing about their lives goes back a long way. Margaret Cavendish wrote of her memoir *A True Relation of My Birth, Breeding and Life*, in 1656:

> I hope my Readers, will not think me vain for writing my life, since there have been many that have done the like, as *Cesar*, *Ovid*, and many more, both men and women, and I know no reason I may not do it as well as they: but I verily believe some censuring Readers will scornfully say, why hath this Ladie writ her own life? since none cares to know whose daughter she was, or whose wife she is, or how she was bred, or what fortunes she had, or how she lived, or what humor or disposition she was of?[13]

As Cavendish may be hinting, it was back then, and still is now, a shot most likely to be fired at women. Gass suggests in his essay that the rise of the narcissistic memoir is partly the fault of the rise of the novel, which was invented "to amuse mainly ladies of the middle class and provide them a sense of importance: their manners, their concerns, their daily rounds, their aspirations, their dreams of romance." The novel infected the discipline of history, he complains, which used to be serious, but then became filled with fripperies, gossip, seduction, and betrayal. Female fiction and female history: the memoir is their freakish and vulgar child. (It'd be nice to think that Gass doesn't really mean any of this, but this is a man who also wrote that women "lack that blood congested genital drive which energizes every great style."[14]) The additional jab at the middle class also appears in Virginia Woolf's 1905 essay "The Decay of Essay Writing." What a flood of personal essays (exhibiting an "amazing and unclothed egoism"[15]) we have these days, Woolf laments, now that the masses have learned to read.

The implication that only men or the highly educated have lives interesting enough to write about and the skill to write interestingly about them is obviously repellent. But even if we removed the sexism and snobbishness, there'd remain something unsavory about the general suggestion that most human lives can't sustain essay-or-book-length treatment. Charles Baxter writes, in defense of memoir, that it's

a perfectly reasonable response to the devaluation and even destruction of personal experience. The memoir (along with journal writing) is one of the few places where experience-memory goes to take shelter and to be increased in value . . . Every memoir argues that a personal memory is precious. No other artistic form makes that argument with the same specificity or urgency.[16]

It's not vain to insist that your experience and voice matter, in a society and economy that often seem arranged to deny that fact. As for self-pity, you can avoid that by taking yourself out of your writing. But another way to do it is simply to avoid fetishizing your afflictions when writing about yourself, a temptation that plenty of memoirists resist.

The charges that memoir is by its nature self-absorbed and exhibitionistic are just as unpersuasive. There's a long history in the autobiographical tradition of writers using themselves not as the end point of examination but as a window into a more general experience or view. Montaigne wrote that "each man bears the entire form of man's estate."[17] While that might be going too far, it's certainly true that in many memoirs the narrator acts as a prism through which to see ideas, ideals, experiences, and phenomena that don't end at the skin of the author. Some memoirs engage directly with major external events—a war, a natural disaster, a political or intellectual revolution. But even those that remain at the small scale of an individual life needn't be primarily focused on the *self* that lives that life, but on the meaning of the events that happened within it, the relationships with other people that structured it, and the more general mysteries and quirks of consciousness and emotion. The experiences of a single life can provide a rich vein for that kind of exploration, which is why the claim that memoirists are all superficial, tasteless attention-seekers is false. Bernard Cooper writes of his memoir: "I'd purposely chosen intimate subjects, not in order to make them public, but because they drove me to probe more deeply the hidden meaning, imagery and metaphors embedded in memory."[18]

These points seem obvious. Why, then, does the charge of narcissism so insistently recur? A central reason may be that many critics of memoir fail to see the genre as an art form, rather than merely a chronicle of events. People don't generally have a problem with poets, fiction writers, and playwrights using personal material, because they see the enterprise not as simple attention-seeking but as art. Why doesn't the same apply to memoir?

Arguably part of the answer to that question is the "feminization" of memoir over the course of the twentieth century. As more women entered the field, the genre's traditional commitments to subjectivity and the exploration of childhood and personal relationships began to be coded as emotional, sentimental, and self-indulgent (as well as naive, unserious, superficial, facile, passive, and "popular"), and contrasted with the *real* art of modernist literary fiction: objective, impersonal, intellectual, ironic, controlled, highly creative, experimental, difficult, and profound—and, by implication, male. In her essay "Just Admit It, You Wrote a Memoir," Rebecca van Laer suggests that this sexist prejudice against the genre is why many contemporary female writers prefer to call what are essentially memoirs "novels from life," "autofiction," "autoanalysis," or "linked essays" instead.[19] (Or, to take it from the other angle, it's why female writers of what are essentially novels prefer to call them fiction rather than "autofiction." Chris Kraus points out that, while people like to slap the autofiction label on female novelists, no one slaps it on *On the Road*, though Sal Paradise is clearly a stand-in for Jack Kerouac—and the same goes for "all of American realism that's written in the first person" by men.)[20] The temptation to disavow memoir is understandable, given that, as Melissa Febos notes elsewhere, female memoirists have "to constantly redirect in interviews away from personal questions or insulting commentary that insinuates we just transcribed our experiences and that's why we were able to publish a book instead of the incredibly arduous work that goes into turning *any* kind of raw material into a book."[21] But in the long run it seems better not to join the pile-on against the genre, but to instead attack the sexist assumptions the narcissism critique is based on.

Another reason for the persistence of the critique may be the unfounded grafting on to memoir of the more general social panic about narcissism—a panic that regularly recurs across generations and hasn't been well borne out by social science.[22]

A final reason is an overgeneralization from a set of legitimate individual targets. The boring and perennial fact is that some memoir is narcissistic and some isn't, just as some novels are masterpieces and some aren't. Whatever we say about particular examples, a genre-sweeping dismissal isn't called for.

Most of us love ourselves too dearly to be autobiographers.

ROY PASCAL[23]

Arguably the best way for a memoirist to avoid the charge of narcissism is to engage in more intense self-exploration and self-confession rather than less. Most people, if they look very intently at themselves and write about what's interesting in their experience with the greatest care, honesty, and beauty they can muster, won't end up appearing vain, self-absorbed, and gratuitously attention-seeking. It's those who skim the surface of themselves that risk that fate. Phillip Lopate suggests that "the trouble with most confessional writing is that it doesn't confess enough."[24]

That seems right, but it raises an interesting ethical question. Extreme self-revelation might be a good guard against the vice of narcissism, but morally troubling for another reason.

Discussions of the ethics of representing real people in art usually focus solely on the risks to people other than the artist. But memoirists don't just write about others: they also, and centrally, write about number one. Number one is a valuable human person, alongside the memoir's other subjects. And number one is vulnerable to several of the same injuries discussed in the previous chapter: harms and incursions on the private sphere from the exposure of sensitive information, breaking of promises, "the exploitation of personal dysfunction for private gain"[25]—even if the agent of such wrongs is the same person as the victim. (Janet Malcolm suggests: "by making himself into a subject, the autobiographer sets himself up for a betrayal no less profound than that invited by the subject of someone else's writing."[26]) So do memoirists have responsibilities to *themselves* not to write about certain subjects, or about certain subjects in certain ways? When does memoir cross the line into wrongful self-disclosure? (Though it's natural to focus here on disclosures about painful, embarrassing, or self-incriminating events, Stendhal's preface to his memoir, *The Life of Henry Brulard*, suggests that memoirists might undermine their own interests by writing about joyful experiences too: "I feared to deflower the happy moments that I have encountered by describing and anatomizing them. Well, that is what I shall not do, I shall jump happiness."[27])

This question about wrongful self-disclosure is rarely asked, maybe because of the strangeness of the idea that someone could have duties to themself. In the seventeenth and eighteenth centuries, moral philosophers widely assumed that we each had moral responsibilities toward our own person. But by the end of the twentieth century, ethicists barely discussed such duties, or if they did, it was only to quickly pass over or dismiss them. Bernard Williams refers to the very idea of duties to the self as "fraudulent."[28]

Why? One reason might be the influence of an argument made by Martin Singer in 1959.[29] Singer's argument draws on three widely accepted claims about the nature of a duty. First, to say that you have a duty to someone is to say that they have a right against you. If Sam has a duty to keep a promise he made to Katia, for instance, Katia has a right that Sam keep it. Second, if you have a right against someone, it's possible for you to release that person from their duty to respect the right. Sam no longer has a duty to keep the promise he made to Katia if she tells him she no longer wants him to keep it. Third, it's impossible for someone to release *themselves* from a duty. Sam can't get out of his promise to Katia just by telling her that he no longer intends to keep it. That's because duties are binding: they have force independently of your will and are designed, in fact, to constrain and curb it. A "duty" that isn't binding in that way isn't a duty at all.

If these plausible claims are true, Singer argues, the idea of a duty to yourself involves a contradiction. If you have a duty to yourself, you have a right against yourself. Moreover, because it's you who have the right, you can waive the right and release yourself from the duty. That, though, is impossible. You can't really be under a duty if you can get yourself out of it at will.

One way to get around this argument is to argue that, despite appearances, when a person has a duty to themself, the person who has the duty and the person who has the right that it's correlated with are not in fact quite the same person—in some special sense. Some philosophers argue, for instance, that each person is made up of a series of distinct temporal parts. You're the set comprised of part-at-time-1, part-at-time-2, part-at-time-3, and so on till your death. If so, the part of you that's active at time 1 can have a duty to the part of you that's active at time 2. (Say, you have a duty not to smoke now, because your later self has a right not to be put at risk of lung cancer.) Time-2-you could in theory waive the right they have against time-1-you ("Sure, go ahead! Give me lung cancer!"). But because time-2-you doesn't exist yet at time 1, they can't *really* waive it. Hence that duty you have at time 1 is genuinely binding. The difficulty with this move is that many people reject the "series of temporal parts" theory of what a person is.

Paul Schofield makes the helpful suggestion here that defenders of duties to self don't need to divide a person into metaphysical parts, but can instead simply distinguish between different perspectives that the same metaphysically unified person can take up.[30] Sister Lucia, for instance, might take up both the perspective of a Catholic nun and the perspective of a wild partier. The interests that the same person has when taking up distinct perspectives can conflict. When Lucia takes up her nun perspective, she may have an interest in staying in at the convent on Friday night; when taking up her partier perspective, she may not. The important point for our purposes is that individual people tend to adopt a succession of different perspectives over the course of their lives. And, Schofield suggests, they can make moral demands, when occupying one perspective at one time, to themselves as occupiers of a different perspective at a later time. Say someone currently occupies the perspective of a happy smoker, for instance. She can nonetheless recognize that, if she keeps smoking, she's likely to later occupy a perspective from which she has painful lung disease. And she can therefore recognize a legitimate moral demand on herself, from that later perspective, to stop smoking. But, again, because she doesn't in fact *yet* occupy the sufferer-of-lung-disease perspective, she's not currently in a position to waive that demand, so the resulting duty isn't the faux kind she can get out of: it really is binding.

If either of these moves work, there's nothing incoherent about the idea of having a duty to yourself. And that would be a good result, because the idea that we do have such duties has a lot going for it.

Most of us accept that we have strong moral reasons to treat people in humane and respectful ways across the board, and it's hard to see why those reasons should dissolve in our own personal case.

Some people, including Singer, have suggested that our reasons to take care of ourselves are a matter of self-interest or prudence only, not morality. If so, while it might be foolish or perverse to harm yourself, it wouldn't be morally wrong. But, as Schofield argues, that way of classing our reasons not to injure ourselves doesn't allow us to say several things about them that we arguably should want to say. For instance, when a person has a moral duty to do something, that duty is meant to weigh very strongly against competing considerations. The duty may not be absolute, but it doesn't just get thrown into the mix to be balanced against other random factors: it has a certain preemptive force. For another, when a moral duty is violated, certain distinctively moral emotions are appropriate: say, guilt and resentment.

If our only reason not to injure ourselves were self-interest, it would be relatively easily outweighed by competing reasons. But that doesn't seem to be the case: we do tend to think we have very compelling reasons to not, say, seriously harm ourselves. Similarly, when we wish we hadn't set back our own interests, we often don't merely *regret* doing it, but also feel at least a little guilty about it and resent our earlier selves for what they've (we've) done.

Say these responses are apt, and we do in fact have duties toward ourselves. If so, what are they? Because little has been written on this subject recently, it's hard to locate a well-developed contemporary account to draw on. It's likely, though, that self-regarding duties will fall into two main categories: a duty not to unjustifiably harm yourself and a duty to properly respect your own dignity and autonomy. You plausibly have a moral duty to yourself not to seriously undermine your own basic welfare interests without very compelling justification, and to avoid lesser harms and hurts to yourself if you can do so without sacrificing anything of comparable moral importance. And you plausibly also have a moral duty to yourself to do what you can to avoid threats to your agency and self-respect from other people and events. It would be wrong, for instance, to voluntarily sign yourself up for genuine slavery, oppression, and domination. (Temporary and constrained play-instances of those things that come with a safe word are different.)

If you really don't like this duty-to-self language—it undoubtedly has an old-fashioned, puritanical ring, though I don't think it needs to—you could put the idea in terms of virtue ethics instead. It's plausible that a virtuous person, Aristotle-style, is one who possesses self-respect and practices what some today call "self-care," alongside the more other-oriented virtues on the standard list.

A lot more needs to be said about all this. (For instance, those who commit suicide or self-harm due to mental illness don't deserve moral condemnation, so what I've said here needs to be qualified to fit the special considerations at issue there.) But if some such duties to self or self-oriented virtues do apply, they'll have implications for memoir. Memoirists will have not just a self-interested, but also a moral, reason to write about themselves with appropriate self-respect and self-concern. This arguably means they should in some cases hold back on the details about very painful, degrading, or self-incriminating events, to protect their own welfare and agency and avoid taking inappropriate advantage of themselves. The sorts of ultraconfessional online personal essays that Laura Bennett criticized in *Slate* as "solo acts of sensational disclosure" that read like "reverse-engineered headlines" might be said to violate this principle.[31]

It's no easy task to weigh self-regarding considerations against the other imperatives of the enterprise—including the aim of avoiding narcissistic vanity preservation that we started with—which may press in the direction of fully frank exposure. As in the case of the other value conflicts in memoir that I've discussed in previous chapters, there's no plausible answer as to which should win out that will cover all cases. My suggestion here is just that self-oriented duties or virtues should be part of the competition. As Alice Kaplan writes, "Writing about yourself is a high-wire balancing act between revelation and a need to set bounds, to respect your own need for privacy and the right to privacy of others. If you achieve what the genre of autobiography asks of you, you may be giving away too much."[32]

The Memoirist as Artist, Scholar, and Moralist

If memoirists aren't driven, as a group, by narcissism, why else might they do what they do? Across the previous chapters we've referred in passing to several more compelling reasons for writing a memoir than exaggerated self-love. Let's recap them here.

One motivation is to make art: to create and share a literary work that is, say, original, resonant, complex, and beautiful. That alone doesn't point in the direction of memoir over other forms of literature or art, but memoir might have certain advantages for some writers. Bernard Cooper writes, for instance:

The very familiarity of autobiographical material freed me up to concentrate on the sensual and emotional effects of language (for me the most pleasurable part of writing) instead of on the invention of story. I'd never flattered myself that my personal history is more exceptional or fascinating than most, but rather have seen it as a readily accessible source from which to write.[33]

In other cases, a memoirist may simply have more inclination and talent for nonfiction than fiction. Some people try writing short stories, but find that their characters are all thinly veiled versions of people they know: sometimes, as they say, your genre chooses you.

Another common motivation is more intellectual than aesthetic. Some memoirists are strongly driven by the desire to discover and record the historical truth, for truth's own sake. Again, fiction can serve something like the same purpose, especially when it's highly researched or strongly autobiographical, but memoir has obvious advantages in the truth department. Some memoirists want to provide a repository for eyewitness accounts of an important social event. Other memoirists are interested in simply discovering the truth about themselves. Self-understanding is an intellectual achievement like any other and can be valued intrinsically. (I discuss some more instrumental reasons for seeking self-understanding below.)

The knowledge that a person gains from writing a memoir may mainly be of value to the memoirist, but memoirists generally hope that others will value the understanding they reach too, and learn from it. In this way, the intellectual motivation can merge into a third motivation (or really, set of motivations) for writing memoir. A large number of memoirists have been driven by a strong moral impulse: a desire to cultivate inner virtue or to promote the interests of others. The inner virtue motivation lies behind the giant corpus of spiritual autobiography in the West. Several branches of Protestant Christianity have traditionally required their followers to write a memoir of sorts (following the sixteenth-century Puritan William Perkins's advocacy of "a narrow examination of thy selfe and the course of thy life"[34]), and several of the great literary autobiographies of the Western canon have taken the form of a conversion narrative or confession. These memoirs are used by their authors as a form of self-exploration and inner accounting, an attempt to detect weaknesses in the writer's soul and fortify them against future temptations. But they can also be offered to others as cautionary tales or inspiring examples of triumph over the forces of sin and suffering.

Many contemporary memoirs still follow this pattern, though they're likely to remove the explicitly religious elements. Stories of recovery from addiction often have an explicit conversion plot line, and the general arc of struggle against adversity crowned with redemption appears more subtly in many other subgenres too. More generally still, the use of memoir as a means of moral reflection is ubiquitous. Arguably every memoir, whether explicitly or not, is an expression of a set of values and priorities, offering a partial picture of what it means to lead (or not lead) a good life. Even if you see yourself as a not especially morally-oriented person, it's arguably impossible to write about your life without at least subtly evaluating, critiquing or justifying it. This is why memoirs, even when they're comic, often have an earnest, even insistent, undercurrent. The writer may be pursuing moral reflection for their own private purposes, but they might also have the interests of their readers in mind. Watching someone else engage in sustained conscience-searching and ethical deliberation can be a prompt to doing it yourself and serve as an example of how to do it bravely and insightfully.

The inner virtue motivation centers on the moral health of the author's (and maybe the reader's) conscience and behavior. But a memoir can also be morally motivated in a different way. A common reason for writing memoir is to provide benefits to readers, of either a personal or a more political kind. On the personal front, memoir benefits readers in three main ways. For one, it provides them with information about how others tick and conduct their lives that may be helpful in the reader's own life. While many other literary genres also perform this role, memoir can do so in a particularly intimate and direct manner. Memoir, at its best, gives us unparalleled access to the inner life of another human, and to the ins and outs of their relationships, projects, failures, and successes.

The second personal benefit of memoir is the sense of intimate connection and companionship it provides. In everyday life, many of the people we interact with, sometimes even our closest friends, are opaque to us. Our inability to understand them, to get at the inner essence of those we love, of anyone, can be a source of deep loneliness and frustration. Virginia Woolf writes in *To the Lighthouse*:

she imagined how in the chambers of the mind and heart of the woman who was, physically, touching her, were stood, like the treasures in the tombs of kings, tablets bearing sacred inscriptions, which if one could spell them out, would teach one everything, but they would never be offered openly, never made public. What art was there, known to love or cunning, by which one pressed through into those secret chambers?[35]

Memoir can offer at least a partial entry, revealing the consciousness of another live human with a bareness that may be unavailable, or unbearable, face to face. Again, other literary forms can do this too. (Knausgaard writes "What is a work of art if not the gaze of another person? Not directed above us, nor beneath us, but at the same height as our own gaze."[36]) But many of us get an extra charge when we know there's a real person not so far behind the scenes. All of us at some time, and some of us all of the time, are starved for this kind of intimacy; it's a morally valuable act to offer it.

The third, related, personal benefit is the sense of solidarity and succor that a memoir can afford those who have undergone or are undergoing suffering or trauma. This is particularly valuable when the book describes the experiences of someone from a marginalized group, whose members often struggle to recognize their experiences in the broader culture or feel heard and seen themselves. Jesmyn Ward's *Men We Reaped* centers on the deaths of five young Black men she knew while growing up in the rural South. She said of the harrowing experience of writing it: "Every time I considered what this story could do for some kid who lives out in the plains of Nebraska, growing up in a neighborhood where there's drug addiction, where there are people dying young, I thought that if I'd had a book like that, it wouldn't have made the pain bearable, but it might have made it so that I was able to continue."[37]

On the political front, memoirs can act as a powerful engine for social change. An intellectual argument about social injustice may be persuasive, but too abstract and impersonal to fire up readers. A personal account that makes the same point through the experience of individual people, especially if it comes in narrative form, will often be more effective. There's a long tradition of memoirs bearing witness to political oppression. Into this category fall narratives written, in the eighteenth century, by refugees from the French Revolution; in the nineteenth, by escaped American slaves; and in the twentieth, by Holocaust survivors. If a political memoir becomes overly argument-driven it turns into history, commentary or propaganda, but it can do its work more subtly. Mike Martin points out that much of the political force of Frederick Douglass's autobiography lies in the writing itself rather than the story told or explicit argument advanced.[38] Douglass's human dignity, intelligence, and moral sensitivity are evident throughout the book, in his masterful use of language and literary devices and his acute and subtle observations. The argument against slavery isn't awkwardly grafted onto the life of this man, but lies both in the life and in its expression.

In his book *The Moral Demands of Memory*, Jeffrey Blustein emphasizes that bearing witness to injustice and tragedy—or to justice, courage, and resilience—can be valuable even if it fails to affect political structures or others' behavior.[39] It's a way of expressing commitment to moral and political ideals, as well as a way of giving voice to those who have been devalued, ignored, or silenced. As such, it's intrinsically valuable and praiseworthy, even if otherwise done in vain. Not every memoirist can hope to have the social impact that, say, Douglass's autobiography had. But any memoirist can do this quieter but still political task of speaking up with conviction against the unjust and tragic and for the beautiful and good.

The Memoirist as Memorialist

One common motivation for making any sort of art is to create a valuable object that will outlast the artist's death, and thereby (in some sense) preserve the artist and the artist's life for eternity. Memoirists might be especially susceptible to this motivation, given that their art is designed to capture their self and experience more directly and comprehensively than most other art forms. Some celebrated practitioners of the form have certainly felt it strongly. Jean Starobinski writes of Montaigne that he reacted to the prospect of his death "not by an act of faith in the divine promise, but by recourse to literature, to art, in order to fashion an image of his life to be bequeathed to posterity. To exist in the pages of a book is better than to vanish into nothingness and oblivion. The *Essays* are to have the value of a *monument*."[40] Similarly, Nabokov wrote in the final chapter of *Speak, Memory*: "I have to have all space and all time participate in my emotion, in my mortal love, so that the edge of its mortality is taken off, thus helping me to fight the utter degradation, ridicule and horror of having developed an infinity of sensation and thought within a finite existence."[41]

Though many memoirists can probably relate to this motivation, it's tempting to dismiss it, for a couple of reasons. One is that it gives off a distinct whiff of the exaggerated self-importance that memoirists are often charged with. Is the memoirist's life really so precious, will its end leave the world so very incomplete, that it demands this sort of verbal taxidermy? Another reason for dismissal is that the project seems ultimately futile. If you're lucky or very lucky, your memoir might get read for a few decades or centuries. But even Montaigne and Nabokov won't be read when, to put it bluntly, the human race inevitably perishes, along with every copy of every book. It makes sense during life to set aside this longer-range cosmic perspective for the most part, since it threatens to sap the point from every human activity. (The reason Alvy Singer gives for not doing his homework in *Annie Hall* is that the universe is expanding and will ultimately disintegrate. His mother replies impatiently: "You're here in Brooklyn. Brooklyn is not expanding.") But explicitly aiming for immortality through art looks like a bad idea.

There's a more sympathetic interpretation of this motivation, though, that doesn't make it seem egotistical or futile. It might be easier to identify in cases where the writer is intent on memorializing another person, rather than themself. People often write memoirs and essays about loved or esteemed people who have died.[42] Why? In many cases the motivation seems to be a desire not to preserve those people for eternity, but instead to *value* them appropriately: to continue to love and honor them through art.[43] The endeavor isn't premised on the thought that the dear departed were so unusually valuable, impartially speaking, that they require special efforts at preservation. Instead it's a heartfelt affirmation that they were significant, that their lives were meaningful and mattered. And making this affirmation can have value, even if the means of expression has a finite future. Something good and beautiful doesn't need to last forever for it to be worthwhile now. If it's true that memorializing the dear departed in memoir makes sense and is valuable in this way, it seems to follow that prememorializing oneself is too. There's nothing inherently self-aggrandizing or pointless about expressing the truth via finite means that your finite existence, like that of others, is a precious thing.

The Memoirist as Self-Healer

The motivations to produce art, gain knowledge, promote moral values, and love or honor the departed are, at least in part, non-self-interested. In each of these cases, the memoirist is aiming at goods whose value is independent of the writer's own good. But memoirists are also, of course, often concerned with their own good in pursuing those goods, as well as others.

Some "prudential" reasons for writing memoir—reasons to do with the writer's own happiness, well-being, or flourishing—are relatively easy to understand and don't need much analysis. Most writers love writing, when they're not hating it. They may also want to share their history with their children or other family members, express gratitude to past benefactors, settle private scores with past antagonists, get paid, or climb up the ladder of a political or literary career. But other prudential motivations for memoir writing are more complex. Chief among these is the desire to heal yourself through your life writing.

There's strong evidence from psychology and medicine that writing about your past can significantly benefit your health and subjective well-being. In the 1980s the psychologist James Pennebaker pioneered a therapeutic technique he named "expressive writing" in which a person writes about a distressing experience in their past for fifteen to twenty minutes, for three to four days. "This very simple exercise," he and his colleague Joshua Smyth report, "has been found to improve people's physical and mental health for weeks, months, and even years when compared to individuals who write about emotionally neutral topics (or other comparison groups)."[44]

WHY WRITE A MEMOIR?

Hundreds of experiments since Pennebaker's initial study have shown positive effects from expressive writing in improving immune function, speeding up wound healing, reducing blood pressure and heart rate, and alleviating symptoms in people with asthma, rheumatoid arthritis, cardiac problems, depression, PTSD, and insomnia. Those who aren't ill but merely experiencing standard human emotions like anger, sadness, grief, shame, and guilt also report reductions in the intensity of those. (It's important not to exaggerate the benefits: expressive writing works best for those with only moderate health problems, its effects don't always persist, and it can backfire if it just inflames distressing emotions without relieving them.)

The empirical record is relatively straightforward. What's more obscure is *why* autobiographical writing has these effects. The general outline seems to be that expressive writing reduces stress and anxiety, and that in turn reduces the risk of stress-related illnesses and distress. But how exactly does writing reduce stress?

Pennebaker and Smyth suggest that a mixture of things may be going on. For one thing, putting an experience into language seems to reduce its emotional intensity. In one of his "affect labeling" studies, psychologist Matthew Lieberman brought a bunch of arachnophobes into his lab and exposed them to a spider.[45] Those who expressed their fear in words while approaching the spider managed to get physically closer to it than those who remained silent. Another study found that when people are asked to describe a picture of a person's face, they're less likely to recognize it afterward.[46] Construing the face in abstract linguistic form seems to blur the subject's mental image of it, decreasing the vividness of the memory of the experience of seeing it (and, presumably, any distress associated with it).

This can't be all of the explanation, though. Studies suggest that merely naming and venting painful emotions doesn't have welfare benefits and can even have adverse effects: mindlessly releasing anger, for instance, just makes you angrier and more stressed.[47] To be beneficial, the expression generally has to be accompanied by a searching attempt to make sense of the emotions at issue, including by thinking about their causes and consequences. This result lines up with the fact that when participants are asked to describe the long-term effects of expressive writing, the majority of them don't merely talk of a feeling of emotional release, but point directly to the self-understanding and insight about their lives they feel they gained. So another link between writing and stress reduction is likely to be the general function of language in organizing, simplifying, and making sense of experience. When people put their past into words, they tend to summarize and order it, which may reduce it to a size and shape that's easier to deal with emotionally.

A further piece may be the fact that writing something down allows people to "externalize" their thoughts about the experience described. Many people tend to either ruminate obsessively over unarticulated trauma or block it from consciousness, both of which take up energy and mental space that might be better used for other things (including sleep, memory, and other cognitive tasks). Insofar as writing involves transferring obsessive or buried thoughts out of the head and onto the page, it can free up this space.

Finally, writing can help people to think more efficiently and constructively about how to solve their emotional problems, by causing them to attend to them at length, in detail and at a slow pace. They can then use those problem-solving results to make positive, stress-reducing changes in their behavior and relationships.

These explanations don't really depend on the act of writing per se, but simply on linguistic articulation: talking might do just as well. But writing may be more readily available and appealing than talking with friends or a therapist.

Memoir writing is rather different from the sort of "expressive writing" used by psychologists and clinicians. Among other things, it takes longer to do, produces more text, and has much broader aims, including literary ones. But the results discussed above are at least suggestive for an analysis of the welfare benefits of memoir, and they track what many memoirists have said about their own writing experiences.

Take Virginia Woolf, whose unfinished "A Sketch of the Past" is as much a reflection on the art of memoir as a memoir itself. In one passage of that book, Woolf suggests the first benefit of memoir mentioned above: that writing about one's experience with the goal of understanding it can serve to emotionally defang it. She writes of certain intense and mysterious experiences she's had since childhood:

As one gets older one has a greater power through reason to provide an explanation; and . . . this explanation blunts the sledge-hammer of the blow . . . It is only by putting it into words that I make it whole; this wholeness means that it has lost its power to hurt me; it gives me, perhaps because by doing so I take away the pain, a great delight to put the severed parts together. Perhaps this is the strongest pleasure known to me.[48]

Why *is* it that the effort to explain an experience via memoir tends to make it less painful? Part of the story is likely to be the sense of power and agency that the effort can produce, a sense that may have been profoundly lacking at the time of the experience described. John Berger writes: "Perhaps this is the true attraction of autobiography: all the events over which you had no control are at last subject to your decision."[49] But it may also be a matter of the analytical detachment that writing involves. Terese Marie Mailhot writes: "You have to remove yourself to write about trauma ... you have to be able to see, *this is better as an end-scene.*"[50] For those memoirists who engage in ongoing note-taking in preparation for future work, this move can help with present as well as past trauma. Melissa Febos reports that "it is easier, the first time after you meet your birth father, who's a career alcoholic, to go park your car in a gas station and take notes while you cry, rather than just cry. It's really like helping with the hors d'oeuvres at a party where you don't know anyone. It's easier to have a job."[51]

Rachel Howard suggests that the control and detachment factors work together: "when you write what you remember of an event, you separate yourself from it. You create a new layer of memory on top of the original one—a memory of you being in control of the old memory."[52]

Elsewhere in "A Sketch of the Past," when discussing writing her autobiographical novel *To the Lighthouse*, Woolf also attests to the second benefit of memoir listed above: the peace a personal narrator can achieve by externalizing painful recurring memories:

Until I wrote [*To the Lighthouse*] out, I would find my lips moving; I would be arguing with [my father]; raging against him; saying to myself all that I never said to him.[53]

I wrote [*To the Lighthouse*] very quickly; and when it was written, I ceased to be obsessed by my mother ... I suppose that I did for myself what psycho-analysts do

for their patients. I expressed some very long felt and deeply felt emotion. And in
expressing it I explained it and then laid it to rest.[54]

Jesmyn Ward says, similarly, that writing *Men We Reaped* helped her
to stop internalizing her trauma and grief and instead "funnel it out-
wards."[55]

It's natural to understand what's going on in all these cases as a
"letting go" of the past. By transforming their past experience into
art, people say, memoirists are able to "release themselves of its grip,"
"leave it behind," and "move on." But things aren't that simple. In
many cases, it's more accurate to say that the memoirist *takes responsibility for* their past.[56] Rather than seeing themself as a passive
victim of purely evil oppressors, or projecting their own flaws onto
others, they acknowledge, maybe for the first time, their active role
in generating or perpetuating significant behavior patterns and relationships. (This isn't to deny that people sometimes are purely passive victims.) The experience can be distressing, but also relieving and
energizing, by virtue of increasing the writer's sense of agency in both
the past and the future. Taking responsibility for the past doesn't involve leaving it behind, but integrating it into one's current sense of
who one is and can be.

Similarly, it's often inaccurate to say that the memoirist comes to
"accept" their past or themself through their writing. Many writers
continue to repudiate their past actions and those of others, and they
may continue to be consumed with shame and self-hatred. It's plausible, though, that many memoirists achieve, if not self-acceptance,
then self-forgiveness, through their writing. While not everything you
take responsibility for is something you should forgive yourself for,
it's also true that you can't forgive yourself for something that you
don't take responsibility for. When self-forgiveness is warranted (and
maybe even when it isn't?), achieving it can massively improve a person's quality of life.

The act of memoir can be an act of self-healing in a number of
other ways, too, ways that may or may not be present in instances of
short-term expressive writing.

For one, sitting down to write can be a way of reasserting your dignity and value in the wake of denials of those things or in the face of
current threats to them. Memoirs written by survivors of abuse or op-

pression, or people living with illness or disability, are often motivated this way. Relatedly, writing a memoir can help traumatized people remember the good in what may at the time (or later) have seemed to be an exclusively bad experience, or help them (re)locate gratitude for love and assistance received during their trials.

For another, memoir writing can help reduce loneliness. I noted above that reading memoirs can be a source of intimate connection and companionship. But writing them can be, too: memoirists can be consoled by the thought of their future or hypothetical audience, and just as much by the thought of their fellow writers, past and present. To narrate your life on the page is to be part of a shared tradition of reasoning and caring about human lives and their literary expression that extends over hundreds of years. Being aware of your own small part in that tradition is a way of feeling less alone in the world.

Finally, writing a memoir can provide the immense psychic relief that comes with presenting yourself as (you believe) you truly are, after possibly decades of isolating secrecy or exhausting dissimulation. Memoirists often claim of writing in order to finally be "seen" by others, and perhaps also by themselves. Saul Friedlander, who was forced to repress his Jewish heritage in occupied France, claimed that *When Memory Comes* derived from "a need for synthesis, for a thoroughgoing coherence that no longer excludes anything."[57] André Gide explained his decision to publish an open account of his life as a young gay man in *Si le grain ne meurt*: "I had the feeling that I could not have died in peace if I had kept all this locked up in me ... I did not want to die without knowing that it is *there*."[58]

As in the case of short-term expressive writing, it's important not to exaggerate the self-healing value of memoir writing. For one thing, while the downstream psychic gain may be large, the writing itself may be emotionally grueling, and not always worth the cost. Although Jesmyn Ward says that writing *Men We Reaped* was ultimately therapeutic for her, she also says that the process of writing it was so awful she'll never write a memoir again.[59] For another thing, the sense of relief can be temporary. Margo Jefferson writes: "I think it's a thing that artists often feel: 'Look I'm an artist, so in some way I have transcended, I have risen above.' And in some ways you can, and then you turn around and you're just another ordinary trapped person. Two hours later: A little sucker."[60]

Finally, if memoir becomes *all* about therapy, its aesthetic value is imperiled. Michiko Kakutani accuses many contemporary memoirists of "the belief that confession is therapeutic and therapy is redemptive and redemption somehow equals art."[61] It doesn't for many reasons, but one is that the willful imposition of an uplifting story arc on your life is a sure route to suppression, simplification, and sentimentality. This may be why some writers, Joan Didion among them, vigorously reject the idea that memoir is healing. That's doubtless true for some memoirists, but, as a general claim, it looks like an overcorrection.

The Memoirist as Self-Seeker

There's good reason to think that writing memoir in many cases reduces stress, improves emotional and physical health, and increases happiness. Those prudential benefits are usually welcome, but they might seem to some memoirists relatively superficial or even wrongheaded. "I'm not writing this thing because it makes me *happy!*" you can imagine a memoirist grumbling. "Even if it does, that's not the point!"

What *is* the point? If it's not art, truth, or morality, two major candidates remain. The one we'll discuss in this section has its most famous exponent in Jean-Jacques Rousseau. Rousseau's *Confessions* was largely motivated by the desire to get clear, for himself and others, on the true nature of his inner self. As noted earlier, such self-understanding can be understood as simply a subcategory of a memoirist's broader intellectual goal to grasp the truth about the world and its inhabitants, period. But it can also be pursued—and was pursued by Rousseau—for an instrumental reason. Rousseau wanted to know what his inner self was chiefly because he wanted to be *in touch* with it, to be *true* to it. He wanted, as we say, to live "authentically": on his own terms, without self-deception, dissimulation, or deference.

It's a motivation we also see in the American transcendentalists of the following century: Thoreau's going to the woods "to front only the essential facts of life"[62] (and write his memoir) away from the distractions and compulsions of society; Emerson's claim in his personal-ish essay "Self-Reliance" that "the only right is what is after my constitution, the only wrong what is against it ... I must be myself."[63] The idea takes full flight in the existentialist tradition (which contains an unusual amount of autobiographical writing for a philosophical school), including the work of Kierkegaard, Nietzsche, Camus, Sartre, and de Beauvoir. To take things up to the present day, we can also detect the theme in Alexander Chee's recent claim that, in memoir, "what you're doing for your reader is riddling through the ways you lie to yourself and others and trying to get at what you actually believe … I engaged in a kind of forensics of the self … I act like a spy on myself, like someone who doesn't love me and is just going to report on me. It's a trust-but-verify relationship to the self."[64] The assumption is that there's a true self in there, that it's hard work to burrow down and find it, and that it's of utmost importance to do so: that an inauthentic life is a terrible thing.

I have mixed feelings about the value of authenticity. I feel it—who reading this book doesn't? Many of us have grown up in a society for which authenticity is a, if not the supreme, value. The goal of being true to yourself is a core part of the legacy of Romanticism and of liberalism, and we continue to have it drummed into us by education, political life, art, therapy, and popular culture. (Be yourself, be real, listen to your inner voice, follow your dreams, let those true colors shine through …) And on the face of it, authenticity is undeniably appealing. How could living via a *fake* self be a good idea? Try that idea on *Oprah* and see how it flies.

Some people reject the ideal of authenticity because they believe that there's no real self to be true to, or else that we can't know its nature even if it exists. We discussed reasons for those beliefs in chapter 2, so I'll set them aside here. My key doubts are ethical and prudential rather than metaphysical or epistemic. Say you do manage to find your true self, perhaps by writing your memoir. What reason would you have to live in accordance with it?

Simon Feldman notes that living "authentically" can be valued for three different reasons: as the best route to well-being, rationality, or moral action.[65] Where well-being is concerned, following your true nature is said to eliminate stress caused by ambivalence and alienation, to promote the peace and happiness that comes with settled conviction, and to enable you to pursue your goals confidently and effectively. As for rationality, an authentic life is claimed to be free of the inconsistencies and cognitive distortions produced by conflicting commitments and unthinking adherence to the beliefs and values of others. And, ethically, it's argued, only a person who guides their life by their own star is able to access their "moral compass," act with self-control and integrity, and take full responsibility for their actions.

In each case, Feldman persuasively argues, the connection between authenticity and the value in question is unreliable and often antagonistic. For instance, ambivalence can be a surer route to well-being than settled conviction, in allowing for a more expansive, open-minded, sensitive, temperate, and flexible approach to life. And sometimes it's better for your welfare that you defer to others rather than yourself, if those others have better ideas. As for rationality, that requires being responsive to reasons, and to reality, rather than running your life exclusively in accordance with your own, possibly misguided, inner promptings. The connection between authenticity and morality is the weakest of all. To whip out the Hitler card: if you're an insane genocidal dictator, being true to yourself is the exact opposite of what morality requires of you. But the point holds even in the more standard-issue cases of authentic sexists, racists, homophobes, narcissists, art monsters, control freaks, cowards, liars, abusers, and sanctimonious bores.

Feldman's general conclusion is that our commitment to authenticity is based on a set of highly dubious assumptions about the nature of welfare, rationality, and morality, and that focusing on the question of what one's true self is tends to distract us from other, better questions that really help us to live well. Given the weight of tradition on the other side, you might need to read his full and detailed argument to be persuaded of that, but I'll just say here that he makes a pretty convincing case.

Nothing in this critique is an argument against seeking your true self via memoir. I agree that autobiographical writing can be a very effective way to gain self-understanding. The sustained examination and interpretation of your dispositions and actions over time that literary self-narration requires, along with the anticipation of a perhaps skeptical audience, can unearth patterns, self-deceptions, and alternative perspectives that would otherwise remain hidden.[66] I also agree that the search for self-understanding is valuable. The journey itself is often interesting, and any knowledge that results from it can be valued intrinsically as well as help you to lead your life and relationships well. (Not always: some self-illusions are beneficial, though studies suggest this is only true of the minor or moderate ones.[67]) The points made above recommend caution, though, against seeking the self—via memoir or otherwise—specifically in order to live in accordance with its nature. While many memoirists have been drawn to that further aim, it's of dubious value.

The Memoirist as Meaning-Seeker

Finally, we come to what's perhaps the most controversial reason for writing a memoir. I suspect that many memoirists mainly write not in pursuit of happiness or authenticity, but in pursuit of meaningfulness—and that in two ways. A direct goal of their work is to search for some kind of meaning in their past experience. And they feel that the search for that meaning via the writing makes their current and future lives more meaningful.

What is it to find meaning in your experience? In part, it's a matter of finding some form or order in it: a recognizable, intelligible shape rather than an indistinct mess. One very common way to do this is to organize the raw material of your life into a story or narrative: an organized representation of a sequence of events, along with an implied evaluative response to them.

As I noted in chapter 2, stories have three core features that render them particularly helpful in making experience intelligible. First, stories are *selective*: they focus on particular agents, events, and settings, out of the mass of material that life provides. Second, they exhibit *unity*: they weave the disparate elements that they select into a cohesive whole, drawing causal or analogical connections between them and situating them within a larger context. Third, they're *isomorphic*: they tend to share certain deep structural features with other stories. The majority of stories people tell about their lives follow the abstract traditional arc of *steady state—complication—rising action—crisis—resolution—coda*, and their substantive content often echoes story lines, themes, and motifs found in earlier stories.

As the first two of these features suggest, stories are effectively models: simplified representations of reality designed to emphasize certain elements. It's unsurprising, then, that stories function to make the world more intelligible to us in much the same way that models in general do. Selectivity results in less material to attend to, opening up space for depth and intensity of treatment. It also clears space for the emphasis on connections between events and the bigger picture that unity supplies. The third feature, isomorphism, assists further by, in effect, supplying models for the model. We use a story's similarity to a familiar set of narrative frames as a shortcut when making sense of new stories. In successful stories, all three features work in concert to produce a sense in the teller or listener of having gained some significant insight about life (difficult as it may be to precisely articulate its content) and an accompanying sense of satisfaction, even if the story's plot is distressing or tragic.

Though stories have these special virtues, other nonnarrative ways of ordering and shaping experience can contribute to intelligibility too. Any selective representation of experience that highlights connections, associations, and recurring motifs or themes can serve to unify and clarify the life it treats, even if it doesn't portray the unfolding of events over time.

Most of us have a natural inclination toward this kind of form-finding, meaning-pursuing activity.[68] Over the past few decades, psychologists have done multiple studies of our collective drive toward personal narration and the connection between that habit and our sense that our lives have meaning.[69] But memoirists, clearly, have a particularly strong case of it. Unlike the average human, who tells stories intermittently throughout the day without thinking much about it, memoirists sit down intentionally and self-consciously to self-narrate at length, and some of them make a lifelong vocation out of it. When explaining why they do this, they often point to the desire to find form and meaning in their experience that I've been pointing to here. Mark Doty writes, for instance:

I wanted to tell the story of my life in order [. . .] to take control of it, to shape some comprehensible element of cause and effect, because the . . . complexity of experience mean that this sense of pattern is always slipping away from us. Memoir is a way of reclaiming, at least temporarily, the sense of shapeliness in a life.[70]

Personal essayists who don't rely on narrative make similar claims. The aim of an essay is often to select some apparently isolated piece of experience and reveal its broader significance, by drawing connections between it and other parts of the author's life, setting it in a larger contextual frame. In some cases, the unifying center isn't a piece of experience but rather a piece of the author: the essayist creates a unified, consistent persona and, by letting it loose on life, creates a patch of coherence and intelligibility in its wake. In both cases, the aim isn't merely to describe, but to order, to explain.

What are people, including memoirists, doing exactly, when they claim to "find" this form and meaning in their experience? Are they genuinely discovering it back there or just making it up? Phillip Lopate suggests the former:

I have a conviction that life itself has forms underneath it: that there are connections to be made between experience and memory that are not purely subjective but that wait patiently to be brought to the surface [. . .] When memoirists or essayists follow closely on the trail of some developing suspense, and discover a through-line, meanwhile cutting away all irrelevancies, we are not fictionalizing, we are serving the innate shape of reality.[71]

Julian Barnes, on the other hand, suggests the latter:

If, as we approach death and look back on our lives, "we understand our narrative" and stamp a final meaning upon it, I suspect we are doing little more than confabulating: processing strange, incomprehensible, contradictory input into some kind, any kind, of believable story . . . I would expect a dying person to be an unreliable narrator, because what is useful to us generally conflicts with what is true, and what is useful at that time is a sense of having lived to some purpose, and according to some comprehensible plot.[72]

Barnes's position reflects the "antinarrativist" version of the fictionalist challenge to memoir that we discussed in chapter 2. The worry is that our attempts to detect a meaningful narrative (or nonnarrative) shape in our experience are merely desperate projections. Life itself has no order or meaning, however much we may wish it did, and our life stories and persona-driven essays are just fictional constructions designed to protect ourselves from that horrifying fact.

I noted back in chapter 2 that I don't find this critique persuasive, for a couple of reasons. For one, antinarrativists tend to move too quickly from the claim that stories are constructions to the claim that they're fictions (in the sense of distortions of reality). A representation can be *made* (all representations are) without being false.

For another, and more importantly here, the claim that life contains no discernable patterns overreaches. Antinarrativists are often motivated by the denial that life has a single, overarching grand purpose of the kind advocated by religious believers. The universe has no author or point, they claim: it's just the chaotic result of randomly operating natural forces. But you can accept *that* claim—I do—without throwing the (lesser patterns) baby out with the (one big cosmic pattern) bathwater.

Individual humans act for reasons, and their actions have consequences, including the imposition of a certain order and pattern on their natural and social environment. We can describe their behavior in terms of atoms moving in the void, sure. But there's another, and equally legitimate, level of explanation that appeals to the values and goals driving that behavior, and its impact on the values and goals of other humans. To give that second kind of explanation is to point to the purpose, significance, and meaning built into human life. A story or essay that tries to offer such an explanation is picking up on real features of the world, not just confabulating. Similarly, it's a genuine feature of humans that we think and act symbolically and associatively: we partake in rituals, gestures, and language with more than surface implications. As a result, a story or essay that appeals to or relies on metaphorical and thematic connections is, again, reflecting, not distorting, human reality.

That said, those who claim that narrative is created, not discovered, are on to something. As Eakin writes, "Repetition of the past is necessarily a supplement to it and never merely a mirror of it . . . *Of course* the repetition adds something; otherwise why write, why bother with reenactment of the past at all?"[73] The truth is that successful personal narrators are *both* discovering and creating. They're doing the difficult creative work of distilling and unifying their experience into a shape that they and others can understand—giving it "the closure, the coherence, the permanence conferred by the stamp of form."[74] And, when they do it successfully, that shape tracks genuine features in the life they've lived.

The search for meaning in your past experience isn't pointless, then: it's possible to find it—though you may need to lower your standards for what counts. Most people's lives don't have a single, unified theme or arc, but exhibit multiple complementary or conflicting ones, none of which is dominant. Joan Didion's essay "The White Album," which records her anxious attempts to find some stable order in the mayhem of 1960s California, concludes with an admission of defeat: "writing has not yet helped me to see what [experience] means."[75] But sometimes the underlying pattern just *is* chaos, and evocatively conveying it—as in this masterfully crafted essay—is a form-finding achievement of sorts. Getting a grip on your lack of a grip is still getting a grip.

Moreover, aiming to discover a *final*, definitive meaning via memoir is probably a bad idea. The meaning of an experience, and of a life, is apt to change as that life is lived. It's not that the past itself changes—we haven't managed that feat yet—but that its significance changes, as it develops a myriad of relationships to later events that hadn't yet happened either at its occurrence or at earlier acts of narration. (Your brief encounter with that guy at Burning Man doesn't mean much at all, say, until he writes to you ten years later and you end up, disastrously, starting an alpaca farm with him.) The past gets new properties as its repercussions proliferate, and our descriptions of what it means get correspondingly richer too.[76] In addition to that, of course, due to any number of reasons (indoctrination, ignorance, love, fear, etc.), we often settle on narratives for our lives that we later come to see as flawed. Many memoirs are themselves in part about this process—also a common theme of therapy—of identifying an earlier false narrative, arduously sloughing it off and replacing it with another. It'd be hubris to think that you can do that just once.

Finding (at least partial and provisional) meaning is possible, then, but why bother with the attempt? Perhaps the best answer is that the search for meaning itself makes one's life more meaningful—though "meaningful" in a somewhat different sense than we've been using so far.

In everyday language, to say that an individual human life is meaningful isn't usually to say that it exhibits an intelligible pattern or shape. Instead it's to say that the life has a certain depth and enduring value, that it's worthy of pride or admiration, that it's worthwhile, not futile. Philosophers have offered different accounts of what it is that gives a life these special qualities. The most popular contemporary account, offered by Susan Wolf, claims that meaning in life is present when "subjective attraction meets objective attractiveness."[77] The life has to contain goods with genuine value (say, loving relationships; intellectual, artistic, or athletic achievements; the pursuit of social justice—whether at a modest or major scale), and the liver of the life has to be deeply invested in and engaged with those goods. A person who's enthusiastically dedicated to relationships, activities, and projects with positive value is living as deep, admirable, and worthwhile a life as we can imagine.

Searching for meaning (in the sense of intelligible shape) in your past experience is one way of making your life meaningful in this broader and more fundamental sense. That's because making your life intelligible to yourself and others contributes to self-understanding and community: just the sorts of objectively valuable and fulfilling goods that Wolf has in mind. We can value those goods intrinsically, as I've suggested in the earlier parts of this chapter, but we can also value them instrumentally, because of the meaning that engagement with them brings to our lives.

That benefit applies to everyone who engages in personal narration, whether in everyday reflection and conversation or in the writing of a memoir. But memoirists have an additional advantage here. Most memoirists don't merely value the *product* of their search for meaning in their past experience: the improved grip they gain on their history and the connections they forge with their readers and fellow writers. They also deeply value the activity of the search itself: simply put, they love writing memoir. And because memoir writing is a highly valuable good, for all the diverse reasons I've canvassed in this chapter, their love is latching on to something that genuinely matters. As a result, if Wolf's account is right, writing a memoir is a paradigmatically meaningful enterprise. Not everyone needs to do it: there are plenty of other valuable goods out there to love and pursue. But if you feel a strong pull toward autobiographical writing and have some talent for it, it's a potential, and possibly potent, source of meaning in life for you.

The relationship of memoir writing to meaningfulness is a complex one, then. Personal narration, done well, doesn't merely recount a life: it transforms it, sometimes in minor, sometimes in dramatic, ways. So writing a memoir can not only reveal meaning in a life, but make meaning in it, too. There's something magic about the idea of creating meaning by the very act of looking for it: it can sound like a kind of trick. But, trick or no, what true memoirist hasn't felt it, known it, and loved it, too?

Acknowledgments

This book involves writing about writing about life, so it's meta twice over (we philosophers love that kind of thing). I'm lucky to have many people to thank at all three of those nested levels.

When it comes to writing about writing about life (and to writing about life in the philosophical mode), I'm grateful to my friends, colleagues, and mentors in the philosophy community, who have taught me so much and enthusiastically supported my evolution from a political philosopher to a philosopher of literature over the past few years. I'm thinking especially of Clare Batty, Joshua Cohen, Phillip Deen, Candice Delmas, Corinne Gartner, Philip Gerrans, Adam Hosein, Alex Rajczi, Agustín Rayo, and my colleagues in the Wellesley philosophy department: Mary Kate McGowan, Alison McIntyre, Erich Hatala Matthes, Julie Walsh, and Catherine Wearing. I'm grateful more generally for Wellesley College, where I've had the privilege of teaching hundreds of smart and passionate students over the past decade. Thanks to all of those students, especially the ones in my Philosophy of Literature class, where I first tried out some of the ideas in this book. I'm very thankful for the generosity of the American Council of Learned Societies, whose Frederick Burkhardt Fellowship allowed me to start and complete this manuscript in the paradisiac environment of Stanford University in 2019–20. Thanks to the philosophy department, and the Philosophy and Literature program, for hosting me in Palo Alto. I'm especially grateful for comments on parts of the book from Lanier Anderson, Joshua Landy, and Antonia Peacocke and for the companionship that year of Rebecca Hasdell, Wendy Salkin, and Kate Vredenburgh.

When it comes to writing about life in the literary mode, I'm grateful to my friends and teachers in the creative writing community. This book wouldn't exist were it not for Howard Axelrod, who first got me thinking about memoir: thanks so much, Howie. Thanks too to the members of my small writing group, Sasha Eskelund and Sharon Horne, who have seen endless drafts of my own memoir writing and given indispensable advice and encouragement for years now: I feel hugely lucky to have you both in my life. Thanks, too, for the same reasons, to my other favorite writer friends, Robyn Autry, Alyssa Proujanksy, and Liz Young. I gained invaluable insight into the nature and value of literature from my summer creative writing instructors Ann Hood, Phillip Lopate, Brenda Miller, Antonya Nelson, and Michelle Tea, along with my too-many-to-list but not forgotten fellow workshop students. One reviewer described this book as, in its defense of the value of the genre, "almost … a self-help book for those who would like to attempt a memoir." I hope that's so, and that it works, because I'd love to return the favor to a community of people who have helped me so much.

When it comes to life, period, I don't know what I'd do without the friends listed already, as well as Leah Abel; Gabrielle Baker; Joanie Berry; Hannah Cook; Jasmine de Bres (my cat); Ellen Eisen; Toby Eskelund; Krista Feichtinger; Sarah Hosein; Erin, Jamie, Ben, and Phoebe Howell; Greg Lee; Katie Potter; Carmen Saracho and Felix Rayo-Saracho; Karen Sawislak; Alison McQueen; Codruţa Morari; Gabriel, Marcel, and Gus O'Malley; and my extended family in New Zealand and England. And the largest thanks of all go to my family— Joris, Angela, and Julia de Bres and Cas Thistoll—for the lifetime of love and joy they've given me and their wholehearted encouragement of my philosophical and creative writing from the beginning. This book is dedicated to all four of them, with all my love.

Finally, my very large thanks to my editor at Chicago, Kyle Wagner, for his enthusiastic support of this project and sound advice throughout, and to Christopher Cowley, G. Thomas Couser, and an anonymous reviewer for their comments on the manuscript.

Notes

Chapter One

1. Paul Fussell, *Class: A Guide through the American Status System*, 15.
2. Daniel Mendelsohn, "But Enough about Me."
3. Friedrich Wilhelm Goethe, *Poetry and Truth, Goethes Werke*, 602.
4. William H. Gass, "The Art of Self."
5. A good book-length example of philosophy *in* memoir is Mike W. Martin, *Memoir Ethics: Good Lives and the Virtues*.
6. One exception is Christopher Cowley, *The Philosophy of Autobiography*.
7. One partial exception here is G. Thomas Couser, *Vulnerable Subjects: Ethics and Life Writing*. Couser's valuable and pioneering discussion of the ethics of self–life writing is both extensive and insightful. However, his book (1) focuses exclusively on ethics, (2) restricts itself to especially vulnerable subjects of memoir, (3) doesn't restrict itself to literary self–life writing, and (4) is intended mainly for fellow scholars.
8. Roy Pascal, *Design and Truth in Autobiography*, 8.
9. Cited in J. Isaiah Holbrook, "Departures and Returns: A Conversation with Sarah M. Broom."
10. Virginia Woolf, *Moments of Being*, 75.
11. Sue William Silverman, *Fearless Confessions: A Writer's Guide to Memoir*.
12. Philippe Lejeune, *On Autobiography*.
13. Woolf, *Moments of Being*, 65.
14. Phillip Lopate, *The Art of the Personal Essay*, is the classic introduction to and anthology of the genre.
15. Michel de Montaigne, *The Complete Essays of Montaigne*, 76.
16. Edward Hoagland, "What I Think, What I Am."
17. Cited in Charles Trueheart, "The Den of the Literary Lions."
18. David Lazar, "Occasional Desire: On the Essay and the Memoir," 106.
19. Cited in Alex Zwerdling, *The Rise of the Memoir*, 126.
20. On essentialism and antiessentialism about literature, see Peter Lamarque, *The Philosophy of Literature*.
21. Arthur Danto, "The Artworld."

22. See David Davies, *Aesthetics and Literature*, 9–16.
23. Sophie Harrison, "Life before Loss."
24. André Maurois, *Olympio: The Life of Victor Hugo*, 157.

Chapter Two

1. Cited in Martha Mulroy Curry, ed., *The "Writer's Book,"* 275–76.
2. Letter to Mrs. J. G. Holland, October 1870, cited in Theodora Ward, ed., *The Letters of Emily Dickinson*, 482.
3. Vivian Gornick, *The Situation and the Story: The Art of Personal Narrative*, 92.
4. This chapter's historical survey of philosophizing about the self draws on the very helpful John Barresi and Raymond Martin, "History as Prologue: Western Theories of the Self."
5. René Descartes, *Meditations on First Philosophy*, 23.
6. See *The Fourth Ennead*, third tractate, in Plotinus, *Ennead VI. 6–9*.
7. John Locke, *An Essay Concerning Human Understanding*.
8. See, inter alia, Galen Strawson, "The Self."
9. Strawson, 425.
10. David Hume, *Treatise of Human Nature*, 252.
11. Friedrich Nietzsche, *The Will to Power*, notes 490, 485.
12. On Buddhist theories of the self, see Mark Siderits, "Buddhist Non-Self: The No-Owner's Manual."
13. Marya Schechtman, *The Constitution of Selves*.
14. Schechtman, 94.
15. The following discussion draws on Stuart Brock and Edwin Mares, *Realism and Anti-Realism*.
16. Phillip Lopate, *To Show and to Tell: The Craft of Literary Nonfiction*, 52.
17. Roland Barthes, *Roland Barthes by Roland Barthes*, 56.
18. Barthes, 1.
19. Goronwy Rees, *A Bundle of Sensations: Sketches in Autobiography*, 9–10.
20. Mary McCarthy, "The Art of Fiction, No. 27," 313.
21. Terry Eagleton, *How to Read Literature*, 69.
22. Malcolm X, *The Autobiography of Malcolm X*, 196. I borrow this example from John D. Barbour, *The Conscience of the Autobiographer: Ethical and Religious Dimensions of Autobiography*.
23. Montaigne, *Complete Essays*, 611.
24. Nancy Mairs, "Trying Truth," 91.
25. Bishop Berkeley, *A Treatise Concerning the Principles of Human Knowledge*.
26. Cited in Susan Haack, *Manifesto of a Passionate Moderate*, 31.
27. Mary Karr, *The Art of Memoir*, 85.

28. On the correspondence, coherence, and verificationist accounts of truth, see Michael Glanzberg, "Truth."

29. "On Keeping a Notebook," in Joan Didion, *Slouching towards Bethlehem*, 136.

30. For an accessible introduction to metaethics, see Russ Shafer-Landau, *The Fundamentals of Ethics*, and Simon Blackburn, *Being Good: A Short Introduction to Ethics*.

31. Stephen J. A. Ward, "Inventing Objectivity: New Philosophical Foundations," 147.

32. Jean-Jacques Rousseau, *Confessions*, 270.

33. For a recent and clear philosophical discussion of self-knowledge, on which the following discussion draws, see Quassim Cassam, *Self-Knowledge for Humans*.

34. Friedrich Nietzsche, *On the Genealogy of Morals*, 1-2.

35. Friedrich Nietzsche, *Beyond Good and Evil: The Philosophy Classic*, 79.

36. Barbour, *Conscience*, 20.

37. See Kathi Baier, "Lying and Self-Deception."

38. Timothy D. Wilson and Elizabeth W. Dunn, "Self-Knowledge: Its Limits, Value, and Potential for Improvement," 498.

39. Daniel L. Schacter, *The Seven Sins of Memory: How the Mind Forgets and Remembers*, 149–53.

40. R. Santioso, Z. Kunda, and G. T. Fong, "Motivated Recruitment of Autobiographical Memories."

41. Richard E. Nisbett and Timothy DeCamp Wilson, "Telling More than We Can Know: Verbal Reports on Mental Processes."

42. On belief-perseverance after evidential discrediting, see Richard E. Nisbitt and Lee Ross, *Human Inference: Strategies and Shortcomings of Social Judgment*.

43. C. McFarland and M. Ross, "The Relation between Current Impressions and Memories of Self and Dating Partners."

44. George Gusdorf, "Conditions and Limits of Autobiography," 41.

45. Cited in Karr, *Art of Memoir*, 6.

46. See Donna Rose Addis, Alana T. Wong, and Daniel L. Schacter, "Remembering the Past and Imagining the Future: Common and Distinct Neural Substrates during Event Construction and Elaboration," and Daniel L. Schacter et al., "The Future of Memory: Remembering, Imagining, and the Brain."

47. Alison Bechdel, *Fun Home*, 71.

48. Ulric Neisser, *Cognition and Reality*, 180–81.

49. Michael Ross and Anne E. Wilson, "Constructing and Appraising Past Selves," 237. See also A. E. Wilson and M. Ross, "From Chump to Champ: People's Appraisals of Their Earlier and Current Selves."

50. Schacter, *Seven Sins*, 6.

51. Cassam, *Self-Knowledge for Humans*, 204.
52. I. M. Begg, A. Anas, and S. Farinacci, "Dissociation of Processes in Belief: Source Recollection, Statement Familiarity, and the Illusion of Truth."
53. See D. C. Rubin, R. W. Schrauf, and D. L. Greenberg, "Belief and Recollection of Autobiographical Memories."
54. I. E. Hyman and J. Pentland, "The Role of Mental Imagery in the Creation of False Childhood Memories."
55. Elizabeth Parker, Larry Cahill, and James McGaugh, "A Case of Unusual Autobiographical Remembering."
56. Cited in Samiha Shafy, "An Infinite Loop in the Brain."
57. Vladimir Nabokov, *Speak, Memory*, 76-77.
58. Barbour, *Conscience*, 44.
59. "The White Album," in Joan Didion, *The White Album*, 13.
60. Russell Baker, "Life with Mother," 38.
61. Nabokov, *Speak, Memory*, 27.
62. Jean-Paul Sartre, *Nausea*, 39.
63. Gornick, *Situation*, 17.
64. Prologue in E. B. White, *Essays of E. B. White*.
65. Hoagland, "What I Think."
66. Nancy Mairs, *Carnal Acts*, 7.
67. Montaigne, *Complete Essays*, 273.
68. Carl H. Klaus, *The Made-Up Self: Impersonation in the Personal Essay*, 21.
69. J. M. Coetzee, *Doubling the Point: Essays and Interviews*, 17-18.
70. Ben Yagoda, *Memoir: A History*, 110.
71. Hayden White, *Metahistory: The Historical Imagination in Nineteenth-Century Europe*, 1973.
72. Noël Carroll, "Interpretation, History and Narrative."
73. Tobias Wolff, *Old School*, 52-53.
74. Carroll, "Interpretation," 161.
75. Lopate, *To Show and to Tell*, 115.
76. Paul John Eakin, *Fictions in Autobiography: Studies in the Art of Self-Invention*, 177.
77. Cited in Raksha Vasudevan, "What the World Demands of You: The Millions Interviews Margo Jefferson."
78. Cited in Alicia Anstead, "The Writer Interview: Margo Jefferson."
79. Geoff Dyer, "The Art of Nonfiction No. 6."
80. G. Thomas Couser, *Memoir: An Introduction*, 33-53.
81. Stacie Friend, "Fiction as a Genre" is an excellent extended discussion of this. Friend emphasizes that what counts as nonfiction or fiction changes over time, as conventions shift (e.g., Tacitus's second-century works on the history of the Roman Empire counted as nonfiction at the time but if published today might count as fiction) and suggests that

the distinction between nonfiction and fiction isn't binary: some works might fall into both genres (just as the same person can be both conformist and nonconformist in different respects).

82. See Hillary Brenhouse, "Porochista Khakpour: Bodily Chaos."
83. Dyer, "The Art of Nonfiction No. 6."
84. Bill Morris, "When We Aspire to Write Like Ourselves: A Conversation with Carl H. Klaus."
85. Lejeune, *On Autobiography*, 131–32.
86. Adam Gopnik, "Little Henry, Happy at Last: The Peculiar Radiance of James's Late Memoirs."

Chapter Three

1. *Publisher's Weekly*, review of John D'Agata's *About a Mountain*.
2. John D'Agata and Jim Fingal, *The Lifespan of a Fact*, 105.
3. D'Agata and Fingal, 108.
4. D'Agata and Fingal, 109.
5. D'Agata and Fingal, 109.
6. D'Agata and Fingal, 109, 110.
7. D'Agata said in an interview about *The Lifespan of a Fact* (Jared Levy, "John D'Agata: In Check") that he didn't intend his stated position in the book to be taken straight: "(W)hen I'm called an asshole by a major media outlet, or a jerk or a liar or a hack or a whatever, it's very clear that these reviewers are reading the persona in that book as me: that I'm behind that figure. Which, for me, proves how we approach nonfiction at a much different level than we approach fiction or poetry or drama: that there's almost no room for metaphor. We expect the 'I' in any nonfiction text to be an autobiographical 'I' when there is a history in the essay of the 'I' being a persona."
8. See Benjamin Wilkomirski, *Fragments: Memories of a Wartime Childhood*, and James Frey, *A Million Little Pieces*, discussed further below.
9. "On Keeping A Notebook," in Didion, *Slouching*, 134.
10. Lamarque, *The Philosophy of Literature*, provides a helpful introduction to the philosophical debate, on which I draw here.
11. Malcolm Bowie, *Proust among the Stars*, 314.
12. Richard Gaskin, *Language, Truth and Literature: A Defense of Literary Humanism*, is a recent defense of the propositional theory.
13. Cited in Joe Fassler, "When People—and Characters—Surprise You."
14. Hilary Putnam, "Literature, Science and Reflection," 488.
15. The position I argue for here is a version of what's known as "cognitivism" in the philosophy of literature. As John Gibson defines that term, cognitivists hold that literature "can be seen as in some significant respect *informative* of extra-textual reality": it corresponds in some way with the world (John Gibson, *Fiction and the Weave of Life*,

82). Gibson, like me, argues that literary works are informative in this way, but not by virtue of transmitting propositional knowledge.

16. Vivian Gornick, "Truth in Personal Narrative," 7–8.

17. "On Keeping A Notebook," in Didion, *Slouching*, 134.

18. Cited in Pascal, *Design and Truth*, 68.

19. See Tracy Kidder and Richard Todd, *Good Prose: The Art of Nonfiction*, 89.

20. John Barth, *Lost in the Funhouse*, 186.

21. Pam Houston, "Corn Maze."

22. Lopate, *To Show and to Tell*, 80–81.

23. Lopate, 80–81.

24. Lamarque, "Literature and Truth," 380.

25. Carmen Maria Machado, *In the Dream House*, 201–4. See also Hope Reese, "'I Was Trapped Forever in This Present Tense': Carmen Maria Machado on Surviving Abuse."

26. Timothy Dow Adams, *Telling Lies in Modern American Autobiography*, 34.

27. I'm grateful to Oded Na'aman for suggesting this point.

28. Mark Doty, "Return to Sender," 157.

29. Dow Adams, *Telling Lies*, 34, 45.

30. Leslie Stephen, *Hours in a Library*, 237.

31. Montaigne *Complete Essays*, 24.

32. Dow Adams, *Telling Lies*, 14–15.

33. David Lazar, "An Introduction to Truth," x.

34. Igor Primoratz, "Lying and the 'Methods of Ethics,'" 54.

35. Francis Hutcheson, *A System of Moral Philosophy in Three Books*, 31.

36. James B. Stewart, *Tangled Webs: How False Statements Are Undermining America*.

37. W. D. Ross, *The Right and the Good*, 21.

38. I discuss the wrong of betrayal at greater length in the following chapter.

39. Colin O'Neill, "Lying, Trust and Gratitude."

40. See Immanuel Kant, "On a Supposed Right to Lie Because of Philanthropic Concerns."

41. Harry Frankfurt, "On Truth, Lies, and Bullshit."

42. Paul Faulkner, "What Is Wrong with Lying?"

43. Immanuel Kant, *Religion within the Bounds of Bare Reason*, 40.

44. Alasdair MacIntyre, "Truthfulness, Lies and Moral Philosophers: What Can We Learn from Mill and Kant?," 315.

45. Sissela Bok, *Lying: Moral Choice in Public and Private Life*, 73–89.

46. Bok, 30–31.

47. Robert Solomon, "Self, Deception, and Self-Deception in Philosophy."

48. A similar argument about *self*-deception appears in Amelie Oksenberg Rorty, "User-Friendly Self-Deception."

49. William Blake, "Auguries of Innocence."
50. Cited in Madeleine Schwartz, interview with Vivian Gornick, *Believer*.
51. Anonymous, in Anonymous, Sonya Huber, and Neil Stuckey-French, "As a Matter of Fact: A Roundtable Discussion about Anonymous' 'The Facts of the Matter' and Truth and Craft in Nonfiction."
52. Karr, *Art of Memoir*, 11.
53. Anonymous, "The Facts of the Matter."
54. Anonymous, Huber, and Stuckey-French, "As a Matter of Fact."
55. Anonymous, Huber, and Stuckey-French, "As a Matter of Fact."
56. Sarah Einstein, "'The Self-*ish* Genre': Questions of Authorial Selfhood and Ethics in First Person Creative Nonfiction."
57. Gornick, "Truth in Personal Narrative," 10.
58. Gornick, 8.
59. Karr, *Art of Memoir*, 10.
60. Anonymous, Huber, and Stuckey-French, "As a Matter of Fact."
61. Couser, *Memoir*, 82.
62. Rigoberta Menchú, *I, Rigoberta Menchú: An Indian Woman in Guatemala*. For an account of the scandal, see Larry Rohter, "Tarnished Laureate: A Special Report; Nobel Winner Finds Her Story Challenged."
63. Bernard Cooper, "Marketing Memory," 111.
64. Irving discusses his Howard Hughes hoax in Clifford Irving, *The Hoax: A Memoir*.
65. Wilkomirski, *Fragments*. Dössekker's book was at first highly acclaimed, and then charged by a Swiss journalist of being a hoax, three years after its publication. Dössekker's literary agency commissioned a historian to investigate further, and the fraud was confirmed. Dössekker, however, continues to protest his innocence. Some have suggested that he genuinely believes his story, as a result of false memories caused by his own actual childhood trauma. If his false claims were unintentional in this way, that would complicate the classing of the book as a hoax per se.
66. Marty Angelo Ministries, Inc., "Christian Prison Evangelist Sides with Oprah Winfrey over 'A Million Little Pieces' Controversy."
67. Andrew Hudgins, "An Autobiographer's Lies."
68. Harry Crews, *A Childhood: The Biography of a Place*, cited in Karr, *Art of Memoir*, 19.
69. Lia Purpura, "On Coming Back as a Buzzard."
70. Einstein, "'The Self-*ish* Genre.'"
71. Henry Adams, *The Education of Henry Adams*, 43.
72. Stendhal, *The Life of Henri Brulard*, 226.
73. Montaigne, *Complete Essays*, 76.
74. Mary McCarthy, *Memories of a Catholic Girlhood*.
75. Beth Kephart, *Handling the Truth: On the Writing of Memoir*.
76. Kephart, 89; Couser, *Memoir*, 74.

77. Oscar Wilde, "The Decay of Lying.".

78. Gibson, *Weave of Life*, 50. Although Gibson may have simply forgotten that literary memoir exists—a common affliction among philosophers of literature—his claim here implies that memoir, by virtue of aiming for truth, is, other things equal, less literary than fiction. That's highly debatable.

79. D'Agata and Fingal, *Lifespan*, 109.

80. Emily Dickinson, *Hope Is the Thing with Feathers: The Complete Poems of Emily Dickinson*, 66.

81. See, inter alia, Noël Carroll, *Art in Three Dimensions*, and Martha Nussbaum, *Love's Knowledge: Essays on Philosophy and Literature*.

82. Nietzsche, *Will to Power*, n962.

83. See Bernard Williams, "Persons, Character and Morality," 18.

84. On the relationship between moral and aesthetic defects, see Noël Carroll, "Moderate Moralism versus Moderate Autonomism."

85. Stefan Maechler, *The Wilkomirski Affair: A Study in Biographical Truth*, 281.

86. Froma Zeitlin, "New Soundings in Holocaust Literature: A Surplus of Memory," 177.

87. Cited in Mendelsohn, "But Enough about Me."

88. Pascal, *Design and Truth*, 92.

89. Judith Barrington, *Writing the Memoir: From Truth to Art*, 28.

90. Charles Eames, design drawings and statement for "What Is Design?" exhibition at the Louvre.

91. The entry on Carl Sandburg in *The Robert Frost Encyclopedia* notes that "it was toward Sandburg that Frost targeted his famous line comparing free verse to playing tennis without a net" (Nancy Lewis Tuten and John Zubizarreta, *The Robert Frost Encyclopedia*, 318).

92. See Bella M. DePaulo, "Lying in Social Psychology."

93. James Patterson and Peter Kim, *The Day America Told the Truth*.

94. See DePaulo, "Lying."

95. See Richard H. Gramzow and Greg Willard, "Exaggerating Current and Past Performance: Motivated Self-Enhancement versus Reconstructive Memory."

96. Karr, *Art of Memoir*, xviii.

97. Marcel Eck, *Lies and Truth*, 160.

Chapter Four

1. Cited in Mendelsohn, "But Enough about Me."

2. One domain of wrongdoing toward subjects of memoir that I don't discuss in this chapter concerns the actions of ghostwriters of "autobiographies" to their subjects. Chapter 3 of Couser, *Vulnerable Subjects*, is a helpful discussion of the ethical issues that arise there.

    I also focus exclusively on wrongs to subjects, rather than to third parties who are connected to them or to the author. Memoirists are sometimes criticized for writing material about their own lives that will, for instance, render their young children vulnerable. Kathryn Harrison's memoir about her sexual relationship with her father was attacked on this ground. The child psychiatrist and author Robert Coles retracted the blurb he'd written for *The Kiss* when he discovered that Harrison had children of her own who would have to deal with the public scandal the book was likely to—and did—cause. (See Paul John Eakin, *How Our Lives Become Stories: Making Selves*, 152.) Similarly, memoirists are sometimes criticized for perpetuating harmful stereotypes about those who share their cultural or social identities. Much of what I say in this chapter is relevant to evaluating these questions about duties to third parties, but other aspects of them lie outside its scope.

3. Joel Feinberg, *Harm to Others: The Moral Limits of the Criminal Law*.
4. Feinberg, 45.
5. Feinberg, 37.
6. Michael Sandel, *Justice: What's the Right Thing to Do?*, 73–74.
7. Feinberg, *Harm to Others*, 187–217.
8. Bok, *Lying*, 72.
9. Edmund Gosse, *Father and Son: A Study of Two Temperaments*, 40.
10. Doty, "Return to Sender."
11. Karr, *Art of Memoir*, 115.
12. Rachel Cusk, *A Life's Work*; Rachel Cusk, *Aftermath: On Marriage and Separation*.
13. Charles Fried, "Privacy."
14. James Rachels, "Why Privacy Is Important."
15. Ruth Gavison, "Privacy and the Limits of Law."
16. Sissela Bok, *Secrets: On the Ethics of Concealment and Revelation*, 21.
17. See, e.g., Catherine MacKinnon, *Toward a Feminist Theory of the State*.
18. Patricia Hampl, "Other People's Secrets."
19. Hampl, 211.
20. Hampl, 213.
21. Hampl, 211.
22. On the ethics of journalism, see Christopher Meyers, ed., *Journalism Ethics: A Philosophical Approach*, the *New York Times'* Ethical Journalism Handbook (available at https://www.nytimes.com/editorial-stan dards/ethical-journalism.html), and the Society of Professional Journalists' Code of Ethics (available at https://www.spj.org/ethicscode .asp).
23. Clifford G. Christians, "The Ethics of Privacy," 210.
24. See Frederick Schauer, "Can Public Figures Have Private Lives?"
25. See Raja Halwani, "Outing and Virtue Ethics."
26. Bill Roorbach, *Writing Life Stories: How to Make Memories into Memoirs, Ideas into Essays and Life into Literature*, 79.
27. Hampl, "Secrets," 220.

28. On exploitation, see Alan Wertheimer, *Exploitation*.
29. Dan Bar-On, "Ethical Issues in Biographical Interviews and Analysis," 20.
30. Shafer-Landau, *The Fundamentals of Ethics*, 169–70.
31. Janet Malcolm, *The Journalist and the Murderer*, 4.
32. Claudia Mills, "Friendship, Fiction and Memoir: Trust and Betrayal in Writing from One's Own Life."
33. Couser offers a sensitive discussion of this case in Couser, *Vulnerable Subjects*, 56–73.
34. Michael Dorris, *Paper Trail: Essays*, 114.
35. Michael Dorris, *The Broken Cord*, 167.
36. Cited in Micah Flores, "Writer Leslie Jamison on Telling Other People's Stories."
37. Abigail Bereola, "A Reckoning Is Different than a Tell-All: An Interview with Kiese Laymon."
38. Maxine Hong Kingston, *Woman Warrior: Memoirs of a Girlhood among Ghosts*, 3.
39. Annette Baier, "Trust and Anti-Trust."
40. Carolyn McLeod, *Self-Trust and Reproductive Autonomy*.
41. Baier, "Trust," 243.
42. Malcolm, *Journalist*, 3–4.
43. Mills, "Friendship, Fiction and Memoir," 105.
44. Doty, "Return to Sender," 156.
45. Hampl, "Secrets," 228.
46. Ruthellen Josselson, "On Writing Other People's Lives: Self-Analytic Reflections of a Narrative Researcher," 62.
47. Cited in Malcolm, *Journalist*, 32–33.
48. Two helpful discussions of the ethics of cultural appropriation are Thomas Hurka, "Should Whites Write about Minorities?," and James O. Young and Susan Haley, "Nothing Comes from Nowhere: Reflections on Cultural Appropriation as the Representation of Other Cultures."
49. Lenore Keeshig-Tobias, "The Magic of Others," 176.
50. Keeshig-Tobias, 177.
51. Ijeoma Oluo, *So You Want to Talk about Race*, 150–51.
52. Phyllis Rose, "Whose Truth?," 35–36.
53. See Aristotle, *Nicomachean Ethics*.
54. Pirkko Lauslahti Graves, "Narrating a Psychoanalytic Case Study," 76.
55. Terri Apter, "Expert Witness: Who Controls the Psychologist's Narrative?," 36.
56. Josselson, "On Writing Other People's Lives," 67.
57. See George Pitcher, "The Misfortunes of the Dead," for a defense of the possibility of posthumous harm and Douglas Portmore, "Desire Fulfillment and Posthumous Harm," for a critique.
58. Rousseau, *Confessions*, 171.

59. William Faulkner, "The Art of Fiction No. 12."

60. Felicia Ackerman, "Imaginary Gardens and Real Toads: On the Ethics of Basing Fiction on Actual People," 144.

61. Calvin Trillin, *Family Man*, 24.

62. Cited in Daniel Mendelsohn, "What's More Appealing: Eight Seasons of 'Suits' or Six Volumes of Karl Ove Knausgaard?"

63. Mendelsohn.

64. Annie Dillard, "To Fashion a Text: Coming of Age in Pittsburgh," 171.

65. Laurie Hertzel, "But Will They Love Me When It's Done? Writing about Family in Memoir."

66. Cited in Hertzel.

67. Karr, *Art of Memoir*, 118.

68. Hertzel, "But Will They Love Me."

69. Rose, "Whose Truth?," 40.

70. See Karr, *Art of Memoir*, 119.

71. Robert Anthony Siegel, "The Ethics of Memoir: An Author Interviews His Mother."

72. Doty, "Return to Sender," 161.

73. Doty, 163.

Chapter Five

1. Cited in Yagoda, *Memoir: A History*, 134. Bell's *Autobiographical Notes* were published after his death, in 1892.

2. Henry James, *Notes of a Son and Brother*, 370.

3. Cited in Leigh Stein, "The Rumpus Interview with Melissa Febos."

4. Gass, "The Art of Self."

5. Jean M. Twenge et al., "Egos Inflating over Time: A Cross-Temporal Meta-Analysis of the Narcissistic Personality Inventory."

6. Jean M. Twenge et al., "Changes in Pronoun Use in American Books and the Rise of Individualism, 1960–2008."

7. Montaigne, *Complete Essays*, 2.

8. Barbour, "Conscience," 11.

9. C. S. Lewis, *Surprised by Joy: The Shape of My Early Life*, 233.

10. Michelle Barrow, "It Happened to Me: My Gynecologist Found a Ball of Cat Hair in My Vagina." The link to this article is expired, but see Maureen O'Connor, "She Had a Cat Hair Ball in Her Vagina—or Did She?"

11. Ralph Waldo Emerson, "Montaigne; or, The Skeptic," 335.

12. Herbert Spencer, *An Autobiography*, 7.

13. Margaret Cavendish, "A True Relation of My Birth, Breeding and Life," 63.

14. William H. Gass, "The Essential Henry Miller, according to Norman Mailer."

15. Virginia Woolf, "The Decay of Essay Writing."
16. Charles Baxter, "Shame and Forgetting in the Information Age," 151.
17. Montaigne, *Complete Essays*, 611.
18. Cooper, "Marketing Memory," 107.
19. Rebecca van Laer, "Just Admit It, You Wrote a Memoir."
20. Alex Clark, "Drawn from Life: Why Have Novelists Stopped Making Things Up?"
21. Melissa Febos and Resham Mantri, "On Facing Your History through Your Art."
22. Kristin Dombek, *The Selfishness of Others: An Essay on the Fear of Narcissism.*
23. Pascal, *Design and Truth*, 187.
24. Cited in Raksha Vasudevan, "Leslie Jamison Is Hauling Out Her Emotional Baggage."
25. J. Antony Lukas, "The Memoir Revolution," 19.
26. Malcolm, *Journalist*, 11.
27. Cited in Pascal, *Design and Truth*, 67.
28. Bernard Williams, *Ethics and the Limits of Philosophy*, 182.
29. Martin Singer, "On Duties to Oneself."
30. Paul Schofield, "On the Existence of Duties to the Self (and Their Significance for Moral Philosophy)."
31. Laura Bennett, "The First-Person Industrial Complex."
32. Alice Kaplan, "Lady of the Lake," 99.
33. Cooper, "Marketing Memory," 112.
34. Cited in Mendelsohn, "But Enough about Me."
35. Virginia Woolf, *To the Lighthouse*, 44.
36. Karl Ove Knausgaard, *My Struggle*, book 2, 535.
37. Cited in Meredith Maran, *Why We Write about Ourselves*, 234–35.
38. Martin, *Memoir Ethics*, 14–15.
39. Jeffrey Blustein, *The Moral Demands of Memory*, 328–37.
40. Jean Starobinski, *Montaigne in Motion*, 35.
41. Nabokov, *Speak, Memory*, 297.
42. Memoirists memorialize places and periods too. Nabokov wrote his intensely elegiac *Speak, Memory* not just to preserve himself but also to recapture the treasured and extinguished world of his childhood before the Russian revolution.
43. Blustein (*Moral Demands*, 240–300) argues that we have a *moral duty* to remember the dear departed for this reason, but you can reject that idea while still agreeing that it's a valuable thing to do.
44. James Pennebaker and Joshua Smyth, *Opening Up by Writing It Down: How Expressive Writing Improves Health and Eases Emotional Pain*, ix.
45. Cited in Pennebaker and Smyth, 39.
46. See J. W. Schooler and T. Y. Engstler-Schooler, "Verbal Overshadowing of Visual Memories: Some Things Are Better Left Unsaid."

47. See Pennebaker and Smyth, *Opening Up*, 29.

48. Woolf, *Moments*, 72.

49. John Berger, *A Fortunate Man: The Story of a Country Doctor*, 158–59.

50. Cited in Monet Patrice Thomas, "The Emotion of the Moment: Talking with Terese Marie Mailhot."

51. Febos and Mantri, "On Facing Your History."

52. Cited in Jennifer Traig, ed., *The Autobiographer's Handbook: The 826 National Guide to Writing Your Memoir*, 155.

53. Woolf, *Moments*, 108.

54. Woolf, 81.

55. Kima Jones, "The Rumpus Interview with Jesmyn Ward."

56. The following discussion draws on Blustein, *Moral Demands*, 57–109.

57. Saul Friedlander, *When Memory Comes*, 114.

58. Linette F. Brugmans, ed., *The Correspondence of Andre Gide and Edmund Gosse, 1904–1928*, 191.

59. Maran, *Why We Write*, 236–37.

60. Cited in Ashley Patronyak, "An Interview with Margo Jefferson."

61. Cited in Mendelsohn, "But Enough about Me."

62. Henry David Thoreau, *Walden*, 135.

63. Ralph Waldo Emerson, *The American Scholar, Self-Reliance, Compensation*, 53, 69.

64. Cited in Amy Gall, "Which Story Will You Tell? A Q&A with Alexander Chee."

65. Simon Feldman, *Against Authenticity: Why You Shouldn't Be Yourself*.

66. See Andrea C. Westlund, "Who Do We Think We Are?," for an excellent discussion of these links between self-narration and self-understanding. Westlund makes the important point that self-understanding via self-narration isn't a static process, but often results in self-transformation. A related idea that I set aside here is that autobiographical writing—or nonwritten self-narration—is a way of *constructing* the self rather than discovering it. Gusdorf writes, for instance: "'To create and in creating to be created,' ... ought to be the motto of autobiography ... [Autobiography] ordinarily fancies that it is restoring this content as it was, but in giving his own narrative, the man is forever adding himself to himself" (Gusdorf, "Conditions and Limits," 44–45). This connects with the narrative conception of the self discussed in chapter 2. Much of what Nehamas writes in *The Art of Living* is relevant and illuminating on this issue, though he focuses exclusively on a small subset of philosophers whom he takes to have successfully "self-fashioned" themselves through their personal-cum-philosophical writing.

67. Timothy D. Wilson and Elizabeth W. Dunn, "Self-Knowledge: Its Limits, Value, and Potential for Improvement."

68. See Galen Strawson, "Against Narrativity," for a detraction.

69. For summaries of recent work in psychology, see Julie Beck, "Life's Stories," and Benedict Carey, "This Is Your Life (and How You Tell It)."

An important early work in this area is Dan P. McAdams, *The Stories We Live By*. For a discussion of recent work in philosophy, see Helena de Bres, "Narrative and Meaning in Life"; what follows draws on that article.

70. Doty, "Return to Sender," 163.
71. Lopate, *To Show and to Tell*, 78–79.
72. Julian Barnes, *Nothing to Be Frightened Of*, 185–86.
73. Paul John Eakin, *Touching the World: Reference in Autobiography*, 46.
74. Eakin, 51.
75. Didion, *The White Album*, 48.
76. See Arthur Danto, *Analytical Philosophy of History*, 155.
77. Susan Wolf, *Meaning in Life and Why It Matters*, 26.

Bibliography

Ackerman, Felicia. "Imaginary Gardens and Real Toads: On the Ethics of Basing Fiction on Actual People." *Midwest Studies in Philosophy* 16: *Philosophy and the Arts* (South Bend, IN: University of Notre Dame Press, 1991): 142–55.

Adams, Henry. *The Education of Henry Adams.* 1906. Boston: Houghton Mifflin, 1918.

Addis, Donna Rose, Alana T. Wong, and Daniel L. Schacter. "Remembering the Past and Imagining the Future: Common and Distinct Neural Substrates during Event Construction and Elaboration." *Neuropsychologia* 45, no. 7 (April 2007): 1363–77.

Anderson, Sherwood. *Sherwood Anderson's Memoirs.* Chapel Hill: University of North Carolina Press, 1969.

Anonymous. "The Facts of the Matter." *TriQuarterly*, October 22, 2012, https://www.triquarterly.org/craft-essays/facts-matter.

Anonymous, Sonya Huber, and Neil Stuckey-French. "As a Matter of Fact: A Roundtable Discussion about Anonymous' 'The Facts of the Matter' and Truth and Craft in Nonfiction." *Brevity*, November 5, 2012, https://brevity.wordpress.com/2012/11/05/as-a-matter-of-fact-a-roundtable-discussion-about-anonymous-the-facts-of-the-matter-and-truth-and-craft-in-nonfiction/.

Anstead, Alicia. "The Writer Interview: Margo Jefferson." *Writer*, October 21, 2018, https://www.writermag.com/writing-inspiration/author-interviews/margo-jefferson/.

Apter, Terri. "Expert Witness: Who Controls the Psychologist's Narrative?" In *Ethics and Process in the Narrative Study of Lives*, edited by Ruthellen Josselson, 22–44. Thousand Oaks, CA: Sage Publications, 1996.

Aristotle. *Nicomachean Ethics.* 340 BC. Cambridge: Cambridge University Press, 2014.

Augustine. *Confessions.* 397–400 AD. Oxford: Oxford University Press, 2009.

Baier, Annette. "Trust and Anti-Trust." *Ethics* 96, no. 2 (January 1986): 231–60.

Baier, Kathi. "Lying and Self-Deception." In *The Oxford Handbook of Lying*, edited by Jorg Meibauer, 203–13. Oxford: Oxford University Press, 2018.

Baker, Russell. "Life with Mother." In *Inventing the Truth: The Art and Craft of Memoir*, edited by William Zinsser, 23–40. Boston: Mariner Books, 1998.

Barbour, John D. *The Conscience of the Autobiographer: Ethical and Religious Dimensions of Autobiography*. London: Palgrave Macmillan, 1992.

Barnes, Julian. *Nothing to Be Frightened Of*. New York: Knopf, 2008.

Bar-On, Dan. "Ethical Issues in Biographical Interviews and Analysis." In *Ethics and Process in the Narrative Study of Lives*, edited by Ruthellen Josselson, 9–21. Thousand Oaks, CA: Sage Publications, 1996.

Barresi, John, and Raymond Martin. "History as Prologue: Western Theories of the Self." In *The Oxford Handbook of the Self*, edited by Shaun Gallagher, 33–56. Oxford: Oxford University Press, 2011.

Barrington, Judith. *Writing the Memoir: From Truth to Art*. 4th ed. Portland, OR: Eighth Mountain Press, 2002.

Barrow, Michelle. "It Happened to Me: My Gynecologist Found a Ball of Cat Hair in My Vagina." *xoJane*, 2015, link expired.

Barth, John. *Lost in the Funhouse*. New York: Bantam Books, 1969.

Barthes, Roland. *Roland Barthes by Roland Barthes*. 1977. New York: Hill and Wang, 2010.

Baxter, Charles. "Shame and Forgetting in the Information Age." In *The Business of Memory: The Art of Remembering in an Age of Forgetting*, edited by Charles Baxter, 141–57. Minneapolis: Graywolf Press, 1999.

Bechdel, Alison. *Fun Home*. Boston: Houghton Mifflin, 2006.

Beck, Julie. "Life's Stories." *Atlantic*, August 10, 2015, https://www.theatlantic.com/health/archive/2015/08/life-stories-narrative-psychology-redemption-mental-health/400796/.

Begg, I. M., A. Anas, and S. Farinacci. "Dissociation of Processes in Belief: Source Recollection, Statement Familiarity, and the Illusion of Truth." *Journal of Experimental Psychology: General* 121, no. 4 (December 1992): 446–58.

Bennett, Laura. "The First-Person Industrial Complex." *Slate*, September 14, 2015, http://www.slate.com/articles/life/technology/2015/09/the_first_person_industrial_complex_how_the_harrowing_personal_essay_took.html.

Bereola, Abigail. "A Reckoning Is Different than a Tell-All: An Interview with Kiese Laymon." *Paris Review*, October 18, 2018, https://www.theparisreview.org/blog/2018/10/18/a-reckoning-is-different-than-a-tell-all-an-interview-with-kiese-laymon/.

Berger, John. *A Fortunate Man: The Story of a Country Doctor*. New York: Knopf Doubleday, 2011.

Berkeley, Bishop. *A Treatise Concerning the Principles of Human Knowledge*. 1710. Oxford: Oxford University Press, 1998.

Blackburn, Simon. *Being Good: A Short Introduction to Ethics*. Oxford: Oxford University Press, 2003.

Blake, William. "Auguries of Innocence." In *Poets of the English Language: Blake to Poe*, edited by Norman Holmes Pearson and Wystan Hugh Auden. New York: Viking Press, 1950.

Blustein, Jeffrey. *The Moral Demands of Memory*. Cambridge: Cambridge University Press, 2008.

Bok, Sissela. *Lying: Moral Choice in Public and Private Life*. Updated ed. New York: Pantheon Books, 1978.

Bok, Sissela. *Secrets: On the Ethics of Concealment and Revelation*. New York: Vintage, 1989.

Bowie, Malcolm. *Proust among the Stars*. New York: Columbia University Press, 2000.

Brenhouse, Hillary. "Porochista Khakpour: Bodily Chaos." *Guernica*, June 13, 2018, https://www.guernicamag.com/porochista-khakpour-bodily-chaos/.

Brock, Stuart, and Edwin Mares. *Realism and Anti-Realism*. Montreal: McGill-Queens University Press, 2007.

Brugmans, Linette F., ed. *The Correspondence of Andre Gide and Edmund Gosse, 1904–1928*. London: Peter Owen Publishers, 1960.

Carey, Benedict. "This Is Your Life (and How You Tell It)." *New York Times*, May 22, 2007, https://www.nytimes.com/2007/05/22/health/psychology/22narr.html.

Carroll, Noël. *Art in Three Dimensions*. Oxford: Oxford University Press, 2012.

Carroll, Noël. "Interpretation, History and Narrative." *Monist* 73, no. 2 (April 1990): 134–66.

Carroll, Noël. "Moderate Moralism versus Moderate Autonomism." *British Journal of Aesthetics* 38, no. 4 (October 1998).

Cassam, Quassim. *Self-Knowledge for Humans*. Oxford: Oxford University Press, 2017.

Cavendish, Margaret. "A True Relation of My Birth, Breeding and Life." 1656. In *Paper Bodies: A Margaret Cavendish Reader*, edited by Sylvia Bowerbank and Sara Mendelson. Peterborough: Broadview Press, 2000.

Christians, Clifford G. "The Ethics of Privacy." In *Journalism Ethics: A Philosophical Approach*, edited by Christopher Meyers. Oxford: Oxford University Press, 2010.

Clark, Alex. "Drawn from Life: Why Have Novelists Stopped Making Things Up?" *Guardian*, June 23, 2018, https://www.theguardian.com/books/2018/jun/23/drawn-from-life-why-have-novelists-stopped-making-things-up.

Coetzee, J. M. *Doubling the Point: Essays and Interviews*. Cambridge, MA: Harvard University Press, 1992.

Cooper, Bernard. "Marketing Memory." In *The Business of Memory: The Art of Remembering in an Age of Forgetting*, edited by Charles Baxter, 106–15. Minneapolis: Graywolf Press, 1999.

Couser, G. Thomas. *Memoir: An Introduction*. Oxford: Oxford University Press, 2011.

Couser, G. Thomas. *Vulnerable Subjects: Ethics and Life Writing*. Ithaca, NY: Cornell University Press, 2003.

Cowley, Christopher, ed. *The Philosophy of Autobiography*. Chicago: University of Chicago, 2014.

Crews, Harry. *A Childhood: The Biography of a Place*. Athens: University of Georgia Press, 1995.

Curry, Martha Mulroy, ed. *The "Writer's Book."* Lanham, MD: Scarecrow Press, 1975.

Cusk, Rachel. *Aftermath: On Marriage and Separation*. London: Picador, 2013.

Cusk, Rachel. *A Life's Work*. London: Picador, 2003.

Cusk, Rachel. *Outline, Transit, Kudo* (series). London: Picador, 2016–18.

D'Agata, John, and Jim Fingal. *The Lifespan of a Fact*. New York: Norton, 2012.

Danto, Arthur. *Analytical Philosophy of History*. Cambridge: Cambridge University Press, 1965.

Danto, Arthur. "The Artworld." *Journal of Philosophy* 16, no. 19 (1964): 571–84.

Davies, David. *Aesthetics and Literature*. London: Continuum, 2007.

de Beauvoir, Simone. *Memoirs of a Dutiful Daughter*. 1958. New York: Harper, 2005.

de Bres, Helena. "Narrative and Meaning in Life." *Journal of Moral Philosophy* 15, no. 5 (October 2018): 545–71.

de Montaigne, Michel. *The Complete Essays of Montaigne*. 1580. Stanford, CA: Stanford University Press, 1958.

DePaulo, Bella M. "Lying in Social Psychology." In *The Oxford Handbook of Lying*, edited by Jorg Meibauer, 436–45. Oxford: Oxford University Press, 2018.

Descartes, René. *Meditations on First Philosophy*. 1641. Cambridge: Cambridge University Press, 2017.

Dickinson, Emily. *Hope Is the Thing with Feathers: The Complete Poems of Emily Dickinson*. Layton, UT: Gibbs Smith, 2019.

Didion, Joan. *Slouching towards Bethlehem*. 1968. New York: FSG, 2008.

Didion, Joan. *The White Album*. 1979. New York: FSG, 2009.

Dillard, Annie. "To Fashion a Text: Coming of Age in Pittsburgh." *Wilson Quarterly* 12, no. 1 (January 1988): 164–72.

Dombek, Kristin. *The Selfishness of Others: An Essay on the Fear of Narcissism*. New York: FSG, 2016.

Dorris, Michael. *The Broken Cord*. New York: Harper Perennial, 1990.

Dorris, Michael. *Paper Trail: Essays*. New York: Harper Collins, 1994.

Doty, Mark. *Firebird*. New York: Harper Perennial, 2000.

Doty, Mark. "Return to Sender." In *The Touchstone Anthology of Contempo-*

rary Creative Nonfiction, edited by Lex Williford and Michael Martone, 152–64. New York: Touchstone, 2007.

Dow Adams, Timothy. *Telling Lies in Modern American Autobiography.* Chapel Hill: University of North Carolina Press, 1990.

Dyer, Geoff. "The Art of Nonfiction No. 6." *Paris Review* 207 (Winter 2013), https://www.theparisreview.org/interviews/6282/the-art-of-nonfiction -no-6-geoff-dyer.

Eagleton, Terry. *How to Read Literature.* New Haven, CT: Yale University Press, 2013.

Eakin, Paul John. *Fictions in Autobiography: Studies in the Art of Self-Invention.* Princeton, NJ: Princeton University Press, 1985.

Eakin, Paul John. *How Our Lives Become Stories: Making Selves.* Ithaca, NY: Cornell University Press, 1999.

Eakin, Paul John. "Introduction: Mapping the Ethics of Life Writing." In *The Ethics of Life Writing*, ed. Paul John Eakin, 1–16. Ithaca, NY: Cornell University Press, 2004.

Eakin, Paul John. *Touching the World: Reference in Autobiography.* Princeton, NJ: Princeton University Press, 1992.

Eames, Charles. Design drawings and statement for "What Is Design?" exhibition at the Louvre, August 29, 1969. Eames Office LLC archives, Santa Monica, California.

Eck, Marcel. *Lies and Truth.* London: Macmillan, 1970.

Einstein, Sarah. "'The Self-*ish* Genre': Questions of Authorial Selfhood and Ethics in First Person Creative Nonfiction." *Assay: A Journal of Nonfiction Studies* 3, no. 1 (Fall 2016), https://www.assayjournal.com/sarah -einstein-the-self-ish-genre-questions-of-authorial-selfhood-and-ethics -in-8203first-person-creative-nonfiction-31.html.

Emerson, Ralph Waldo. *The American Scholar, Self-Reliance, Compensation.* New York: American Book Company, 1893.

Emerson, Ralph Waldo. "Montaigne; or, The Skeptic." In *The Annotated Emerson*, edited by David Mikics. Cambridge, MA: Harvard University Press, 2012.

Fassler, Joe. "When People—and Characters—Surprise You." *Atlantic*, November 3, 2015, https://www.theatlantic.com/entertainment/archive/2015 /11/by-heart-mary-gaitskill-tolstoy-anna-karenina/413740/.

Faulkner, Paul. "What Is Wrong with Lying?" *Philosophy and Phenomenological Research* 75, no. 3 (October 2007): 535–57.

Faulkner, William. "The Art of Fiction No. 12." *Paris Review* 12 (1956), https:// www.theparisreview.org/interviews/4954/the-art-of-fiction-no-12-will iam-faulkner.

Febos, Melissa, and Resham Mantri. "On Facing Your History through Your Art." *Creative Independent*, June 17, 2019, https://thecreativeindependent .com/people/writer-melissa-febos-on-facing-your-history-through-your -art/.

Feinberg, Joel. *Harm to Others (The Moral Limits of the Criminal Law)*. Oxford: Oxford University Press, 1987.

Feldman, Simon. *Against Authenticity: Why You Shouldn't Be Yourself*. Lanham, MD: Lexington Books, 2015.

Flores, Micah. "Writer Leslie Jamison on Telling Other People's Stories." *Daily Campus*, Southern Methodist University, November 29, 2018, https:// www.smudailycampus.com/ae/writer-leslie-jamison-on-telling-other -peoples-stories.

Frankfurt, Harry. "On Truth, Lies, and Bullshit." In *The Philosophy of Deception*, edited by Clancy Martin, 37–48. Oxford: Oxford University Press, 2009.

Frey, James. *A Million Little Pieces*. London: John Murray, 2003.

Fried, Charles. "Privacy." *Yale Law Journal* 77, no. 3 (January 1968): 475–93.

Friedlander, Saul. *When Memory Comes*. Madison: University of Wisconsin Press, 2003.

Friend, Stacie. "Fiction as a Genre." *Proceedings of the Aristotelian Society* 112, no. 2 (2012): 179–209.

Fussell, Paul. *Class: A Guide through the American Status System*. New York: Touchstone, 1992.

Gall, Amy. "Which Story Will You Tell? A Q&A with Alexander Chee." *Poets and Writers*, April 17, 2018, https://www.pw.org/content/which_story _will_you_tell_a_qa_with_alexander_chee.

Gaskin, Richard. *Language, Truth and Literature: A Defense of Literary Humanism*. Oxford: Oxford University Press, 2013.

Gass, William H. "The Art of Self." *Harper's Magazine*, May 1994; republished online December 7, 2017, https://harpers.org/2017/12/the-art-of-self/.

Gass, William H. "The Essential Henry Miller, according to Norman Mailer." *New York Times*, October 24, 1976, https://www.nytimes.com/1976/10 /24/archives/the-essential-henry-miller-according-to-norman-mailer .html.

Gavison, Ruth. "Privacy and the Limits of Law." *Yale Law Journal* 89, no. 3 (January 1980): 421–71.

Gibson, John. *Fiction and the Weave of Life*. Oxford: Oxford University Press, 2007.

Glanzberg, Michael. "Truth." In *The Stanford Encyclopedia of Philosophy*, edited by Edward N. Zalta (Fall 2018 ed.), https://plato.stanford.edu /entries/truth/.

Goethe, Friedrich Wilhelm. *Poetry and Truth, Goethes Werke*, edited E. Trunz. Hamburg: Christian Wegner Verlag, 1955.

Gopnik, Adam. "Little Henry, Happy at Last: The Peculiar Radiance of James's Late Memoirs." *New Yorker*, January 10, 2016, https://www.newyorker .com/magazine/2016/01/18/little-henry-happy-at-last.

Gornick, Vivian. *Fierce Attachments*. 1987. New York: FSG, 2005.

Gornick, Vivian. *The Situation and the Story: The Art of Personal Narrative*. New York: FSG, 2002.

Gornick, Vivian. "Truth in Personal Narrative." In *Truth in Nonfiction: Essays*, edited by David Lazar, 7–10. Iowa City: University of Iowa Press, 2008.

Gosse, Edmund. *Father and Son: A Study of Two Temperaments*. 1907. London: Penguin, 1986.

Gramzow, Richard H., and Greg Willard. "Exaggerating Current and Past Performance: Motivated Self-Enhancement versus Reconstructive Memory." *Personality and Social Psychology Bulletin* 32, no. 8 (August 2006): 1114–25.

Graves, Pirkko Lauslahti. "Narrating a Psychoanalytic Case Study." In *Ethics and Process in the Narrative Study of Lives*, edited by Ruthellen Josselson, 72–79. Thousand Oaks, CA: Sage Publications, 1996.

Gusdorf, Georges. "Conditions and Limits of Autobiography." 1956. In *Autobiography: Essays Theoretical and Critical*, edited by James Olney, 27–48. Princeton, NJ: Princeton University Press, 1980.

Haack, Susan. *Manifesto of a Passionate Moderate*. Chicago: University of Chicago Press, 1998.

Halwani, Raja. "Outing and Virtue Ethics." *Journal of Applied Philosophy* 19, no. 2 (December 2002).

Hampl, Patricia. "Other People's Secrets." In *I Could Tell You Stories: Sojourns in the Land of Memory*, 208–30. New York: Norton, 2000.

Harrison, Sophie. "Life before Loss." *Guardian*, August 29, 2008, https://www.theguardian.com/books/2008/aug/30/fiction4.

Hertzel, Laurie. "But Will They Love Me When It's Done? Writing about Family in Memoir." *TriQuarterly*, March 8, 2016, https://www.triquarterly.org/craft-essays/will-they-love-me-when-it%E2%80%99s-done-writing-about-family-memoir.

Hoagland, Edward. "What I Think, What I Am." *New York Times*, June 27, 1976, https://www.nytimes.com/1976/06/27/archives/essay-what-i-think-what-i-am-the-guest-word.html.

Holbrook, J. Isaiah. "Departures and Returns: A Conversation with Sarah M. Broom." *Rumpus*, August 7, 2019, https://therumpus.net/2019/08/the-rumpus-interview-with-sarah-m-broom/.

Houston, Pam. "Corn Maze." *Hunger Mountain*, accessed July 17, 2020, http://www.hungermtn.org/corn-maze/.

Hudgins, Andrew. "An Autobiographer's Lies." *American Scholar* 65, no. 4 (Autumn 1996): 541–53.

Hume, David. *Treatise of Human Nature*. 1739. Oxford: Clarendon Press, 1888.

Hurka, Thomas. "Should Whites Write about Minorities?" In *Principles: Short Essays on Ethics*, 2nd ed., 183–86. San Diego: Harcourt Brace, 1999.

Hutcheson, Francis. *A System of Moral Philosophy in Three Books*. 1755. Cambridge: Cambridge University Press, 2015.

Hyman, I. E., and J. Pentland. "The Role of Mental Imagery in the Creation of False Childhood Memories." *Journal of Memory and Language* 35, no. 2 (1996): 101–17.

Irving, Clifford. *The Hoax: A Memoir.* New York: Open Road Integrated Media, 2014.

James, Henry. *Notes of a Son and Brother.* New York: Scribner, 1914.

Jones, Kima. "The Rumpus Interview with Jesmyn Ward." *Rumpus,* October 10, 2013, https://therumpus.net/2013/10/the-rumpus-interview-with-je smyn-ward/.

Josselson, Ruthellen. "On Writing Other People's Lives: Self-Analytic Reflections of a Narrative Researcher." In *Ethics and Process in the Narrative Study of Lives,* edited by Ruthellen Josselson, 60–71. Thousand Oaks, CA: Sage Publications, 1996.

Kant, Immanuel. "On a Supposed Right to Lie Because of Philanthropic Concerns." In *Critique of Practice Reason and Other Writings in Moral Philosophy,* 346–50. Chicago: University of Chicago Press, 1949.

Kant, Immanuel. *Religion within the Bounds of Bare Reason.* 1793. Indianapolis: Hackett, 2009.

Kaplan, Alice. "Lady of the Lake." In *Tell Me True: Memoir, History and Writing a Life,* edited by Patricia Hampl and Elaine Tyler May, 98–114. Saint Paul: Minnesota Historical Society, 2011.

Karr, Mary. *The Art of Memoir.* New York: Harper Collins, 2015.

Keeshig-Tobias, Lenore. "The Magic of Others." In *Language in Her Eye: Views on Writing and Gender by Canadian Women Writing in English,* ed. Eleanor Wachtel, Sarah Sheard, and Libby Scheier, 173–77. Toronto: Coach House Press, 1990.

Kephart, Beth. *Handling the Truth: On the Writing of Memoir.* New York: Avery Publishing, 2013.

Khakpour, Porochista. *Sick: A Memoir.* New York: Harper Perennial, 2018.

Kidder, Tracy, and Richard Todd. *Good Prose: The Art of Nonfiction.* New York: Random House, 2013.

Kingston, Maxine Hong. *Woman Warrior: Memoirs of a Girlhood among Ghosts.* 1976. New York: Knopf, 2010.

Klaus, Carl H. *The Made-Up Self: Impersonation in the Personal Essay.* Iowa City: University of Iowa Press, 2010.

Knausgaard, Karl Ove. *My Struggle,* Books 1–6. New York: FSG, 2003–19.

Lamarque, Peter. "Literature and Truth." In *A Companion to the Philosophy of Literature,* edited by Garry L. Hagberg and Walter Jost, 367–84. Hoboken, NJ: John Wiley and Sons, 2015.

Lamarque, Peter. *The Philosophy of Literature.* Hoboken, NJ: Wiley, 2008.

Lamb, Charles. *Essays of Elia.* 1823. Iowa City: University of Iowa Press, 2003.

Langham, Jill. *How I Became the Dancing Queen of Palm Springs: A Memoire of Body, Mind and Spirit Transformation.* Scotts Valley, CA: CreateSpace, 2018.

Larson, Thomas. *The Memoir and the Memoirist: Reading and Writing Personal Narrative.* Athens, OH: Swallow Press, 2007.

Laymon, Kiese. *Heavy: An American Memoir.* New York: Scribner, 2018.

Lazar, David. "An Introduction to Truth." In *Truth in Nonfiction: Essays*, edited by David Lazar, ix–xiii. Iowa City: University of Iowa Press, 2008.

Lazar, David. "Occasional Desire: On the Essay and the Memoir." In *Truth in Nonfiction: Essays*, edited by David Lazar, 100–13. Iowa City: University of Iowa Press, 2008.

Lejeune, Philippe. *On Autobiography*, edited by Paul John Eakin. Minneapolis: University of Minnesota Press, 1989.

Levy, Jared. "John D'Agata: In Check." *Interview Magazine*, April 17, 2012, https://www.interviewmagazine.com/culture/john-dagata-the-lifespan -of-a-fact.

Lewis, C. S. *Surprised by Joy: The Shape of My Early Life*. Orlando, FL: Harcourt Brace Jovanovich, 1955.

Locke, John. *An Essay Concerning Human Understanding*. 2nd ed. 1694. London: Penguin, 1998.

Lopate, Phillip. *The Art of the Personal Essay: An Anthology from the Classical Era to the Present*. New York: Anchor, 1995.

Lopate, Phillip. *To Show and to Tell: The Craft of Literary Nonfiction*. New York: Free Press, 2013.

Lukas, J. Antony. "The Memoir Revolution." *Authors Guild Bulletin*, 1997.

Machado, Carmen Maria. *In the Dream House*. Minneapolis: Graywolf Press, 2019.

MacIntyre, Alasdair. "Truthfulness, Lies and Moral Philosophers: What Can We Learn from Mill and Kant?" The Tanner Lectures on Human Values, Princeton University, 1994, https://tannerlectures.utah.edu/lecture-lib rary.php.

MacKinnon, Catherine. *Toward a Feminist Theory of the State*. Cambridge, MA: Harvard University Press, 1989.

Maechler, Stefan. *The Wilkomirski Affair: A Study in Biographical Truth*. Translated by John E. Woods. New York: Schocken Books, 2001.

Mairs, Nancy. *Carnal Acts*. New York: Harper Collins, 1990.

Mairs, Nancy. "Trying Truth." In *Truth in Nonfiction: Essays*, edited by David Lazar, 89–92. Iowa City: University of Iowa Press, 2008.

Malcolm, Janet. *The Journalist and the Murderer*. New York: Vintage, 1990.

Maran, Meredith. *Why We Write about Ourselves*. New York: Plume, 2016.

Martin, Mike W. *Memoir Ethics: Good Lives and the Virtues*. Lanham, MD: Lexington Books, 2016.

Marty Angelo Ministries, Inc. "Christian Prison Evangelist Sides with Oprah Winfrey over 'A Million Little Pieces' Controversy," January 18, 2006, http://www.prweb.com/releases/2006/1/prweb334484.htm.

Maurois, André. *Olympio: The Life of Victor Hugo*. New York: Harper, 1956.

McAdams, Dan P. *The Stories We Live By*. New York: Guilford Press, 1993.

McCarthy, Mary. "The Art of Fiction, No. 27." In *Writers at Work: The Paris Review Interviews, Second Series*, edited by George Plimpton. New York: Viking Press, 1963.

McCarthy, Mary. *Memories of a Catholic Girlhood.* San Diego: Harcourt, 1957.

McCourt, Frank. *Angela's Ashes.* New York: Scribner, 1996.

McFarland, C., and M. Ross. "The Relation between Current Impressions and Memories of Self and Dating Partners." *Personality and Social Psychology Bulletin* 13 (June 1987): 228–38.

McLeod, Carolyn. *Self-Trust and Reproductive Autonomy.* Cambridge, MA: MIT Press, 2002.

Menchú, Rigoberta. *I, Rigoberta Menchú: An Indian Woman in Guatemala.* 2nd ed. London: Verso, 2010.

Mendelsohn, Daniel. "But Enough about Me." *New Yorker,* January 25, 2010, https://www.newyorker.com/magazine/2010/01/25/but-enough-about -me-2.

Mendelsohn, Daniel. "What's More Appealing: Eight Seasons of 'Suits' or Six Volumes of Karl Ove Knausgaard?" *New York Times,* September 24, 2018, https://www.nytimes.com/2018/09/24/books/review/karl-ove-knausga ard-my-struggle-book-six.html.

Meyers, Christopher, ed. *Journalism Ethics: A Philosophical Approach.* Oxford: Oxford University Press, 2010.

Miller, Brenda, and Suzanne Paola. *Tell It Slant.* 3rd ed. New York City: McGraw Hill, 2019.

Mills, Claudia. "Friendship, Fiction and Memoir: Trust and Betrayal in Writing from One's Own Life." In *The Ethics of Life Writing,* edited by Paul John Eakin, 101–20. Ithaca, NY: Cornell University Press, 2004.

Moore, Dinty W. *Crafting the Personal Essay: A Guide for Writing and Publishing Creative Nonfiction.* Cincinnati: Writer's Digest Books, 2010.

Morris, Bill. "When We Aspire to Write Like Ourselves: A Conversation with Carl H. Klaus." *Millions,* January 14, 2011, https://themillions.com/2011 /01/when-we-aspire-to-write-like-ourselves-a-conversation-with-carl-h -klaus.html.

Nabokov, Vladimir. *Speak, Memory.* 1951. New York: Vintage, 1989.

Nehamas, Alexander. *The Art of Living.* Berkeley: University of California Press, 1998.

Neisser, Ulric. *Cognition and Reality.* New York: W. H. Freeman, 1976.

Nietzsche, Friedrich. *Beyond Good and Evil: The Philosophy Classic.* 1886. Hoboken, NJ: Wiley, 2020.

Nietzsche, Friedrich. *The Genealogy of Morals.* 1887. Mineola, NY: Dover Publications, 2012.

Nietzsche, Friedrich. *The Will to Power.* 1901. Edinburgh: T. N. Foulis, 1913. https://www.gutenberg.org/files/52915/52915-h/52915-h.htm.

Nisbett, Richard E., and Timothy DeCamp Wilson. "Telling More than We Can Know: Verbal Reports on Mental Processes." *Psychological Review* 84, no. 3 (1977): 231–59.

Nisbitt, Richard E., and Lee Ross. *Human Inference: Strategies and Shortcomings of Social Judgment.* Upper Saddle River, NJ: Prentice Hall, 1980.

Nussbaum, Martha. *Love's Knowledge: Essays on Philosophy and Literature.* Oxford: Oxford University Press, 1990.

O'Connor, Maureen. "She Had a Cat Hair Ball in Her Vagina—or Did She?" *The Cut,* September 3, 2015, https://www.thecut.com/2015/09/she-had -cat-hair-in-her-vagina-or-did-she.html.

Oluo, Ijeoma. *So You Want to Talk about Race.* Berkeley, CA: Seal Press, 2019.

O'Neill, Colin. "Lying, Trust and Gratitude." *Philosophy & Public Affairs* 40, no. 4 (2012): 301–33.

Parker, Elizabeth, Larry Cahill, and James McGaugh. "A Case of Unusual Autobiographical Remembering." *Neurocase* 12, no. 1 (February 2006).

Pascal, Roy. *Design and Truth in Autobiography.* 1961. Abingdon-on-Thames: Routledge, 2015.

Patronyak, Ashley. "An Interview with Margo Jefferson." *Bookslut,* March 2016, http://www.bookslut.com/features/2016_03_021406.php.

Patterson, James, and Peter Kim. *The Day America Told the Truth.* Upper Saddle River, NJ: Prentice Hall, 1992.

Pennebaker, James, and Joshua Smyth. *Opening Up by Writing It Down: How Expressive Writing Improves Health and Eases Emotional Pain.* 3rd ed. New York: Guilford Press, 2016.

Pitcher, George. "The Misfortunes of the Dead." *American Philosophical Quarterly* 21, no. 2 (1984): 183–88.

Plato. *Phaedo.* 360 BC. Oxford: Oxford University Press, 2009.

Plotinus. *Ennead VI. 6–9.* 250 CE. Cambridge, MA: Harvard University Press, Loeb Classical Library, 1988.

Portmore, Douglas. "Desire Fulfillment and Posthumous Harm." *American Philosophical Quarterly* 44, no. 1 (2007): 27–38.

Primoratz, Igor. "Lying and the 'Methods of Ethics.'" *International Studies in Philosophy* 16, no. 3 (1984): 35–57.

Publisher's Weekly. Review of John D'Agata's *About a Mountain,* 2009, https://www.publishersweekly.com/978-0-393-06818-4.

Purpura, Lia. "On Coming Back as a Buzzard." *Orion,* August 24, 2009, https://orionmagazine.org/article/on-coming-back-as-a-buzzard/.

Putnam, Hilary. "Literature, Science and Reflection." *New Literary History* 7, no. 3 (1976): 483–91.

Rachels, James. "Why Privacy Is Important." *Philosophy & Public Affairs* 4, no. 4 (Summer 1975): 323–33.

Radtke, Kristen. *Imagine Wanting Only This.* New York: Pantheon, 2017.

Rees, Goronwy. *A Bundle of Sensations: Sketches in Autobiography.* London: MacMillan, 1961.

Reese, Hope. "'I Was Trapped Forever in This Present Tense': Carmen Maria Machado on Surviving Abuse." *Longreads,* November 2019, https://long reads.com/2019/11/07/interview-with-carmen-maria-machado/.

Rohter, Larry. "Tarnished Laureate: A Special Report; Nobel Winner Finds Her Story Challenged." *New York Times,* December 15, 1998, https://

www.nytimes.com/1998/12/15/world/tarnished-laureate-a-special-re
port-nobel-winner-finds-her-story-challenged.html.

Roorbach, Bill. *Writing Life Stories: How to Make Memories into Memoirs,
Ideas into Essays and Life into Literature.* Cincinnati: Writer's Digest
Books, 2008.

Rorty, Amelie Oksenberg. "User-Friendly Self-Deception." *Philosophy* 69, no.
268 (April 1994): 211–28.

Rose, Phyllis. "Whose Truth?" In *Truth in Nonfiction: Essays,* edited by David
Lazar, 31–41. Iowa City: University of Iowa Press, 2008.

Ross, Michael, and Anne E. Wilson. "Constructing and Appraising Past
Selves." In *Memory, Brain and Belief,* edited by Daniel Schacter and
Elaine Scarry, 231–58. Cambridge, MA: Harvard University Press, 2000.

Ross, W. D. *The Right and the Good.* 1930. Oxford: Oxford University Press,
2002.

Rousseau, Jean-Jacques. *Confessions.* Oxford: Oxford University Press, 2000.

Rubin, D. C., R. W. Schrauf, and D. L. Greenberg. "Belief and Recollection of
Autobiographical Memories." *Memory and Cognition* 31, no. 6 (2003):
887–901.

Sandel, Michael. *Justice: What's the Right Thing to Do?* New York: FSG, 2010.

Santioso, R., Z. Kunda, and G. T. Fong. "Motivated Recruitment of Autobiographical Memories." *Journal of Personality and Social Psychology* 59,
no. 2 (1990): 229–41.

Sartre, Jean-Paul. *Nausea.* 1938. New York: New Directions, 1964.

Sartre, Jean-Paul. *The Words.* 1963. New York: Vintage, 1981.

Schacter, Daniel L. *The Seven Sins of Memory: How the Mind Forgets and Remembers.* Boston: Houghton Mifflin, 2001.

Schacter, Daniel L., Donna Rose Addis, Dennis Hassabis, Victoria C. Martin,
R. Nathan Spreng, and Karl K. Szpunar. "The Future of Memory: Remembering, Imagining, and the Brain." *Neuron* 76, no. 4 (2012): 677–94.

Schauer, Frederick. "Can Public Figures Have Private Lives?" *Social Philosophy and Policy* 17, no. 2 (June 2000): 293–309.

Schechtman, Marya. *The Constitution of Selves.* Ithaca, NY: Cornell University Press, 2007.

Schofield, Paul. "On the Existence of Duties to the Self (and Their Significance
for Moral Philosophy)." *Philosophy and Phenomenological Research* 90,
no. 3 (May 2015).

Schooler, J. W., and T. Y. Engstler-Schooler. "Verbal Overshadowing of Visual
Memories: Some Things Are Better Left Unsaid." *Cognitive Psychology*
22 (1990): 36–71.

Schwartz, Madeleine. Interview with Vivian Gornick, *Believer,* March 24,
2014, https://believermag.com/logger/2014-03-24-we-knew-we-were
-not-liberated-and-were-never/.

Sedaris, David. *When You Are Engulfed in Flames.* Boston: Little, Brown and
Company, 2008.

Shafer-Landau, Russ. *The Fundamentals of Ethics*. 2nd ed. Oxford: Oxford University Press, 2012.

Shafy, Samiha. "An Infinite Loop in the Brain." *Spiegel Online*, November 21, 2008, https://www.spiegel.de/international/world/the-science-of-me mory-an-infinite-loop-in-the-brain-a-591972.html.

Siderits, Mark. "Buddhist Non-Self: The No-Owner's Manual." In *The Oxford Handbook of the Self*, edited by Shaun Gallagher, 297–315. Oxford: Oxford University Press, 2011.

Siegel, Robert Anthony. "The Ethics of Memoir: An Author Interviews His Mother." *Harvard Review Online*, July 12, 2019, https://www.harvard review.org/content/the-ethics-of-memoir-an-author-interviews-his -mother/.

Silverman, Sue William. *Fearless Confessions: A Writer's Guide to Memoir*. Athens: University of Georgia Press, 2009.

Singer, Martin. "On Duties to Oneself." *Ethics* 69, no. 5 (April 1959): 202–5.

Slater, Lauren. *Lying*. London: Penguin, 2000.

Solomon, Robert. "Self, Deception, and Self-Deception in Philosophy." In *The Philosophy of Deception*, edited by Clancy Martin, 15–36. Oxford: Oxford University Press, 2009.

Spencer, Herbert. *An Autobiography*. London: Williams and Norgate, 1904.

Starobinski, Jean. *Montaigne in Motion*. Chicago: University of Chicago Press, 1985.

Stein, Gertrude. *The Autobiography of Alice B. Toklas*. 1933. New York: Vintage, 1990.

Stein, Leigh. "The Rumpus Interview with Melissa Febos." *Rumpus*, February 27, 2017, https://therumpus.net/2017/02/the-rumpus-interview-with -melissa-febos-2/.

Stendhal. *The Life of Henri Brulard*. 1890. New York: New York Review Books, 2002.

Stephen, Leslie. *Hours in a Library*. Vol. 3. London: Smith, Elder and Co., 1892.

Sterne, Laurence. *The Life and Opinions of Tristram Shandy, Gentleman*. 1759. Oxford: Oxford University Press, 2009.

Stewart, James B. *Tangled Webs: How False Statements Are Undermining America*. London: Penguin, 2011.

Strawson, Galen. "Against Narrativity." *Ratio* 17 (December 2004): 428–52.

Strawson, Galen. "The Self." *Journal of Consciousness Studies* 4, no. 5 (1997): 405–28.

Thomas, Monet Patrice. "The Emotion of the Moment: Talking with Terese Marie Mailhot." *Rumpus*, May 11, 2018, https://therumpus.net/2018/05 /the-rumpus-interview-with-terese-marie-mailhot/.

Thoreau, Henry David. *Walden*. 1854. London: Penguin, 1983.

Traig, Jennifer, ed. *The Autobiographer's Handbook: The 826 National Guide to Writing Your Memoir*. New York: Henry Holt and Company, 2008.

Trillin, Calvin. *Family Man*. New York: FSG, 1999.

Trueheart, Charles. "The Den of the Literary Lions." *Washington Post*, April 25, 1987, https://www.washingtonpost.com/archive/lifestyle/1987/04/25/the-den-of-the-literary-lions/21e91f51-b8f3-420e-a0ff-3b19fd81a904/.

Tuten, Nancy Lewis, and John Zubizarreta. *The Robert Frost Encyclopedia*. Westport, CT: Greenwood Publishing Group, 2001.

Twenge, Jean M., W. Keith Campbell, and Brittany Christine Gentile. "Changes in Pronoun Use in American Books and the Rise of Individualism, 1960–2008." *Journal of Cross-Cultural Psychology* 44, no. 3 (2003): 406–15.

Twenge, Jean M., Sarah Konrath, Joshua Foster, and Brad J. Bushman. "Egos Inflating over Time: A Cross-Temporal Meta-Analysis of the Narcissistic Personality Inventory." *Journal of Personality* 76, no. 4 (2008): 875–902.

van Laer, Rebecca. "Just Admit It, You Wrote a Memoir." *Electric Literature*, May 25, 2018, https://electricliterature.com/just-admit-it-you-wrote-a-memoir/.

Vasudevan, Raksha. "Leslie Jamison Is Hauling Out Her Emotional Baggage." Interview with Leslie Jamison, *Electric Literature*, September 23, 2019, https://electricliterature.com/leslie-jamison-is-hauling-out-her-emotional-baggage/.

Vasudevan, Raksha. "What the World Demands of You: The Millions Interviews Margo Jefferson." *Millions*, September 26, 2018, https://themillions.com/2018/09/what-the-world-demands-of-you-the-millions-interviews-margo-jefferson.html.

Ward, Stephen J. A. "Inventing Objectivity: New Philosophical Foundations." In *Journalism Ethics: A Philosophical Approach*, edited by Christopher Meyers, 137–52. Oxford: Oxford University Press, 2010.

Ward, Theodora, ed. *The Letters of Emily Dickinson*. Cambridge, MA: Belknap Press of Harvard University Press, 1986.

Wertheimer, Alan. *Exploitation*. Princeton, NJ: Princeton University Press, 1996.

Westlund, Andrea C. "Who Do We Think We Are?" *Philosophy and Literature* 43, no. 1 (2019): 173–91.

White, E. B. *Essays of E. B. White*. New York: Harper Collins, 1977.

White, Hayden. *Metahistory: The Historical Imagination in Nineteenth-Century Europe*. Baltimore: Johns Hopkins University Press, 1973.

Wilde, Oscar. "The Decay of Lying." In *Intentions*. Portland, OR: Thomas B. Mosher, 1904.

Wilkomirski, Binjamin. *Fragments: Memories of a Wartime Childhood*. New York: Schocken, 1997.

Williams, Bernard. *Ethics and the Limits of Philosophy*. Cambridge, MA: Harvard University Press, 1986.

Williams, Bernard. "Persons, Character and Morality." In *Moral Luck*, 1–19. Cambridge: Cambridge University Press, 1981.

Wilson, A. E., and M. Ross, "From Chump to Champ: People's Appraisals of

Their Earlier and Current Selves." *Journal of Personality and Social Psychology* 80 (2001): 572–84.

Wilson, Timothy D., and Elizabeth W. Dunn. "Self-Knowledge: Its Limits, Value, and Potential for Improvement." *Annual Review of Psychology* 55, no. 1 (February 2004): 493–518.

Wolf, Susan. *Meaning in Life and Why It Matters.* Princeton, NJ: Princeton University Press, 2010.

Wolff, Tobias. *Old School.* New York: Vintage, 2003.

Woolf, Virginia. "The Decay of Essay Writing." In Virginia Woolf, *Selected Essays*, 3–5. Oxford: Oxford University Press, 2009.

Woolf, Virginia. *Moments of Being.* San Diego: Harcourt Brace, 1985.

Woolf, Virginia. *To the Lighthouse.* 1927. Oxford: Oxford University Press, 2006.

Wordsworth, William. *The Prelude.* 1799. London: Penguin Classics, 1996.

X, Malcolm. *The Autobiography of Malcolm X.* 1964. New York: Random House, 2015.

Yagoda, Ben. *Memoir: A History.* New York: Riverhead Books, 2010.

Young, James O., and Susan Haley. "Nothing Comes from Nowhere: Reflections on Cultural Appropriation as the Representation of Other Cultures." In *The Ethics of Cultural Appropriation*, edited by James O. Young and Conrad G. Brunk, 268–89. Hoboken, NJ: Wiley Blackwell, 2012.

Zeitlin, Froma. "New Soundings in Holocaust Literature: A Surplus of Memory." In *Catastrophe and Meaning: The Holocaust and the Twentieth Century*, edited by Moishe Postone and Eric Santer, 173–208. Chicago: University of Chicago Press, 2003.

Zwerdling, Alex. *The Rise of the Memoir.* Oxford: Oxford University Press, 2017.

Index